**Susanne James** has enjoyed creative writing since childhood, completing her first—sadly unpublished—novel by the age of twelve. She has three grown-up children who were, and are, her pride and joy, and who all live happily in Oxfordshire with their families. She was always happy to put the needs of her family before her ambition to write seriously, although along the way some published articles for magazines and newspapers helped to keep the dream alive!

Susanne's big regret is that her beloved husband is no longer here to share the pleasure of her recent success. She now shares her life with Toffee, her young Cavalier King Charles spaniel, who decides when it's time to get up (early) and when a walk in the park is overdue!

**Recent titles by the same author:**

BUTTONED-UP SECRETARY, BRITISH BOSS
THE MASTER OF HIGHBRIDGE MANOR
THE BOSELLI BRIDE
THE PLAYBOY OF PENGARROTH HALL

**Did you know these are also available as eBooks?
Visit www.millsandboon.co.uk**

**Helena forced herself to concentrate, and tried to ignore the faint, musky drift of Oscar's aftershave.**

Clearing his throat, the solicitor continued, 'To my beloved great-nephew Oscar Iannis Theotokis I leave one half of the property known as Mulberry Court.' Adjusting his spectacles, he went on, 'And I also bequeath one half of the said property to Helena Lingston. All and everything to be shared equally between the two aforesaid parties.'

*What* had he just said? Immediately shocked beyond belief, Helena gasped and almost stood up. This isn't right, she thought wildly. Not Mulberry Court! There had to be some mistake!

If she'd been struck by something hurtling from outer space Helena couldn't have felt more stunned. There was complete silence for a few moments, then Helena pulled herself together and looked across at Oscar's stern profile, trying to stem the hot tide of feeling that was rippling through every nerve and fibre of her body.

# THE THEOTOKIS INHERITANCE

BY
SUSANNE JAMES

All the characters in this book have no existence outside the imagination
of the author, and have no relation whatsoever to anyone bearing the
same name or names. They are not even distantly inspired by any
individual known or unknown to the author, and all the incidents are
pure invention.

First published in Great Britain 2012
by Mills & Boon, an imprint of Harlequin (UK) Limited.
Harlequin (UK) Limited, Eton House, 18-24 Paradise Road,
Richmond, Surrey TW9 1SR

© Susanne James 2012

ISBN: 978 0 263 89053 2

Harlequin (UK) policy is to use papers that are natural, renewable
and recyclable products and made from wood grown in sustainable
forests. The logging and manufacturing process conform to the
legal environmental regulations of the country of origin.

Printed and bound in Spain
by Blackprint CPI, Barcelona

# THE THEOTOKIS INHERITANCE

# CHAPTER ONE

Just before three o'clock on a chilly April afternoon, Helena drew into the crowded car park of Dorchester solicitors Messrs Mayhew & Morrison, and glanced at her watch. She was five minutes early for her appointment—so she'd made good time on her journey from London.

As she'd left the motorway and joined the quieter country roads, the usual wave of nostalgia had run through Helena. Dorset was home territory—and she'd stayed away too long this time. In fact, she realized, she hadn't returned since her father's funeral four years ago.

Opening her bag, she took out the solicitor's letter and looked at it again. It merely confirmed the date of today's meeting when the will of the late Mrs Isobel Theotokis would be discussed. As she slipped the letter back into its envelope, Helena's eyes moistened briefly. Mrs Theotokis, who'd been her father's long-time employer, had obviously not forgotten Helena, nor her promise all those years ago that the precious porcelain figurines which had so fascinated the child would one day be hers.

Helena checked her appearance briefly in the car's

interior mirror. Her generously fringed, widely spaced blue eyes seemed to glitter in certain lights, and someone had once said that they belonged in a stained glass window. She had regular features and a small nose, and her milky skin, though typically English rose, reacted well to the sun's rays so that most summers she looked prettily tanned. And today she had chosen to wind her thick blonde hair up on top into a coiled knot.

She got out of the car and presented herself at the solicitor's office. The girl at the reception desk looked up and smiled.

'Ah, yes—Miss Kingston? Good afternoon.' She stood up and immediately led Helena towards an inner door. 'Mr Mayhew is waiting for you.'

As Helena was ushered inside, John Mayhew, the senior partner, stood up at once and came forward to greet her. He was a short, affable man with white bushy eyebrows and a moustache to match and he shook Helena's hand warmly.

'Thank you for making the trip, Helena,' he said kindly, and the girl's throat tightened briefly. She was known to John Mayhew because her father's modest affairs had also been handled by this firm, and the last time she'd been here was to finally settle everything up—and it hadn't taken long.

'Do take a seat,' the man said, adding, 'The other… interested party…has been delayed slightly. But he should be here any minute.'

Even as he spoke, the door opened and Helena turned her head, colour rising rapidly in her cheeks, leaving her breathless as the layers of her memory peeled away.

She was suddenly weightless, floating backwards in space…she was in free fall!

Oscar! Helena formed the name silently under her breath. Oscar…

This was Isobel's great-nephew whom Helena, three years his junior, had once worshipped…Oscar, who had initiated her into the first heady delights of romantic love. But that had been more than ten years ago…a lifetime away.

She forced herself to try and breathe normally as she looked up at him.

It was no surprise that he was still the most mind-numbingly handsome man she had ever seen—or would ever see—wearing his overt sensuality like a permanent badge of office. Helena gripped her hands together tightly. Why hadn't she thought that they might possibly meet again—and under these particular circumstances? But it had not crossed her mind, and she'd not been ready for it. But she met his gaze levelly as he looked down at her.

His glossy black hair was styled more formally than she remembered, but the chiselled, dark-skinned features, the expansive brow, the firm uncompromising mouth—that had closed over hers so many times—were still as enchanting as they had always been.

He was wearing a formal suit perfectly designed to do justice to his lean, powerful physique, but he had no tie on, his crisp white shirt partially open at the front, revealing the merest glimpse of dark bodily hair at the throat. Helena swallowed over a dry tongue as he looked down at her.

John Mayhew broke the few moments' silence. 'I

am sure you two must have met in the past,' he said, 'but let me introduce you again…'

Before he could go on, Oscar cut in, the familiar voice rich and evocative, with only a trace of his cruelly seductive native tongue. 'No need for that, John,' he said slowly. 'Helena and I know each other from when I used to visit my great-aunt at holiday times.' He paused, moving forward slightly, extending a strong brown hand in greeting. Then, 'How are you, *Heleena*?' And Helena's heart quickened. Because that had been Oscar's occasional, special pronunciation of her name. And hearing it again made her inner thighs tingle.

'I am well, thank you,' Helena responded coolly, half-standing to meet his outstretched hand. His long, sensitive fingers curled against her own, making her colour rise again. 'And you…Oscar?'

'Good, thank you,' he said briefly. He sat down on one of the big leather armchairs opposite John Mayhew's desk, and glanced briefly at Helena again. Pale, sometimes wistful, Helena had become a stunning, sophisticated female, exhibiting all of nature's attributes, he thought. She was wearing a dark blue, fine woollen suit and cream shirt and very high heeled shoes, her slender legs clad in sheer dark tights. As she looked across at him, her lips were slightly parted as if she was about to say something, but it was her eyes, those blue, blue eyes which had once known the touch of his lips, their charisma remained, unique, unforgettable. Oscar straightened up and turned his attention to the solicitor.

After all the usual polite greetings had been exchanged, John Mayhew opened a large file in front of him and began to read.

"'This is the last will and testament of Isabel Marina Theotokis of Mulberry Court in the county of Dorset...'" he read out, before proceeding to chant the detailed formalities. Watching him with her hands clasped in her lap, Helena was relieved that her heart rate was returning to something approaching normality. She wondered how many times in his life John Mayhew would have performed this task. Probably too many to count, she thought, hoping that the interview wouldn't last long and she could escape. The room was beginning to feel warm as afternoon sunlight filtered in through the high windows, and she automatically leaned forward, forcing herself to concentrate, and trying to ignore the faint musky drift of Oscar's aftershave.

Clearing his throat, the solicitor continued.

"'To my beloved great-nephew Oscar Ioannis Theotokis I leave one half of the property known as Mulberry Court in the county of Dorset together with all its contents, goods and chattels.'" Adjusting his spectacles, he went on, "And I also bequeath one half of the said property known as Mulberry Court with all its contents goods and chattels to my dear longtime friend Helena Kingston. All and everything to be shared equally between the two aforesaid parties.'"

*What* had he just said? Immediately shocked beyond belief, Helena gasped and almost stood up. This isn't right, she thought wildly. It was Isobel's coveted figurines in the library which she had promised would one day be Helena's...not the *house*! Not Mulberry Court! There had to be some mistake!

If she'd been struck by something hurtling from outer space Helena couldn't have felt more stunned... And she was not going to look across at Oscar because—if this *was* true, and she quickly realized that it obviously had to be—she had virtually been given half his birthright! How on earth was he going to accept that? That the daughter of his great-aunt's gardener was to receive such wealth! It was preposterous!

She forced herself to listen as the names of all the other beneficiaries were read out. There was a very long list, including a substantial sum of money for Louise, her housekeeper, and countless charities and local organizations were included, but it was clear that the two main beneficiaries were Helena and Oscar.

'As in many cases, there are one or two details which have been added at the end,' the solicitor said. 'For your information, Mrs Theotokis has given some instructions.' There was a long pause before he went on. 'She asks that Mulberry Court is not put up for sale until one year from the date of her death, and she asks that, if possible, prior consideration be given to a couple with a family.' He looked up. 'I happen to know that it was a matter of great regret to Isobel that she and Mr Theotokis never had children of their own.' He smiled. 'Maybe she is hoping that, one day, childish noise and chatter may echo through the rooms and grounds of Mulberry Court,' he said, 'and if it ever does,' he added kindly, 'I am quite sure that she will hear it all from her well-deserved place in heaven.'

Hearing those words made a painful lump form in

Helena's throat. Isobel Theotokis had been a gracious, kind and loving woman to everyone who'd crossed her path, and her final act of generosity to Helena was to actually give her part of the home she'd loved so much. What an incredible gift, an incredible honour! It was totally unbelievable, but in the short term how was it going to affect her? And just as important—what was it going to mean to Oscar? He wouldn't want to waste any time here—or anywhere else—that might distract him, even temporarily, from the famous Theotokis family business empire.

There was complete silence for a few moments, then Helena pulled herself together and looked across at Oscar's stern profile, trying to stem the hot tide of feeling that was rippling through every nerve and fibre of her body.

'Although I feel almost totally overwhelmed,' she began, trying to sound normal, 'it would be wrong of me not to say how very…grateful…I feel to have been remembered in such a way by Mrs Theotokis.' She hesitated, hoping she was saying all the right things. 'I shall, of course, do whatever is considered necessary to…well…to assist in any way I can,' she added, wondering what on earth anyone did when suddenly coming into a fortune that included a massive property full of treasures.

For the following few minutes Helena could barely concentrate on what the other two were saying, but presently, after some further formalities had been dealt with, the solicitor handed over two large bunches of keys, and Helena stared down at the set in her hand— her very own keys to Mulberry Court! And the way she was feeling at the moment, they might have been a ticking time bomb!

They all got to their feet, and as Helena looked up into Oscar's eyes—which were glittering like ice-cold granite—she couldn't begin to imagine what was going through his mind. The revelation that they were now joint owners of his great-aunt's home must have been as great a shock to him as to her, she thought—that she, Helena, was going to be playing an important part in his life, at least for the next year. Then, lifting her head, she thought—well, it wasn't her fault, and they were both going to have to make the best of whatever lay ahead.

After they'd been assured of Mayhew & Morrison's wish to be of further service when necessary, the two left the building together, and in the late afternoon sunshine stood outside briefly.

'Well—' Oscar shrugged and looked down at her with half-narrowed gaze. 'That was something of a surprise,' he said. *And that remark was something of an understatement*, Helena thought. *For both of them.* 'Still,' he went on, 'I'm sure we can come to some arrangement that suits us both.' The comment was casually made—as if he was merely referring to one of life's irritating necessities—and, before Helena could reply, he went on, 'I'll get someone to value the place in the first instance, give us some idea of value until we sell next year.' He shook his head briefly. 'Isobel requesting a delay is obviously going to hold us up. It would have been more convenient to have got things done and out of the way as soon as possible.'

Helena looked up at him, still feeling shattered, still

finding it hard to take all this in. Was she *really* here again with Oscar—about to embark on a serious business venture? Oscar, who'd been the true love of her life when she'd been on the cusp of womanhood. Oscar, who had shown her what desire, and being desired, meant? Their romantic meetings, many of them under the graceful branches of the willow tree beyond the orchard—their special willow tree—were indelibly imprinted in her memory, as was the way it had all ended so abruptly...as *he* had ended it so abruptly, with little explanation. After one of his visits, Oscar had simply walked away—and taken her heart with him. She bit her lip thoughtfully. Had their relationship ever crossed his mind since? she wondered. Had he ever felt anything at all—regret or remorse, or even sadness at losing something which had once been precious? Probably not, she thought realistically. She would only be one in a very long list of women who'd experienced his particular craft in the romantic stakes.

She swallowed hard, forcing herself to stop thinking along these lines. There was no point in digging up the past, even mentally, and she had quite enough on her mind—not counting today's revelation—to focus on. To sort out.

Looking up at Oscar, she realized that he hadn't expressed one word of appreciation that his great-aunt had remembered him in this way, but then, why would he? He was a bona fide member of the fabulously rich Theotokis dynasty, with vast worldwide business concerns. Mulberry Court and 'all its goods and chattels' would be no more than a blot of ink on Oscar's personal portfolio, and he was no doubt thinking that he could well do without this annoying interruption in his life, especially as it was going to include someone else—*her*! She lifted her chin.

'First of all, I think we need to discuss one or two things,' she said calmly. She paused. 'I happen to know that Isobel's personal belongings were tremendously important to her, and we should consider that point very carefully.' Mulberry Court was full of treasures—as well as those priceless figurines—which Isobel Theotokis had brought home from all the travelling she'd done in her life.

'Oh, valuers—experts in the trade—will deal with all the paintings and antiques. They'll ensure that everything's sold appropriately,' Oscar began. 'At least we can start to sort that out straight away.'

Helena frowned briefly. How typically masculine! He had no problem with Isobel's cherished belongings being handed over to complete strangers to 'deal' with, without a thought as to what everything had meant to the old lady. Well, Helena wasn't having that. She had spent so many happy hours at Mulberry Court when she'd been growing up—had almost been like the child Isobel had never had.

'I don't think that's a good idea,' she said. 'I think that that part of the equation should be our responsibility alone, without the input of strangers.'

Oscar raised his eyebrows—more in surprise that Helena had voiced her opinion than what she'd actually said. He shrugged.

'Well, yes, perhaps,' he said reluctantly, accepting for the first time that they both had to agree on everything before any action could be taken. 'But I'm afraid my time here is very limited. I'm due back in Greece by the end of the month, though I expect to be in the London office until then.' He paused. 'What about your own commitments?' he asked. 'I remember Isobel mentioning that you live and work in London.'

Helena nodded. 'I head the team at the Harcourt Employment Agency at the moment,' she said, 'but I have started looking for something else.' She bit her lip. So far, she'd found nothing which offered anything comparable with her present salary, nor the lovely mews cottage she was renting as part of the deal.

'You're not happy there?' Oscar asked briefly.

Helena paused before answering. 'It's just…just that I think it's time for a change,' she replied guardedly.

There was silence for a moment, then, 'I could come back this weekend—if you're free as well,' Oscar said. 'A couple of days should be enough to give us a clear picture of what has to be done.'

'As it happens I am free, and it would be a start,' Helena said, 'but it's bound to take some time, and we shouldn't rush things.' She paused. 'I intend to take the matter very seriously—and do my utmost for Isobel… in her memory,' she added.

She began walking across to where she'd parked her car, with Oscar following, and she opened her bag. 'In the meantime,' she said, 'if you think you need to contact me, here's my card.'

He glanced at it briefly, then withdrew his own from his wallet and handed it to her, and without even looking at it Helena slipped it into her bag.

'I must get back,' she said, glancing at her watch.

'The roads are going to be a lot busier than they were this morning.'

He held open her door for her, and as she got in she looked up at him through the open window, wondering if she should apologize for the situation they'd found themselves in—the situation that he'd been landed in. But before a single word had formed on her lips, Helena checked herself. She had nothing to say sorry for. Isobel Theotokis had every right to dispose of her property in whichever way she wanted.

'So—I'll come back down on Friday night,' she said, 'and that'll give us Saturday and Sunday to have a proper discussion and look over the house.' She switched on the engine. 'I'll book myself a room locally,' she added.

'I'll have to stay somewhere myself,' he said casually, 'so I'll see to it. I'll leave you a message to let you know the arrangements.'

'Oh… OK. Fine. Thanks,' Helena said, and with a brief wave of her hand she began driving slowly out of the car park, glancing in her rear-view mirror to see Oscar standing there, watching her go. She'd love to have been able to read his mind! So far he'd been cool, almost impassive, at their news, and once or twice she'd caught him staring at her with an inscrutable expression on his face. But it was good that there'd been no obvious sense of awkwardness between them, she thought, though there wasn't much doubt that he was wishing he was now the sole owner of Mulberry Court.

As she began her journey back to London, Helena felt mightily relieved to be alone with her thoughts. She, Helena Kingston, had just been left a fortune, and it was like winning a lottery she'd never entered. But was she prepared for such wealth? Her beloved father, a widower for many years, having lost his wife when Helena had been just ten, had left a very modest inheritance for his only child. Money which she had put aside for the day when she might need it for something special. And so far she never had, thanks to her successful career.

But quite apart from everything else—apart from even the amazing legacy she had just received—there was another problem she had to face: she and Oscar were going to have to spend time together again under totally bizarre circumstances. This wasn't ten years ago when they'd both been young and carefree and so in love, something which had been so important then, but which would be utterly embarrassing to even mention now. Did he remember any of it? she wondered. Did he remember all the time they'd spent walking, talking, kissing and enjoying spending time with each other? How could either of them pretend it had never happened? Helena made a face to herself. If he did remember any of it, he'd also have to remember how he'd dumped her—but then, he'd probably dumped so many other women since, she was just another note on whatever mental record he kept of his love life.

As Oscar got into his own car, his feelings were in turmoil. Because it had given his emotions a huge and undeniable jolt to see Helena today.

His handsome brow creased into a frown and his hands, tense on the steering wheel, became pale under his grip as he sat there for a few moments, deep in thought.

What had he done to her? What had he done to himself, to them both? Why had he allowed fate to rule their lives? Because when he had looked down into her wide, misty eyes, he was aware of his heart exploding into a million painful fragments of regret. The heart which had taken so long to heal had shattered again, renewing his sense of loss.

Over time, Oscar had managed to convince himself that he would probably never see Helena again. But he'd thought about her often enough, wondered who she'd married, how many beautiful children she might have. And while trying to concentrate on what was going on around them today, he'd automatically noted that there was no gold band on her ring finger and every male instinct he possessed had urged him to pull her up towards him, to enfold her, to taste her mouth again.

But he knew that would not have gone down very well. Why would she ever want him near her again? A nerve clenched in his strong jaw as his thoughts ran on.

Of course, it was not unexpected that he should be named as a beneficiary in his great-aunt's will because he was now the only member of his generation left—he'd never had siblings and his two cousins had been killed in a multiple car crash. But although he'd always known that Isobel had been very fond of Helena, the will *had* taken him by surprise, he admitted. Not that he cared a jot about having to share the value involved; that was irrelevant. Great wealth had never interested him in a personal sense. It was only the continuing suc-

cess of the family firm that was important—ever since
he'd realized that it was his destiny.

*Destiny.* Oscar's lip curled briefly. There was still
one, more vital, personal expectation of him which he
had so far not fulfilled. To find himself a suitable wife.
And if his father—Georgios—had his wish, a wife
from the rich Papadopoulos family, who had important financial ties with the Theotokis clan.

'It is about time you married and settled down,
Oscar,' Giorgios frequently said. 'A good Greek wife
would be a wonderful support, a wonderful investment!
Would bless you with many children! There are those
two beautiful daughters just waiting for you to make
up your mind! Either of them would make you a happy
man! What is your problem?'

The 'problem' was, Oscar knew he did not love either
Allegra or Callidora Papadopoulos, desirable though
they were. And no other woman, yet, had made him
want to commit to lifelong love and loyalty. Because
when he did find such a woman—if she existed—that
was how it must be. For ever. And Oscar knew he would
never view any wife as an 'investment'—as his father
clearly did. Profit and loss were not part of the equation.
Unconditional love was the only thing that mattered.

Now, straightening his shoulders, Oscar switched
on the engine and prepared to drive away. For the fore-
seeable future he had a more immediate matter to re-
solve—the disposal of Mulberry Court and its contents.
And it would be unavoidable that he and Helena would
be spending a great deal of time together and that she
was going to have to be consulted every step of the way.

* * *

Oscar had already decided which accommodation they'd be using and now, leaving Dorchester, he drove rapidly towards the Horseshoe Inn, an out-of-town up-market establishment a few miles away. It was small but well-appointed, and discreet—somewhere they could talk and get this business sorted without too many distractions. Vast hotels had never had any appeal for Oscar and he never used them if he could help it. And when in London he always used his private apartment, where he looked after himself and where this car—a favourite among the several others he owned—could be safely garaged.

Now, as the sleek grey Italian sports car took him swiftly to his destination, he remembered how confidently Helena had manoeuvred her own vehicle out of the overcrowded car park and he tilted one eyebrow thoughtfully. Her car was obviously not new, but in reasonable condition—and probably perfectly adequate for London use, he thought.

Although in recent years his aunt had often spoken of Helena—and always in glowing terms—he didn't really know anything about her career. His eyes narrowed slightly as a thought struck him. Perhaps he could pay her off, give her far and away more than the combined value of the house and all its assets and leave the business of disposing of everything to him? Surely it would be tidier all round if just one of them was involved. Wouldn't she find that far less hassle than having to spend time down here? Then he made a face to himself, discounting the thought almost at once. Helena—obviously very confident and self-assured—had given every indication that she intended being full-on in the whole assignment. He groaned inwardly. *Aunt Isobel*, he thought, *I always loved you, but why have you done this to me?*

# CHAPTER TWO

AFTER a fairly tedious journey home, Helena made herself some toast and a mug of hot chocolate, then undressed and went into her bathroom for a shower. As the warm water began drenching her body and releasing the tension in her tired muscles, she kept reliving every moment of that incredible afternoon. Her life had changed! The world had changed! Well, it was certainly going to be different.

But Helena knew that all the formalities of the day, and the enormous significance of inheriting a fortune, were as nothing compared with the overpowering feelings she'd experienced at meeting Oscar again. Lifting her hair from the nape of her neck, she soaped her skin languidly, smoothing the sponge across her shoulders and down her arms, conscious that even thinking of him made her feel sensuous, dangerously sensitive. She remembered how her face had flamed crimson red as his brilliant dark eyes had bored into hers, how her pulse had raced, her tongue had dried as he'd stared down at her. She had wanted to look away, to escape from his entrapping gaze, but she hadn't been able to. She'd been transfixed by his nearness, helpless beneath his scrutiny, and she'd wanted to scream out in protest that she was no longer a young, inexperienced, naïve teenager! She'd grown up and moved far, far away from his sphere of influence! Her need for him had long since dissipated, had been replaced by all of life's other imperatives, like standing on her own two feet, holding down a good job that earned her enough money to survive in London's fast track world. And to make and keep friends, form relationships...to just *be*. Without *him*.

Yet now, it seemed, she was being forced to stand within his aura of light once again. But this time in a business capacity. How was she going to live through that?

Helena sighed as she reached for a towel, just thinking of business bringing her back down to earth and her present problems—the problems she'd been facing before today's revelations. Her problems with relationships.

Her split with Mark had happened two months ago—unexpectedly and painfully. And the trouble was that she kept bumping into him with the new 'love of his life', as he'd described her, both of them looking blissfully happy. That was bad enough, but then almost at once Simon Harcourt had started getting amorous towards her. Lately his attentions had become so annoying that Helena felt she would have no alternative but to leave the job, soon. Even if it did mean having to give up the cottage that went with it.

What she'd really like to do, Helena thought savagely, was to emigrate and get right away from everyone she knew in London and live in a completely different environment. Just until she got into calmer emotional waters.

Then, even as the unlikely thought of emigration crossed her mind, another amazing one struck her and she stared at her own reflection in the steamed-up mirror for a second. Could *Isobel* have given her an unexpected lifeline, an escape? Could such an impossible, fleeting idea work?

If she were to go and stay—well, live—just for a short time at Mulberry Court, she could reassess things and take stock of her situation. For the first time she would be in her very own home—well, partly her very own home—and find some peace to really recover from the emotional switchback she'd been riding lately. It would make it easy to give Simon her notice because she could tell him, quite truthfully, that her circumstances had changed and that for the next year she was needed in Dorset.

A wave of excitement swept over Helena as she considered all this. It really could be a temporary answer, she thought. She had enough money saved to pay for her immediate needs and anyway there was sure to be temping work she could find in Dorchester when she needed to.

She bit her lip thoughtfully. The big question was— what would Oscar think of her taking up residence, even temporary residence? Would he be agreeable to that? Wouldn't he think it opportunistic of her...or even inappropriate?

Presently, as she slipped into her nightdress, her mobile beeped, indicating a text message from Oscar: *'Horseshoe Inn bkd wk end. Meet Fri nt O.'*

Helena snapped the phone shut, wondering where he was now. What was he doing, and was he thinking about her at all? Was he feeling as confused about the afternoon's bombshell as she was? No, of course he wasn't, on either count, she decided at once. This would be a pretty insignificant affair to him, just another small and inconvenient detail in his important life which had to be sorted out. And everything in his attitude towards her had suggested that she, Helena Kingston, was merely part of that unwelcome inconvenience.

She slid gratefully into bed and pulled the duvet up around her shoulders, wondering whether she'd ever be able to get any sleep. She wished she had someone close that she could share her news with, a brother or a sister—it was far too late to ring her best friend, Anna. But still, she was used to steering her own way through life's sometimes turbulent waters without anyone's hand to hold on to. And she was certainly not going to let this particular tsunami sweep her under the waves.

Snuggling down, she tried to shut everything from her mind, to calm herself into believing that it would all seem straightforward in the morning. But how could it? Because behind her closed lids all she could see were Oscar's intense black eyes in their pools of startling white, gazing at her with that heart-stopping expression that had always sent shivers down her spine.

On Friday evening, Helena had no trouble in finding the Horseshoe Inn, though it was unknown to her. Situated on a private road and nestling amongst trees, the Grade II listed building backed on to open country, and after her long drive it looked like heaven.

Inside, the tall, bearded man standing in the small reception area by the crowded bar smiled at her enquiringly. 'Hi there,' he said. 'I'm Adam—can I help?'

'I believe accommodation has been booked for me for a couple of nights,' Helena said. 'I'm Helena Kingston.'

'Of course—yes.' The man glanced at the huge calendar in front of him. 'Room numbers two and five have been allocated, one for Mr Theotokis and one for yourself,' he said, smiling again. He paused. 'Would you like something to drink before I show you to your room? The chef's on duty until midnight if you'd like a meal,' he added.

Immediately, Helena felt completely at ease. The inn had a sophisticated air, yet was welcoming and reassuring, its ambience the sort she imagined Oscar would approve of—though what his opinions, likes and dislikes were she actually had no idea of at all. Not now, not any more. But, hopefully, they might have just enough in their shared pasts to make this unlooked for alliance reasonably pleasant. Helena certainly hoped so, even though his reaction to the news had been slightly ambivalent.

'I'd love a pot of tea in about ten minutes, and perhaps a sandwich?' Helena said, glancing over to the lively-looking restaurant area at the far end. She picked up the small case she'd brought with her, then hesitated. 'Is Mr Theotokis about?'

'Haven't seen him—and he hasn't booked in yet,' Adam said, taking a key from one of the pegs on the wall. 'Let me show you the way,' he said, taking Helena's case from her.

Her charmingly rustic bedroom with every conceivable mod con was going to suit her very well, Helena thought as she looked around her. She'd be quite happy to stay here for a couple of nights. Sitting on the edge of the huge double bed for a moment, she glanced at her watch. It was getting late and she'd imagined Oscar to have been here by now, and she wasn't sure what to do next. Would he expect her to wait around for him until he turned up, or could she go to bed after she'd had her tea?

At that exact moment her mobile rang. It was Oscar. 'Helena, I'm sorry to be this late,' he said. Then, 'I take it you found the place OK?'

'I did, and my room is excellent—thanks.'

There was a pause. 'I'm not far away, so I should arrive in twenty minutes or so.'

'Shall I… Would you like me to order something for you?' Helena asked. 'I'm told the chef's still on duty.'

'You can order me a whisky—but nothing to eat, thanks,' Oscar said, and without another word he rang off.

By the time he arrived almost half an hour later, Helena had eaten the sandwiches she'd ordered for herself, and was sitting in a quiet corner of the still busy bar with her glass of wine and Oscar's whisky already on the table. He came straight over and sat down opposite her.

'Hi,' he said briefly, then picked up his glass and took a generous swallow. '*You* obviously got here with no difficulty,' he said, sitting down, and feeling fleetingly pleased to be with someone he knew—or knew once. And she was looking good—amazing, in fact—in her jeans and striped sweater, her hair tied back in a long ponytail.

Helena couldn't help noting the dark expression on his features, and an uncomfortable chill ran through her. He was obviously thoroughly annoyed at being so late, she thought—or maybe he wasn't appreciating having to be here at all—with her. Helena's spirits sank at the thought of what lay ahead of them, of how he might view everything to do with their shared legacy. And, now that he'd had time to mull it over, how he was viewing her significant presence in the whole affair. Was he going to expect her to meekly see his point of view—to kowtow just because of who he was? And would she ever have the nerve to put her suggestion to him about staying at the house? He certainly didn't seem in a particularly positive mood at the moment, she thought.

'Anyway, it's rather late for us to discuss anything tonight,' he said briefly. 'So we'll have an early breakfast in the morning, then spend the rest of the day at Mulberry Court and catalogue all the items that need disposing of.' He took another drink. 'The quicker we make a start, the better.'

Helena finished her wine and picked up her bag. 'I'm aware that you have a very busy life, Oscar,' she said firmly, 'but…' She paused. 'I would really like to spend some time just looking around Isobel's home, revisiting something of my past, perhaps,' she said. 'I knew Mulberry Court so well when I was growing up, but it is such a long time since I was there—I wasn't even able to make the funeral—which upset me a lot. And Isobel's death was so sudden—so totally unexpected.' She paused.

'Yes, I thought you'd been forgotten,' Oscar said, 'that your name had somehow been omitted from the long list of my aunt's friends and acquaintances who would have been informed of her death.'

'No, I wasn't forgotten—and I did explain later, with my apologies,' Helena said carefully. 'I was actually ill in bed with a horrendous attack of flu,' she added, surprised that her attendance at what would have been a very crowded occasion had been missed by anyone— especially Isobel's ambitious great-nephew. She stood up.

'Well, then, I'll see you in the morning,' she said, and Oscar stood as well, looking down at her briefly.

'Yes, and tomorrow you can have your little trip down memory lane,' he said obliquely.

After she'd gone, Oscar bought himself another whisky and sat back down, relieved that the golden liquid was beginning to calm him, bringing him back to normal. The reason behind his lateness had been an accident that had shaken him up quite badly. In all the countless hours of driving he'd done, he'd never been caught up in anything like it—and he hoped he never would again. One of the first on the scene, and having to rescue two young kids from the back of a car that had seemed ready to burst into flames, had been a shattering experience. But the emergency services had arrived in an impressively short time and had been ful-some in their praise of Oscar's quick thinking—which, when he thought about it now, had been purely instinctive. He drank quickly again. It was a miracle that no one had been killed or badly hurt, though the young mother who'd been driving had clearly been in deep shock. Thank God he'd been there at just the right moment to be of some use.

After a while, his thoughts turned to his reasons for being here. In the few days which had elapsed since the reading of the will, he'd had time to think things over and had to accept that its contents—and instructions—were hardly Helena's fault. But one thing was certain—it was going to be a major inconvenience for both of them. Though, from what she had said just now, she was going to take her time. Well, if there was too much procrastination he'd have to hurry her up a bit, he decided.

He fingered his glass thoughtfully, that other idea occurring to him again. Could he get her to agree to sell him her share straight away? She might be glad of some quick money—living in London was expensive, and she could certainly do with a new car.

He drained his glass and went over to the bar for the key to his room. Adam looked up and smiled. 'Everything all right, Mr Theotokis?' he asked.

'I certainly hope it's going to be,' Oscar said enigmatically.

'No, no, *no*! You can't do this to me…it isn't fair! You *shan't* have them…you can have the house, you can have everything…but these are mine! Isobel promised!' And then a low, pitiful scream followed as the figurines fell to the floor and shattered into a thousand pieces.

Helena sat bolt upright in bed, putting her hand to her

mouth. Had she screamed out loud just then—had anyone heard her? That was one of the most awful, vivid
dreams she'd ever had in her life. But this dream—
this nightmare—had been so strong it had actually felt
physical. She had felt Oscar's hands holding hers in an
iron grip as they'd both struggled for possession of the
beautiful ornaments. Pushing and pulling each other
like demented creatures. But Helena had been no match
for his masculine strength and with that cry of despair
she had released her hold and watched her precious
figurines destroyed before her eyes.

As the early dawn light filtered in through the
slightly parted curtains at the window, Helena allowed herself a shaky smile as she waited for her heart
rate to return to normal. Thank goodness for dreams,
she thought, because that was all they were—mythi-
cal wanderings of a half-awake mind. Her figurines
were not smashed, they were still safely in their place
at Mulberry Court, but could her dream have been a
warning? she wondered. A warning to stand her ground
with Isobel's nephew and not let herself be intimidated
by the fact that he was a true blood relative and she a
complete outsider?

Oscar had decided that they should start the day early,
and Helena made her way downstairs to the restaurant
for breakfast as early as possible.

He was already seated reading a morning paper, a
large cafetière of coffee in front of him, and he stood
up as Helena came in and glanced down at her. She
was wearing slimline black trousers and a pale blue
shirt, her hair tied back away from her face, which

was devoid of make-up. She looked rather wan today, he thought, and for the merest second he saw again the lovely, innocent girl of long ago. He pulled out a chair for her to sit down.

'I'm impressed,' he said. Then, 'I didn't expect to see you for at least another hour.'

Helena shot him a look as she took her seat. 'I'm used to getting up early,' she said. She wasn't going to tell him that it was the horrible dream she'd had which had woken her at dawn.

Declining Oscar's invitation to share his coffee, Helena decided to order a pot of tea for herself, feeling very thankful that he, too, seemed to need little to eat. She had never been a breakfast person.

Later, driving rapidly in Oscar's car, they arrived at Mulberry Court and as they made their way along the broad, curved drive, Helena felt her stomach churn. This was now her house—partly her very own property. The much loved building she'd privately thought of as home all those years ago was legally hers! She still felt it too incredible to believe as she sat with her hands clasped in her lap, looking around her.

There, to one side, and out of sight of the main entrance, were the two semi-detached staff cottages, one each for the housekeeper and the gardener, and Helena turned her head to gaze back as they went past. After her mother had died, Helena and her father had come from their rented house in Dorchester to live in the gardener's cottage and for the following eight years, until she'd gone to university, she had lived what she now thought of as a charmed life, roaming free in the wonderful Dorset countryside and the extensive grounds of Mulberry Court, where her father had been the full-time gardener and general factotum. Louise, a local woman, had been Isobel's housekeeper and cook, and Helena would frequently drop in next door to enjoy her company—and share her wonderful home-made cakes.

As for Paul Theotokis, Isobel's husband, Helena had barely seen him at all. He had been a rather shadowy figure, constantly away looking after his business interests, but when Helena was about thirteen Paul had died suddenly, and the impressionable child had been amazed at the extravagant funeral arrangements and the hundreds of people who'd attended. Huge, glistening cars arriving, one after the other.

'Who lives in our...I mean...who lives in the gardener's cottage now?' Helena asked curiously.

Oscar glanced across at her. 'Benjamin. He joined the "firm", as my aunt liked to call it, a month or so after your father died,' he said shortly.

'And Louise? I know she's still here, isn't she?'

'She is. She's been keeping everything ticking over until...well, until the future becomes clearer,' Oscar said. 'But she's having a few days away in Durham with a cousin at the moment, I believe,' he added.

Poor Louise, Helena thought. Mulberry Court—and her little cottage—had been her home for so many years. Now there was the prospect of no home, and no employment, either.

Oscar drew the car slowly to a halt outside the entrance door to Mulberry Court, and they both got out and went into the house. And as soon as she stepped over the threshold, the smell of the place filled Helena with a warm rush of welcome. She took a deep breath, feeling almost faint for a second as a wave of nostalgia rippled through her.

'It's been such a long time,' she said quietly. 'Although Isobel very kindly arranged a small reception here for my father's funeral, it was held in the conservatory...and, anyway, I was so...distraught...I hardly knew where I was at the time.'

Oscar gave her a sidelong glance. 'I haven't been here myself much, either,' he admitted. 'There just never seems to be the time...or a suitable opportunity.'

Together, and not saying much, they wandered through the rooms on the ground floor, Oscar making notes as they went, though Helena didn't bother to follow suit. To her this was all so familiar, and little seemed to have changed, she noticed happily.

The glistening, well appointed kitchen was exactly as she knew it would be—the Aga still comfortingly warm and, in the dining room next door, the huge polished rosewood table was graced by the customary massive fresh flower arrangement in its centre. Helena smiled inwardly. Louise had obviously been determined that standards wouldn't be allowed to drop just because Isobel was no longer there.

The main sitting room leading into the conservatory was still furnished exactly the same, though the heavy ivory-coloured curtains at the full-length windows were new, she noted. The smaller occasional room next door was where Helena and Isobel had spent many evenings together playing Scrabble or watching television.

Further along was the library, which had always been Helena's favourite place, and now, as they went inside, she was stupidly relieved to see that her figurines were still there in their usual softly lit alcove.

But dominating the room on the opposite wall was the amazing gold-framed portrait of Isobel, and Helena had to put her hand over her mouth to stop her lips from trembling.

The painting was so touchingly real that it felt as if Isobel might get up from the chair she was seated in and step forward to greet the two of them in the room. She was shown wearing a soft, loosely fitting dress in a delicate shade of pink, her luxuriant silver hair elegantly coiffed on top, her large grey eyes smiling that gentle smile that Helena knew so well.

As with the other rooms, every available space was taken up to display all the ornaments to best effect and, as they turned to go, Oscar clicked his tongue, looking back briefly.

'My aunt was some collector,' he remarked obliquely. He refused to acquire much for his own homes, preferring to keep his space empty and clutter-free—much like his life.

'Yes—but there are collectors, and collectors,' Helena said, immediately on the defensive. 'Every single thing here is exactly right for its situation. Isobel had an eye for such things and she had wonderful taste—and it shows.' She paused, her head on one side. 'I don't know what you intend…I mean…I don't know what your opinion is, but I think it's best if everything is left exactly as it is for the time being—until after the sale of the house, I mean. I don't think we should move a thing. After all, any prospective buyer is going to be far more impressed when viewing a property that looks lived-in…loved…cared for.' She looked up at Oscar earnestly. 'Once everything's gone, the house will be just an empty shell. Lifeless.' The fact was, she admitted, she couldn't bear to see Isobel's beloved home broken up and sold off in bits and pieces, even though it was inevitable one day. To Helena, it would seem like the ultimate betrayal.

A nerve pulsed in Oscar's neck as he looked down at her, and he was aware of a certain hunger he hadn't felt for a very long time.

'We'll have to think about that,' he said, averting his gaze. Then, 'By the way, as far as I'm concerned, you're welcome to have anything you want… Take it now.' He paused. 'I don't need any of this,' he added.

Helena looked up at him seriously. No, I don't expect you do need anything, she thought. And did she, Helena, *need* anything? Despite her prospective inheritance, she could never envisage a time when she'd eventually settle somewhere which would happily house such wealth.

'I don't want to think about what I want, or don't want or need,' she said coolly. 'Not now. Not yet.' She paused, her gaze lingering on the figurines for a second. 'Only those over there—the shepherd and shepherdess—they are the only things that I would love to have.'

'Feel free to take them, but it'll all have to go eventually,' Oscar said firmly. 'Putting off the inevitable is just procrastination.' And procrastination hinders progress, he thought. He avoided procrastination wherever possible.

Presently, Helena followed Oscar up the wide staircase to the first floor. Immediately ahead, there were the four bedrooms, and around the corner to the next wing were two more, all with en suite bathrooms, the long windows on this generous landing lighting up the pattern on the richly carpeted floor.

Helena caught her breath as her memories kept flooding in. This was the first time in over nine years that she had been upstairs at Mulberry Court and she had to resist the temptation to run along and throw open the door of the room at the far end which had been 'hers'—the one in which she had stayed on the few occasions that her father had had to go away.

'Isobel had so many friends…I remember she was always entertaining, always having people to stay. These rooms were never empty for long,' Helena said, adding, 'I stayed here once or twice.'

'And…this was my room,' Oscar remarked, throwing open the door to the one they'd come to. He paused, looking around him. 'I used to enjoy my visits,' he added, and Helena's heart missed a beat. Could he actually have forgotten what his visits had meant to *her*—to both of them? Had he completely obliterated those times from his memory? Had they meant nothing?

After a few more minutes they went outside to wander through the grounds. The kitchen garden at the back was still flourishing and well-kept, Helena noticed, trying not to feel too sad that someone else was now in charge there. Though Benjamin didn't seem to be around today.

Nothing had changed outside, either, she thought, her eye drawn towards the secluded wooded path that led to their willow tree and, even after all this time,

Helena could feel her senses swim at the memory of the intoxicating moments she and Oscar had experienced together. Yet they were walking here now as if none of it had ever happened. As if they were two strangers in a foreign place…

Without her realizing it, Oscar had been looking down at her as they walked, his eyes following her gaze as she'd been reminiscing, and abruptly, as if he'd had enough of all this, he stopped and turned.

'I need to get back to the Inn,' he said briefly. 'I want to check my emails, and I'm expecting an important phone call.' He glanced at his watch. 'Anyway, it's gone one o'clock—you're probably ready for some lunch, aren't you?'

To her surprise, Helena wasn't feeling at all hungry, despite having had no breakfast. But another of Adam's delicious sandwiches suddenly seemed attractive.

'OK,' she said casually as they walked towards the car. 'And, actually, perhaps I ought to phone my boss. He hasn't been in the office for a few days, but I know he's back this weekend. Perhaps there's something he needs to tell me before Monday morning.'

As they drove back to the Horseshoe, something made Oscar decide to try his luck. He'd been thinking about it for the last hour or more, but he knew he'd have to pick his words carefully.

'Look, if it would be any help to you, Helena…I'd be more than happy for us to get a true valuation of Mulberry Court, the contents, everything,' he said carefully, 'and, allowing for inflation, to pay you a very generous half of the total, now. It would relieve you of all responsibility, and you've said you don't want anything for yourself…other than those figurines.' He turned to glance at her as she sat beside him impassively. 'It would save you a great deal of trouble…'

There was complete silence from Helena, and he went on, 'Of course, the sale can't proceed for a year, as we both know, but if you agree, at least one of us will be spared considerable interruption to our life. John Mayhew would sort out the transaction for us, I'm sure,' he added.

He drew into the car park and looked across at Helena, noting her flushed features.

'You've forgotten what I said, Oscar,' she said, staring straight ahead. 'I've already told you—I want to be able to play my part in making sure that we deal sensitively with all the material possessions which Isobel held dear.'

Now she did look at him, her eyes almost crackling with distaste. She knew what his game was—he wanted her out of the way! For his own convenience, not hers. She was an unnecessary encumbrance! Although he may have cared for her once, he didn't care about her now and he didn't care about Isobel's lovely things, either, which he'd make sure went to the highest bidder.

She opened her door, then looked back at him squarely.

'I am grateful for your concern at the "interruption" to my busy life,' she said, 'but…thanks, but no thanks, Oscar. Mulberry Court and I have a very long way to go before we're through.' And with that she got out of the car and walked swiftly towards the entrance to the Inn.

\* \* \*

Back in his room, Oscar took his laptop from the wardrobe and threw it down on the bed, admitting to feeling unusually distracted. Exploring Mulberry Court this morning had ruffled his memories more than he'd expected and he'd felt his aunt's presence in every corner. He knew he had always felt closer to her than to his own parents, and her wise gaze as she'd looked down at him from that portrait had unnerved him slightly.

He shrugged. Anyway, he'd probably blown any chance of Helena agreeing to his perhaps unrealistic proposal. It had obviously been the wrong moment to have mentioned it, he thought. If ever there was to be a right one. He remembered enough about her to know that she had a mind of her own, and would not easily be persuaded into making decisions she might later regret.

But what to do with the house and its contents was a totally insignificant matter compared with the far more vital one to be handled, he thought. Because he had the distinct feeling that he'd been awakened from a hundred-year sleep and by the most desirable woman he'd ever known. Or was ever likely to know. But had he woken up in time?

# CHAPTER THREE

TRYING to subdue her somewhat ruffled feelings, Helena went into her bathroom to wash her hands and put a brush through her hair.

The morning had been a rather emotional experience, she thought. At certain points it had seemed to her as if she and Oscar were trespassing, which was obviously silly because Mulberry Court was legally theirs. But Isobel's presence had seemed to follow them as they'd wandered through her home, and it seemed wrong to Helena that she hadn't been there as well.

But what was really getting to her now was Oscar's proposal that she should wash her hands of their present situation and leave him to it. Even if it would obviously mean that straight away a very considerable amount of money would come her way. She sighed briefly. He wouldn't have the sensitivity to understand her feelings—the look on his face had said everything. But she felt, acutely, that Isobel had left this assignment to the pair of them, to be handled with dignity, obviously thinking that two heads were better than one.

Helena frowned as she dwelt on all this. Perhaps she was being mean, not giving Oscar the benefit of the doubt. Perhaps he really *did* have her interests at heart.

Then she shook her head, responding to that thought. No, this was all about him, wanting to go it alone without the handicap of someone else possibly having an opinion that didn't match his. He was, after all, a cut-throat businessman—he had to be, surely, as the head of the Theotokis dynasty? Sentiment didn't come into it because everyone knew that there was no room for sentiment in business.

With her head beginning to throb with all these teeming thoughts, Helena decided that for the moment she'd had enough. Taking her mobile from her bag, she dialled his number.

'Oscar, I've developed rather a bad headache,' she said calmly. 'So I'm going to have a lie down. Perhaps we can continue our...discussions...later. At supper?'

There was barely a pause as he responded snappily—she'd obviously interrupted something. 'Fine. I'll book a table downstairs for eight.' And, after a moment, 'If you think you'll have recovered by then.'

Helena could imagine him raising his eyes impatiently at what she'd just said. Then she sighed. She didn't usually have negative thoughts about people, about anyone, but somehow, she and Oscar... It had to be the disparity in their positions which had ignited the latent inferiority complex which she occasionally had to battle with, she thought. Well, thanks to Isobel, for the moment she was now exactly on a par with him. There was no need for her to feel that he had any advantage over her at all, and she must keep reminding herself of that. For one year, they were to be partners.

'Oh, I'll be fine by then,' she reassured him. 'I'll see you at eight.' And with that she rang off. Anyway, she thought, he wouldn't be sorry to have some time to concentrate on far more important things.

As he drank his glass of whisky in the bar, Oscar had to accept that the morning hadn't gone as he'd expected. He'd fondly imagined that he and Helena could have had a straightforward discussion about his aunt's possessions—to make a list of what they wanted to take away with them, wanted to sell, to at least have made a beginning. He'd fully expected Helena to want some of the contents of Mulberry Court for herself, maybe a picture or two, or a small chair or some books, things that would easily fit into her car to take away. Arrangements could be made for anything else she might fancy to be delivered to her place later. But apparently she didn't wish for anything at all except those ornaments, and she'd made it clear where her instincts lay—to leave it all in situ.

Helena was just lying on the bed reading her book and sipping the last of her coffee when her mobile rang. As she answered it, Simon Harcourt's voice met her ears and she frowned slightly. 'Oh—hello, Simon,' she began, then listened for several minutes while he explained the reason for his call.

Interrupting at last, Helena said, 'Actually, Simon, I won't be available to come to the conference with you that weekend because…I'm afraid I shall actually be giving you my notice on Monday,' and before he could say anything, she went on quickly, 'I've learned that I've just inherited a property in the country, and it's not a straightforward matter, so I need to leave London almost at once.' She swallowed, hard. Well, she'd burned her boats as far as Simon was concerned. Where she stood with Oscar was another matter!

Helena slipped into her simple knee-length three-quarter-sleeve aubergine dress—which she'd decided at the last moment to bring with her—and glanced at herself in the mirror. The garment was still a favourite item in her wardrobe, and whenever she wore it she always made a point of sweeping her hair up on top, which she felt suited the low boat-shaped neckline. Her only make-up was her light foundation and a slick of eyeshadow. Her long pearl-quartz earrings completed the picture.

As the ancient clock on the landing chimed eight, she made her way downstairs. Oscar was standing at the bar, talking to Adam, and both men looked up as she approached, Oscar with a heightening of his pulse, which he tried to ignore.

As Helena approached, she smiled quickly, noting Oscar's undeniably sexy appearance. He was dressed in light trousers and designer jacket and open-neck shirt; his hair had been newly washed, the dark, determined jaw obviously clean-shaven. A perfect model for any advertisement, she thought instinctively.

Immediately, Adam came from behind the bar, two large menus in his hands, and beckoned the two to follow him, leading them over to a table in the far corner of the restaurant.

Holding Helena's chair out for her, he said, 'Tonight's special dish is seared sea bass—caught this morning,' he added proudly. Then he took the just-opened bottle of wine from the ice bucket on the table and filled their glasses. 'I'll be back for your order as soon as you've decided,' he said.

'He seems to run a very tight ship here,' Oscar commented, glancing at the man's retreating figure. 'By the way, I hope you approve of this...of my choice,' he said, picking up his glass.

How could Helena not approve? It was vintage champagne. She put the glass to her lips and sipped at the frothy bubbles, looking across at him steadily. 'Is this by way of a celebration?' she asked enigmatically.

Oscar raised a brow. 'If you like,' he said casually. Well, they had just been left a fortune. 'I hope you don't have a problem with champagne?'

Helena smiled briefly. 'I've only had it twice before—at weddings,' she said. 'And while I'm no connoisseur, I always found it a very...special...drink.' She paused. 'Thank you,' she added.

A muscle pounded in Oscar's jaw as he gazed across at her. She looked so unutterably lovely he couldn't keep his eyes off her. Her hair was shining, its thick bands glinting like gold in the flickering candlelight, but she did look pale, and he said briefly, 'Are you feeling OK now...has your headache really gone?'

'Absolutely,' Helena said lightly. 'And, as a matter of fact, I'm feeling quite hungry,' she added. She picked up her menu, hoping he didn't notice it trembling slightly between her fingers. In a thousand lifetimes could she ever have imagined she'd be so close to Oscar again? To breathe the same air that he was breathing? To watch that firm mouth with the immaculate teeth, white against his suntan? He wasn't merely good-looking, not merely handsome; he had that stunning, sultry, Mediterranean charisma that turned every gullible female heart to jelly.

As they gave Adam their order and waited for their meal to arrive, Oscar said, 'I've had time to think things over this afternoon and I can't help wondering if it's the right thing to be leaving the house unoccupied for so long.' He drank from his glass. 'There's a big problem with squatters taking over empty premises—certainly in London at the moment—and I understand that once they're in, it's difficult to get rid of them.' He frowned thoughtfully. 'Of course, I know that Benjamin and Louise will always be close at hand, but that wouldn't stop determined individuals from gaining entry on a dark night—and if that did happen it would certainly add to our problems.' He paused. 'Maybe we should consider a short-term let,' he added, 'as a safety measure.'

Helena could hardly believe what she'd just heard Oscar say. This could clinch it for her! Play right into her hands! Had her guardian angel—who'd been somewhat absent lately—decided to put in an appearance?

Presently, enjoying their meal—they'd both selected the sea bass with salad—Oscar said bluntly, 'So, perhaps we ought to catch up. What's been happening to you in the last ten years or so?' He speared a cherry tomato expertly with his fork. 'Isobel informed me that you got a place at a top London university.'

'Yes. Amazing, wasn't it?' Helena said lightly. 'Amazing that a modest secondary school in the sticks can take students to such elevated places.' She looked down quickly, hoping that hadn't sounded like a dig at his private boarding school education which had taken him to Cambridge, and later to Harvard.

She went on hurriedly. 'Anyway, I got a respectable degree in Economics and International Business Studies, and my present job is with the Harcourt Employment Agency,' she added, 'but, as I've mentioned, I hope to soon be on the move.'

'So, where next, then?' he enquired.

Without looking at him, Helena said, 'I'm not sure yet because I haven't made up my mind. I want to give myself time to really look around before deciding. And in the meantime, of course, temporary employment is not hard to find in the city.'

There was silence for a moment, then he said, 'You live alone?'

'Yes,' Helena replied promptly.

'So, no man in your life…no marriage ties on the horizon for you?'

Helena shook her head quickly. 'No.' She decided to lob the ball back to him. 'And you, Oscar? No wife and children at your beck and call?'

That familiar tilt of his upper lip. 'No,' he said flatly. 'I have a feeling that that's a rather unlikely scenario,' he added, before resuming his meal.

That remark didn't surprise Helena. He was obviously not the marrying kind, though there must be a permanent and very hopeful queue of women at his disposal. From his lofty perch in life he could look down, take his pick and walk away. Besides, mistresses were a far more convenient answer to the emotional needs of men like him, weren't they? No need to commit himself in any way.

He interrupted her thoughts. 'I can't help wondering why you're still free and single,' he said. 'London is a big city with plenty of men after beautiful women. How have you managed to escape their clutches?'

Helena felt a rush of pleasure at the remark—because it implied the sort of compliment she hadn't expected from Oscar. Not any more.

Then, feeling unusually relaxed, she went on, 'Not long after my father died, I did meet Jason, and we were together for some time.' She paused. 'He was a great help at the time and seemed to understand how I was feeling, how much I was missing not being able to ring my dad, tell him the latest news.' She sighed. 'When I look back, I realize Jason must have listened for hours to me feeling sorry for myself.' She looked across at Oscar quickly. 'Perhaps I should have grown up by then,' she added.

Oscar made no comment, but his eyes had softened at her words, realizing how much he was loving watching her mouth, the fleeting expressions on her face as she'd spoken. He'd always known that Helena's mother had died years ago, and that Daniel and his daughter had been extremely close, so it was natural that Daniel's death would have hit her hard. And, despite all outward appearances, he recognized that touching vulnerability about Helena that had always stirred him.

'Big cities can be very lonely places,' he said briefly.

Helena kept her eyes on her plate. She wasn't going to say anything at all about Mark, who she'd thought she'd been deeply in love with—and who she'd imagined had returned her feelings. Their unexpected breakup had hurt, and the split, when it happened, had come as a total shock. She didn't want to think about it ever again, or the fact that he'd cheated on her with an old mutual friend. But, even worse, Mark had told Helena that he found her cool and distant. He hadn't mentioned the word frigid, but the implication was there, and she was still finding it hard to accept.

'Anyway,' Helena went on, touching her lips with her napkin, 'eventually I realized that I was using Jason just as a shoulder to cry on, and that was hardly fair because I felt nothing for him, not really. He was nice, and very kind, but nothing more. It was time to let him go and stop wasting any more time on me.' She paused. 'And I still feel terribly guilty about it.'

She took a sip from her glass, then smiled briefly. 'But I needn't have worried about him. He soon found someone else, and I think they're engaged to be married.'

Oscar raised an eyebrow. 'Jason was obviously a man with a single-track purpose,' he said. And, after a moment, added, 'Each to his own, I suppose.'

Helena made no comment. Being a settled family man was never going to be on Oscar's agenda, she thought. How could she ever have thought otherwise?

As they were finishing the last of the meal, he said casually, 'My aunt was very upset about your father's death at the time… He'd been a valued member of her staff for so many years.' He paused. 'And he was still comparatively young, wasn't he?'

'He was fifty-nine,' Helena said shortly. 'I had already begun planning a party for his sixtieth birthday.'

There was quite a long silence after that, then Helena

said, in a deliberately bright tone, 'And your parents, Oscar? How are they?'

He paused before answering. 'My father no longer works…hasn't done for a long time. He and my mother live permanently in their place in Bermuda.' He reached across to refill their glasses. 'My uncle—my father's remaining brother—has also retired, so I am the only working family member left.'

The significance of what Oscar had just said didn't need to be spelt out. That he was the last in a long line and that, although it was unthinkable that the firm would ever founder, if he had no heirs the family name would inevitably die out.

'And of course Isobel was the last of her generation?' Helena asked.

'Yes, she was, and the only Englishwoman—the only "foreigner"—to infiltrate our community, our enclave,' Oscar replied. 'It had never been done before. But all the family loved her and, in spite of all the places she could have lived around the world, her base was always Mulberry Court. Though of course she travelled extensively when my uncle was alive.'

'Yes, I know,' Helena said. 'I was always fascinated by her description of all the places she'd seen. She made it all so real.'

By now, her third glass of champagne was having its effect on Helena—she seldom drank, and was unused to alcohol of this quality. She certainly hadn't expected to feel as comfortable as this with Oscar, not after all this time. Taking a grape from the cheese tray in front of them, she nibbled it thoughtfully and looked across at him.

'So, where do you live—usually, I mean?' she asked.

'Oh, here, there and everywhere,' he said casually. 'I've an apartment in London, a place in Greece and an apartment on the Upper East Side, New York, but I don't stay anywhere for long. I've never felt settled enough to put down any roots. I'm travelling so much all the time, but I suppose my place in Athens is my useful bolt-hole.'

Helena immediately remembered when he had promised to take her to his homeland one day, but she didn't voice her thoughts.

They'd finished their coffee and Helena picked up her almost full glass of champagne, drinking it down to the last drop. Then, after a few moments, she said slowly, her brow slightly furrowed in thought, 'You know, you may have a point about a possible squatter problem at Mulberry Court.' She paused. 'And I think I might have a solution to that, Oscar.'

'Oh?'

'Well...' She spoke carefully. 'I could arrange to come and stay at the house myself for a short while... Well, a month or so, at least.'

Oscar raised his eyebrows. 'Would that be possible?' he enquired. 'I mean—your present arrangements in London, your job...your current home?''

'Actually, it would fit in rather well,' Helena said casually. 'When I switch jobs—which I intend to do almost immediately—it'll mean I'm homeless because my cottage belongs to Simon Harcourt.' She hesitated. 'I feel I need a sort of breathing space in my life at the moment, and I'd certainly like to get out of London— even if it is just temporarily.'

Oscar pursed his lips, thinking about this for a second. 'The house is rather isolated, isn't it... Are you sure you like the idea of being there on your own?' he said.

Helena smiled briefly. 'I'm used to being on my own,' she said. 'Besides, the cottages are less than a minute's walk away...I'd always have Louise for company—and Benjamin is obviously always about as well.'

Oscar nodded slowly, feeling slightly surprised at Helena's suggestion, but agreeing that it would be a useful move for the moment. He shrugged.

'Well, why not?' he said. Mulberry Court belonged to Helena now, he thought—she had a perfect right to stay if she wanted to. 'When do you anticipate that this plan could be put into action?' he asked.

'By the beginning of May,' Helena said at once—there was no need to tell Oscar she'd already given in her notice. She looked up at him, her eyes shining at how easily her hopes had materialized. 'And I can always get temping work in Dorchester if I run short of funds.'

Oscar was about to offer some interim financial input—then thought better of it. Helena was an independent woman with clearly a very firm hold on her private affairs. And she'd already turned down one offer he'd made, in no uncertain terms.

'Just think—I shall be Mistress of Mulberry Court!' Helena said. 'It'll be like the games I used to play when I was a child...pretending, imagining things!' She knew she still felt totally overwhelmed at all that had happened in the last few days, and being here with Oscar

was the most overwhelming thing of all! An excited
giggle almost turned into an attack of hiccups as she
pointlessly picked up her empty glass, then put it down
again. And at once, seeing her flushed cheeks and realizing that Helena had no head for alcohol, Oscar got
up and came round to her side of the table to help her
to her feet.

'It's been a long day, and I think it's time you were
in bed, Helena,' he said shortly.

Helena stood rather shakily and picked up her bag
and, with Oscar's hand under her elbow, they made
their way upstairs, pausing outside Helena's door for a
second while she searched for her key. And with every
masculine impulse urging him, Oscar was acutely
aware of a treacherous warm tide of feeling in his groin.
In any other circumstances, with any other woman, it
would have been a foregone conclusion that he spent
the night in her bed. With his hand lightly on the small
of her back, he said, 'You're quite sure about all this—
about staying by yourself at Mulberry Court?' He hesitated. 'If you change your mind, we can always get John
Mayhew to find a suitable tenant.'

'There's absolutely no need for anyone else to live in
our…in the house—not yet,' Helena said quickly, looking up at him, painfully conscious of his dark, magnetic
gaze as he looked down at her in the subdued lighting.
'It's going to all work out *perfectly*,' she added. 'I just
know it is.'

And in an insanely impulsive, grateful reflex action,
she raised her head and kissed him lightly on the cheek
before turning away, but not before Oscar's hand was at

the back of her neck, pulling her around towards him firmly, pulling her face closer to his own.

But with every warning bell ringing in her head, Helena avoided his lips, her hands shaking so much that she dropped her key. She stooped quickly to pick it up, then unlocked her door and glanced back at him, smiling tremulously.

'Goodnight, Oscar,' she said.

Inside, Helena closed the door behind her and stood with her back against it for a few moments, waiting for her heart to stop almost leaping from her chest. She must have been *mad* to have kissed Oscar like that, she thought, because he'd obviously read something into it which she hadn't meant! She'd only given him a brief peck on the cheek, that was all! A sort of normal thing to someone she'd known for such a long time…

But with her skin tingling at the thought, Helena knew that Oscar had wanted to kiss her! She kept repeating the thought over and over in her mind… He'd wanted to kiss her and somehow, *somehow*, she'd managed to turn away! She'd managed to avoid the very dream she had so often relived in her mind. How had she managed to stop herself from collapsing into those strong arms, feeling the weight of him against her, letting that manly, musky smell of him ignite all her primitive instincts…?

But she *had* managed it. Because she'd been there before, she reminded herself bleakly—and she was never going to risk another unhappy ending like the one which had driven her to unimaginable despair.

* * *

In his own room two doors away, Oscar stood by the window for a few moments, clenching his jaw. He'd just had the unique experience of being turned down by a woman!

The sensuous mouth twisted as he let his mind dwell on the what-might-have-been... He would now be slowly undressing her, he thought, caressing her, using all his natural abilities to inflame her, to make her want him as much as he had wanted her.

He turned away abruptly. In the bathroom, he had a cold shower then dried himself briskly, drawing the huge towel back and forth across his tanned shoulders, his glistening muscles flexing and hardening with the effort. Catching a sight of himself in the mirror, he leaned forward thoughtfully. His brow seemed to be developing more lines every time he looked, he thought.

As for Helena...Helena was still as dove-soft, as flawless, as she had been on the first day he'd set eyes on her.

# CHAPTER FOUR

HELENA woke the following morning having had the most blissful night's sleep she could ever remember. A night full of dreams in which she'd lain in Oscar's arms, felt his lips claim hers over and over again, felt his hands trace the curves of her body...the sort of dreams which she had stopped having a very long time ago. But last night it had been so wonderful, so real, she had awoken, her heart drumming wildly, and had fully expected to see him there, raised above her, his eyes alight with desire...

Now, she sat up and rested her head on her knees. It was so stupid of her to have given him that peck on the cheek, she told herself again. And what hot-blooded, alpha male—especially one like Oscar Theotokis— ever resisted an opportunity? Yet Helena was honest enough to admit that another millisecond, and she would have been helpless in his arms. Because, in spite of everything, she knew she probably still loved Oscar, was still in love with him, even after all these years. And the pathetic position she was in was dangerous, because he didn't love her, not any more, and he probably never had. Lust and love were two entirely different things—everyone knew that—and it was lust undoubtedly fuelled by that amazing champagne that he must have been feeling last night. Even so, she acknowledged a shiver of pleasure at the thought.

She got out of bed and went into the bathroom, groaning at the sight of herself. Her hair was all over the place and needed immediate attention if she was to face Oscar with no telltale signs of the restless night they had shared—if only in her dreams! She'd be sitting opposite him in an hour, having breakfast and making desultory conversation—and hoping that nothing in her eyes or manner would reveal the emotion still simmering just below the surface of her thoughts.

With rugged determination, Helena forced herself to concentrate on the present. One good thing was, she'd be able to tell Simon tomorrow that she was definitely leaving his employment. She made a face as she recalled her boss's persistent, unwanted attentions. No, she wouldn't be sorry to leave the Harcourt Agency, she thought. Though she would miss the other girls, plus the salary, she had to admit.

It was funny, she thought, as she smoothed lotion over her arms and body, that although she'd come to accept that she'd been left a considerable inheritance, she just couldn't take it in, or what it might eventually mean to her when the house was sold. She certainly did not want any money in the meantime, as Oscar had suggested, because until the sale of the house, there really wasn't any. Not really. It was still all on paper.

The far more important reason for her to feel almost dizzy with excitement was that Oscar had seemed quite happy for her to stay at Mulberry Court for a while. It would have been *so* embarrassing if he'd found a reason to object. But he hadn't.

Suddenly, a wave of optimism ran through Helena. She had just taken a very big step to tread a new path. And somehow she felt it was the right thing to do at this particular point. And now she had the prospect of spending spring and early summer in the place she loved best in all the world. Could it get any better?

She got ready and presently went downstairs to the restaurant. Oscar was already there, and when he saw her approach he stood up without smiling, and Helena coloured slightly. Did he remember their brief encounter last night? His undeniable gesture of familiarity? If he did, his expression gave nothing away. He was wearing casual trousers and a jacket, his round-neck, fine grey T-shirt exhibiting taut, well-toned muscles, and she deliberately avoided looking at him.

'Hello... Did you sleep well?' he said slowly, his voice seductively smooth, even at this early hour. Helena sat down on the chair he'd pulled out for her, tucking a stray frond of hair behind her ear.

'Very well, thank you,' she said, surprised at how easy it was to tell a blatant lie. She picked up the breakfast menu even though she didn't feel like much to eat. 'You?' she enquired.

'I seldom sleep more than four, maybe five hours,' he said. 'So I've been able to get some work done.' He shrugged briefly. 'As a matter of fact it looks as if I have to go back to Athens tomorrow. I'd hoped to be in the UK until the end of April... So if there's anything at all that we can sort out today, that would help,' he added, omitting to make the point that they could have done quite a lot if Helena had fallen in with his wish to more or less empty the house of its contents straight away.

He raised a hand to summon the waiter to take their breakfast order. 'We can at least talk with Benjamin about the grounds,' he went on, 'because it's obvious that he needs to be retained until further notice, and it would have been good to have seen Louise, too... Whatever happens, the property must be adequately maintained for the next twelve months.'

Helena adjusted the knife beside her plate carefully and picked up her napkin. It was obviously back to business this morning, she thought. That spontaneous, fleetingly amorous gesture of Oscar's last night hadn't meant anything at all—and he'd obviously completely forgotten about it. Well, that was no surprise—and that was good—wasn't it?

Later, as Oscar drove smoothly out of the car park, Helena settled herself back into the luxurious passenger seat and stared out of the window. So far, not a single mention had been made of her wish to stay at Mulberry Court. She hoped that he wasn't regretting it—or maybe he'd forgotten about that too, she thought.

But, as if reading her thoughts, he said, without looking at her, 'So, there are obviously going to be quite a few details of your own to sort out, Helena... What are you going to do about your personal belongings, your furniture?'

'Oh, I don't have very much at all,' Helena assured him quickly. 'I've only ever lived in furnished accommodation,' she explained, 'and before the cottage I shared with Anna, my friend from university. But she got married last year.'

Helena paused before going on. 'So, apart from books—rather a lot of books, I must admit—and clothes and bedding—and a few pictures, of course,' she went on, 'that's about it. It's only a few things so I'll be travelling very light,' she added.

Oscar smiled inwardly. He could already picture the sight of Helena's elderly car crammed to the roof with her 'few things'. And judging by everything he'd seen her wearing so far—including today's choice of a soft jade cashmere knit over skinny jeans—the contents of her wardrobe would probably take up most of the space.

They eventually came to the narrow road which led to Mulberry Court, and almost at once the cottages came into view and Helena leaned forward excitedly.

'Oh, look—Louise is there in the garden!' she exclaimed.

'She must have got back yesterday afternoon,' Oscar said, 'and there's Benjamin coming down the path—with Rosie, his adored hound,' he added.

Helena felt a surge of happiness at seeing the black Retriever bounding around the gardener's feet. The cottage wouldn't be the same without a dog, she thought. The fact that Bella, their black Labrador, had had to be put down just a couple of weeks before Daniel had died so suddenly had only added to Helena's sense of loss at the time. It was as if her father and the dog had refused to be separated.

Oscar drew the car to a halt, and he and Helena got out. At once Louise turned in surprise, then ran up and threw her arms around Helena's neck, hugging her tightly.

'Well, what a *wonderful* surprise to see you—and you, Mr Oscar,' she added, smiling up diffidently.

'I didn't expect that we'd see you this weekend, Louise,' Oscar began, and Louise cut in.

'No, well, I wasn't going to come back until Tuesday, but I don't like the house to be unattended for too long, and anyway I was beginning to feel homesick—isn't that silly?' Louise's open, friendly face broke into another grin and Helena thought—no, that's not silly. That's not silly at all.

By this time Rosie was determined to be noticed, winding her body around and around Helena's legs and barking, and Helena immediately bent to make a fuss of the dog.

'What a lovely animal,' she said, trying to avoid a very wet kiss on the nose.

Oscar spoke again. 'Helena, let me introduce you. Benjamin—this is Helena... Her father was my aunt's right-hand man for many years, doing the job you're doing. Before Helena went away to university she lived here in the cottage, so there isn't anything she doesn't know about Mulberry Court and its surroundings.'

Benjamin, a tall man, with a mass of unruly greying hair, shook Helena's hand warmly. 'Louise has told me all about your father, Helena, and I can only hope to keep up the standards he set here.'

Helena flushed with pride. 'We were walking in the grounds yesterday, Benjamin, and everything looked wonderful,' she assured him.

Louise pulled Helena towards her again. 'What are

we standing out here for?' she demanded. 'Come in, and let me make us all some coffee.'

'Thanks, but I must be getting on,' Benjamin said, clicking his fingers for the dog to follow him, and after they'd made their farewells the others went into Louise's warm and cosy cottage.

Presently, as they sat drinking their coffee, Oscar said, 'Have you been informed of the terms of my great-aunt's will, Louise?'

Louise looked away, her expression troubled. 'Only that I'm to receive a very generous sum of money,' she said. 'And also that I've been asked to stay on here until the…um…future of the house is decided.' She sighed. 'It will be so terrible to think of new owners taking over,' she added. 'But I know it's got to happen, and everyone has to face unpleasant changes from time to time.'

'Well, you needn't worry about that yet,' Oscar said. He paused, clearing his throat. 'Actually, my aunt has left the entire estate jointly between Helena and myself, but there is to be no sale for a year. And…' he shot a quick glance at Helena '…as a matter of fact, in a few weeks' time Helena will be coming to live at Mulberry Court herself.'

Louise's face lit up with delight. 'Well, I shall sleep easy for the first time since Mrs Theotokis died,' she said firmly. 'I hate not knowing what's going on—and Benjamin has been worried, too. We'd imagined we'd be packing our bags by now.'

Oscar put his cup down and stood up. 'Although we were up at the house yesterday, we need to take another look around today,' he said, looking down at Louise. 'Something might occur to us that could be done now.'

'I've been up there most days since Isobel died,' Louise said. 'Opened all the windows and kept the dust down.'

'Yes, we thought everything looked as perfect as ever, Louise—' Helena broke in '—including the lovely flower arrangement on the dining room table.'

Louise nodded. 'You'll have noticed that I've kept the Aga going—well, Benjamin and I take it in turns,' she added. Then, 'I emptied the fridge but not the freezer—and I haven't gone through the kitchen cupboards, either.' She hesitated. 'I didn't really know how much I should do for the time being. Mulberry Court has felt rather like a ship without a captain,' she added.

'Well, we'll be more of a crew now, Louise,' Helena said, 'as soon as I've settled things up in London. I should be back in three, four weeks at the most.'

Oscar and Helena left the cottage and after a second Louise followed them. 'Here—you'll want to make yourselves a drink up there,' she said, handing Helena a pint of milk. 'And if there's anything you need, just shout.'

As they drove slowly up the drive towards the house, Helena glanced across at Oscar. 'Isobel was lucky to have such a loyal person working for her all that time, wasn't she?'

Oscar tilted his head to one side. 'My aunt obviously appreciated her very much.' He narrowed his eyes briefly, thinking that it was good that Louise would be staying on at the cottage because it would be company for Helena while she was staying here.

He drew the car smoothly to a halt, and they both got out and started walking towards the main entrance of the house. The weather was bright with a high wind, making Helena's loosely tied hair fly wildly, almost covering her face for a second or two. As they got to the large oak front door, she tucked her hair safely behind her ears and reached into her bag for the keys to the house.

'My turn to open up today,' she said lightly, glancing up.

Inside, every corner of the place was lit up by shafts of strong morning sunlight and, as Oscar followed Helena into the kitchen, he said, 'I'll go and find Benjamin, tell him he'll be needed here for the next twelve months.' He paused. 'Of course, the new owners may decide to keep him on when the time comes. Left unattended, the place would be a wilderness in no time,' he added.

Helena didn't need reminding of that. It had always been a full-time job for her father, who'd only ever hired extra help in the autumn for harvesting the fruit.

She put her bag and the bottle of milk down and glanced up at Oscar. 'I liked him—Benjamin,' she said. 'He seemed really nice, and he and Louise seemed happy enough, relaxed enough, together, didn't they? It could have been really difficult if they hadn't got on—living next door to each other.' She smiled. 'And that lovely dog…Benjamin obviously worships her,' she added.

Oscar nodded. 'Yes, his luck really changed when my aunt interviewed him.'

Helena looked up curiously. 'Oh?'

'Apparently he had lost his job in the city and was staying with a friend in the area who told him about the vacancy at Mulberry Court. When Isobel heard his story she considered that Benjamin's genuine longing to be out in the open air—and his determination to learn quickly and to work hard if she'd give him the opportunity—were sufficient reasons to employ him.'

'What caused all the problems?' Helena asked.

'Oh, it was a common scenario…successful city trader is unexpectedly made redundant, loses his wife and his home all at the same time…' Oscar said. 'There are apparently two children involved as well, who he doesn't get to see very often. So Isobel decided that Mulberry Court might be just the thing for him to turn his life around. And from all outward appearances, she seems to have been right,' he added.

Oscar turned and went towards the door. 'I shan't be long,' he said, not looking back.

After he'd gone, Helena stood looking around her and marvelled again that this all now belonged to *her*… well, almost…and not just the house, but everything in it! And although it was to be only for one year, she was going to make the most of every second of the time she'd be staying here. And finding her way around the kitchen again would be a good start.

As Louise had said, the fridge was empty and had been turned off, but the freezer was still reasonably full of the usual staple items, none of which had yet exceeded their sell-by date, Helena noted, as she searched through the contents. This would still be OK for her own use when she returned in what she hoped would only be a couple of weeks.

The numerous cupboards held everything she'd need to keep herself fed while she was living here, and she could always shop for more, she thought, as she looked along the shelves. All the basic ingredients necessary for simple cooking were there, neatly arranged in Louise's usual way. Helena smiled briefly. She was looking forward to having some time to cook for herself here in this wonderful kitchen, where all that time ago Isobel's housekeeper had shown her most of the tricks of the trade.

After a while, she left the kitchen and wandered again through the rooms on the ground floor, before going slowly up the wide staircase. She paused for a moment to gaze out of the long landing windows at the garden beyond, biting her lip. It was really difficult to think of this place as belonging to her, she thought, whatever it said in Isobel's will. This was a Theotokis property—Oscar was a Theotokis so it was obviously different for him. But she was the outsider. And once the house was sold next year, there would never be a reason for her to come near the place ever again.

Back down in the kitchen, Helena glanced up at the big clock on the wall. It was almost lunch time, and Oscar still hadn't come back. She suddenly remembered the food she'd seen in the freezer and there were several packets of unopened staples in the cupboard, and they could have tea or coffee with the milk Louise had given them. Enough for a simple meal, Helena thought, setting the things out on the table. She wondered, idly, when he intended going back to London...

He obviously wouldn't be leaving it late because he'd said he would be flying back to Greece tomorrow, and anyway, she herself needed to leave in an hour or so. She wanted to be in the office early tomorrow, to start clearing her desk and tying up ends.

She decided to make some tea—she was certainly ready for some, she realized. She put out two mugs and plates and knives, then went over to fill the kettle, her mind going over and over all her hopes and plans and trying to keep her developing feelings for Oscar firmly out of her thoughts.

She stood waiting for a couple of minutes until the kettle came to boiling point, then she picked it up and was just starting to pour when Oscar returned, a sudden gust making the back door slam behind him loudly, and Helena automatically jumped, turning quickly, before letting out a shriek of pain as a stream of boiling water coursed over her hand and arm, almost making her drop the kettle on the floor. 'Ow... Oh... Ow!' she cried desperately. *'Ow!'*

Immediately seeing what had happened, Oscar cursed out loud.

*'Heleena!'* he exclaimed, reaching her in three long strides, and taking the kettle from her. Then, turning the cold tap on full, he grasped her hand and held it under the gushing water while Helena winced in agony.

For several minutes they both just stood there, Oscar not letting go of Helena's hand from under the running water, looking down at her, his eyes intense with concern as Helena tried hard to take control of herself.

'That was the most idiotic thing I've done in a long time,' she wailed, almost crying with the unbelievable pain. She automatically leaned into Oscar, who had put his arm tightly around her waist to support her, and presently the anguish began to lessen and he gently let her go, passing her some tissues from the box on the counter top. He bent his head to examine her reddening flesh, muttering incomprehensible oaths under his breath.

'Oh…*agapi mou*,' he said softly, and Helena closed her eyes at the memory of that expression of endearment she hadn't heard for so long, and even after all this time it sent a tremor of warmth through her thighs right down to her toes.

After a few moments, seeing how shocked it had made her, he led Helena over to the table to sit down, glancing at the few things she'd laid out for their lunch. 'You really shouldn't have gone to all this trouble,' he joked.

She dabbed her hand very cautiously with the tissues, not looking at him. Her skin wasn't broken, she noted gratefully. But it was bright red and the incident had given her a horrible fright, making her tremble visibly. And Oscar had seen it.

Without saying any more, he went over to make the tea, before bringing it across to Helena. 'Here,' he said gently, 'drink this—it'll help.'

After a few cautious sips, Helena pulled herself together and glanced up at him. 'So…you obviously saw Benjamin,' she said, trying to act normally, and Oscar nodded.

'Yes, he was more than happy to be here for another year. At least he's being given time to come to terms with the prospect of yet another dramatic change in his personal circumstances.'

As she tried to nibble at a biscuit, Helena said, 'And we know that he and Louise will take good care of Mulberry Court for the time being,' she added.

Oscar took a mouthful of some of the food Helena had prepared before speaking. 'Have you seen anything in the house that you might want to take away with you, I mean eventually, apart from the figures?' he asked, and Helena cut in.

'No, nothing. Anyway, I shall have more time to consider it when I come back,' she said. 'I intend returning to London early this afternoon…after I've picked up my things and paid my bill at the Inn,' she added.

'I've already settled our bill there,' Oscar said casually, and Helena looked at him quickly. She hadn't realized he'd already paid for their stay.

'How much do I owe you?' she asked, reaching for her bag.

Oscar paused. 'I've forgotten,' he said, taking another biscuit from the plate. 'but I remember thinking it was very reasonable.'

Helena opened her purse. 'Well, then, try and remember,' she said firmly. He needn't act Mr Philanthropist, she thought, just because he was unbelievably rich. She had more than enough money to pay her own way.

'Forget it,' he said. 'It's not important.'

Helena sighed, but decided to let the matter drop. She wasn't in the mood for any arguments—and anyway, she'd never win one with Oscar. She sipped at her tea again, aware that they were now sitting so close their knees and thighs were touching under the table. She knew she could have moved away slightly, but she didn't want to. The warmth of him was comforting… more than comforting…and she had to choke back the sensuous thoughts that would come bubbling up every time she was anywhere near him. Fate had been kind— and cruel—at the same time, she decided. She had been left an inheritance she could never have dreamed of, but it meant that the drop dead gorgeous Greek who'd long ago stolen her heart was here with her again, temporarily part of her life. And she didn't need it, because he didn't want her—or any woman. Helena swallowed at the depth of her own feelings. She had to face facts. Whatever their present circumstances, there was never going to be a future for her and Oscar, so she must try and deal with the here and now sensibly… *Sensibly?*… What part did sense play where matters of the heart were concerned?

Realizing that they hadn't spoken for several moments, he took her hand and said softly, 'Is it still hurting very much, *Heleena?*' And as she looked up at him Helena wanted to say, *Oh, yes, it still hurts… You'll never know how much, Oscar…* But instead she attempted a cool reply.

'No…no—I can hardly feel anything at all now,' she said, wiping a stray tear from her cheek. 'Just a very slight burning sensation, that's all.' And admitting the double meaning in those words made Helena's blue eyes limpid with hopelessness.

Then, as his unflinching gaze enslaved her once more, Oscar slowly raised her hand and pressed it gently to his lips. 'There,' he said huskily, looking down at her, 'let me make it feel better...'

In the next few moments of suspended silence, broken only by the gentle ticking of the clock, nothing could have prepared Helena for what was about to happen, because, with time standing still, Oscar slowly got to his feet, scraping back his chair, and pulled her up towards him, closing his mouth over her parted lips with expert precision. She gasped, the unexpectedness of what was happening taking her completely by surprise, and something vital, electrical, leapt from her at the urgency of his kiss...leaving her breathless.

'Oscar...' she faltered—this was not happening! Not again! She must not let it! She couldn't bear it!

But it was too late. Much too late. She was in his arms, surrendering to his lithe, powerful physique, helpless and ecstatic. Then, frightened at what was happening to her, she managed to pull away slightly and look up at him, at his dark eyes, aflame with desire, boring into hers...

'Oscar...this is not...I must leave...' Helena began, but as she tried to protest he took advantage of her open mouth to claim it again and again, his kisses deep, penetrating, leaving her breathless with longing.

'Heleena...kardia mou.' The dark passion in his voice sounded like the guttural growl of an animal about to claim its prey, and Helena pulled away properly, stepping back, her eyes full of fear.

'It's too late, Oscar,' she whispered. 'For us it's much, much too late.'

* * *

An hour later, they drove back to the Inn to collect their belongings, Helena sitting silently, choking back tears.

As Oscar had kissed her so thoroughly she had been in paradise—a paradise once lost, and so briefly regained. But wait a minute, she was not the inexperienced female she had once been, she told herself again—this was *now*! And there was no going back. That kiss had been a gesture—a gesture born of fleeting male sympathy—but then, being Oscar, it had very quickly become something much more. More vital, more intense, and yes, more thrilling. It would be wrong to deny it, wrong to pretend that she hadn't wanted it to go on and on. She had not known another man who could match his sensitive, sensual, unforgettable technique.

She cast a fleeting glance at him, at the stern profile, the determined chin, and her shoulders drooped. For him, she thought, it would have been merely a case of déjà vu, something to be enjoyed for old times' sake...

Today had been a bad mistake, a terrible mistake, she thought, and now she couldn't wait to be by herself. Away from temptation, away from him.

And Oscar, keeping his concentration on the road ahead, had arrived at one of his usual, unequivocal decisions. Time was precious, and limited. Time was finite, and life was short and he didn't intend to waste any more of it. Using every ounce of ingenuity, he would have to make her understand. And trust him. But love him?

Oscar allowed himself an inward smile. Oh, yes, he knew he could make her love him again. The memory of the way she had responded to his ardour proved that Helena was still the warm, passionate female she'd always been. And would be again…with him.

# CHAPTER FIVE

THREE weeks later, very early in the morning, Oscar took a brief glance around his large air-conditioned office high above the bustling streets of Athens, before packing his essential belongings into the large business holdall that went everywhere with him. His secretary had arranged for a car to be outside to take him to the airport where his private jet would be waiting, and now he walked swiftly towards the lift. He knew he would have to return again on Monday, but now there were other things than business on his mind. Or, rather, another person on his mind. And he knew that today she was returning to Dorset.

As the jet flew him rapidly across the ice-blue skies towards Heathrow Airport, Oscar gazed thoughtfully out of the window. Since meeting Helena again, it seemed to him that the planet had tilted somewhat on its axis, throwing things into slight confusion. He leaned back in the luxurious chair, stretching out his legs in front of him. Whatever else was happening to the world, the one thing he was certain of was that he needed to be with Helena… Being away from her was solving nothing, and he'd been away for far too long. Ten years too long.

\* \* \*

It was turning out to be a very warm day, and Helena pushed up the sleeves of her top and went on vacuuming the carpets, before taking a final look around the cottage to make sure everything was clean and tidy, and to check that she was not leaving anything behind.

Her last weeks in the office had gone better than she could have hoped because Simon had hardly been there at all, and all the other girls had been happy for her—if rather envious at her news. They'd had a very jolly farewell lunch together, with Helena giving them the address she'd be staying at—and them threatening to visit her en masse—and as she'd waved them a last goodbye, she had to admit to a mixture of feelings. From the safety of normality and routine, she was about to tread an unknown path...and she fervently hoped she was doing the right thing.

But filling her mind and overriding every other thought was the way that Oscar had kissed her that afternoon. She'd tried to stop thinking about it ever since, tried to convince herself that it hadn't meant anything to him. But did she want it to mean anything? Was she kidding herself that any relationship that might fleetingly blossom between them now, under these particular and very unusual circumstances, would end any differently than the last time? Helena sighed. She knew the answer to that. She knew she must force herself to be realistic.

She stopped what she was doing for a moment, wiping her forehead with the back of her hand, remembering how, later, after picking up their belongings from the Inn, they hadn't said much, making a very casual departure in their separate cars, with Oscar merely saying a brief, 'Take care,' to her through her open window. And she'd only heard from him once since— a rather hurried phone call, obviously from his office because she'd heard men's loud voices raised in the background. It was a rather blunt request that he be 'informed' when she expected to take up residency at Mulberry Court. She shrugged as she thought about that. Well, he did have a vested interest in the place, she thought, and was clearly anxious for it not to be unoccupied for too long. So, by going to live there temporarily, she was doing them both a favour, she told herself firmly.

Now, she picked up her duvet and went outside to put it in the back of the car, which by now was crammed to the roof. She hadn't realized just how much she'd accumulated since she'd been living here, but at least her bedding would help to keep everything safe, she thought, as she tucked it firmly around her belongings. Her cases and bags of clothes were in the boot, and she'd wrapped towels around her few pieces of china and glassware, but she'd had to use the passenger seat and the floor-well for most of her books and CDs. It had been something of a major exercise to pack everything, she admitted, pushing back a tendril of hair from her flushed forehead.

She locked up for the last time, determined to go without a backward glance. She *had* been happy living here, she thought, but that part of her life was in the past and she had somewhere else to go now—just for a bit—and London would still be here waiting for her when she returned.

With her heart doing somersaults of excitement—

and a little apprehension—she switched on the car's engine, her eyes widening in concern at the response. Instead of roaring into life—which, despite its age, it usually did—there was only a sort of wheeze, a cough…and nothing! Oh, *no!* The car had been so good-tempered of late. *Please, not today of all days*, she implored it. She waited a few seconds before trying again—she'd once been told that was what you should do—but the result was almost the same, except this time it didn't even cough, and the wheeze was only a gentle breathy whisper of protest.

Since her experience of car maintenance was nil, Helena knew that she had one option—she'd have to call the road service people and hope that someone could arrive soon because, apart from wanting to get going on her journey, the inside of the car was becoming like an oven.

She took her mobile from her bag and, after a few abortive tries, she got through to someone who told her that, unfortunately, it was unlikely anyone could arrive for about two hours. The fact that she was not stranded on an isolated road and was actually outside her own front door seemed to weigh against her, Helena thought, as she gave an exasperated sigh. She rang off, biting her lip, annoyed that she hadn't bothered to get the car serviced; she knew she should have done it by now, but it was usually so reliable and it was one of the things she'd let slip. Well, there'd been a lot on her mind lately, she excused herself, resting her head back against the seat.

Suddenly her mobile rang and she jumped, her spirits rising. Perhaps someone could come now after all.

It was Oscar! And although just to hear his voice sent her heart soaring, Helena made a face to herself. She'd have to tell him her present position, and for some reason she didn't want to, didn't want to sound pathetic. She should have been on her way by now.

'Helena—have you arrived?' The deep voice sent Helena's nerves all over the place, as usual.

She swallowed. 'Oh…hello…no, not yet,' she said, clearing her throat. 'My car refuses to start, and no one can come to sort me out for a couple of hours so I'll just have to sit it out until…'

'Where are you?' Oscar cut in abruptly.

Helena gritted her teeth. She'd have to own up. 'I'm outside my front door—my ex-front door,' she said. 'I haven't been able to move as much as a yard up the road. I'm sitting here surrounded by all my stuff… In fact, there's only just room for me,' she added, keeping her voice deliberately light. She didn't want to make a fuss—and anyway, she was sure to get to Mulberry Court by nightfall.

There was barely a moment's pause before he said breezily, 'Oh, well, that's life.' And with that he ended the call, and Helena smiled briefly. He really was determined to make sure he knew what was going on, she thought, but it was really good to hear from him, she admitted.

Presently, she glanced at her watch. It was gone two and, feeling thirsty, she reached for the bottle of water she'd packed and took a long drink. Surely someone should be here soon, she thought, sitting back and closing her eyes.

Even with all the windows open it was hot and sultry in the car with not even a breath of air to relieve the humidity. After a few minutes, despite all her efforts to stay awake, Helena's eyelids began to droop. Once or twice she made herself sit up straighter, before relapsing again into a state of torpor, until at last she couldn't stop herself from drifting off, her semi-consciousness full of thoughts tumbling in on more thoughts and through it all the sound of Oscar's voice, gentle but insistent. Her lips tilted in a smile as she heard him apologizing, over and over again, for disturbing her.

Then, more strongly, 'It does seem a shame to disturb you, *Heleena*,' the voice repeated, 'but we have places to go, things to do...'

Suddenly, Helena woke up properly and with a gasp of amazement she found herself looking up into Oscar's amused eyes. Several seconds passed before she gained possession of her senses and was able to speak.

'Oscar... What on earth? I mean...why are you? What are you doing here? Why aren't you in Greece?' she stuttered foolishly.

'Because I'm here to make sure you get safely to Mulberry Court...today, if possible,' he added wryly.

Helena gazed up at him unbelievingly. If you thought someone was hundreds of miles away and suddenly he appeared in front of you like an apparition, it was distinctly unnerving, she excused herself.

'I flew in early today,' he said. 'I needed to see someone in the London office and thought I'd check up on you, see if you were OK,' he added casually.

Helena got out of the car, then saw the four-by-four parked alongside and, before she could say anything,

Oscar said, 'I knew we'd never get all your belongings in the Ferrari so I hired this instead.' He peered into Helena's car. 'And I think I did the right thing,' he added bluntly.

Helena looked at him, slightly mystified. 'But...what are we going to do about my car?' she said. 'We just can't leave it here—and what about the person who's supposed to be coming?'

'Ring the company again now,' Oscar instructed her. 'Tell them you've left the keys at your local dealers—they're only half a mile away from here—and then they can either drive it or tow it there. We'll arrange for the garage to keep the car there until further notice and pick it up at some point in the future.' He glanced at his watch. 'In the meantime, I'll start loading up.'

Feeling extremely thankful—though rather dazed—at the formidable way Oscar was taking over, Helena rang the road organization again, who seemed more than ready to do as she asked, especially as it meant that now there was less urgency for them to send out a mechanic.

She snapped her mobile shut, then began passing things to Oscar as he deftly fitted everything neatly into the four-by-four. As she started heaving one of the heavy boxes of books from the passenger seat of her car, he came up quickly behind her, taking it from her.

'I remember you saying you had rather a lot of books,' he said, smiling down at her briefly.

Helena took a deep breath, intensely conscious of him standing so close to her. He was wearing designer jeans and a cream rugby shirt, and his hair, shining black and glossy, had fallen forward onto his forehead, making him look boyish and carefree—just as she remembered him...

Later, with everything safely stowed in the larger vehicle, Oscar began driving slowly away from the area. He glanced across at her. 'Did you have a fairly smooth exit from the job?' he enquired briefly.

'Yes, there was no problem,' Helena replied, remembering Simon's very formal last few words to her in front of everyone. Still, that was all in the past, she thought, her spirits lifting at the thought of the immediate future and what lay ahead.

'I don't suppose you've been able to have anything to eat yet, have you? It's well past lunch time... Would you like to stop somewhere?'

Helena glanced at him quickly. 'What about you?'

He shrugged. 'I had quite a serious meal on the flight,' he began, and Helena interrupted.

'I'm not a great fan of on-board food,' she said. 'What did they give you?'

Oscar half smiled. 'They gave me what I ordered,' he said briefly and, without looking at her, 'I was using the company jet,' he added.

Helena looked out of her window, annoyed at her stupidity. Of course. Did she imagine that Oscar Theotokis would have been mixing with the rest of humanity on a routine morning flight? Even if it would have been first class? No, he'd arrived on his very own aircraft. She sighed, her hands clasped tightly in her lap. It must be weird, she thought, to have access to such incredible wealth, to give any instruction, any order, and know that money would buy it.

'So, shall we stop for something to eat?' he asked.

'No, I'd rather go on,' Helena said quickly. 'And, anyway, I did pack a picnic. Maybe we can stop and have it later.'

They drove in silence for a while, each with their own thoughts, Oscar headily aware of how beautiful Helena was looking, dressed in a pair of white jeans and a golden yellow top, her hair tied back in one long ponytail. She always appeared so effortlessly chic, he thought, licking his top lip briefly.

Three long weeks had passed since he'd held her in his arms, since he'd felt her soft lips mould with his. Despite everything else going on, she had never left his thoughts…his desperate thoughts of wanting her. So how much longer was it going to be…? How much longer was he prepared to wait? But strategy was everything, he reminded himself, and if he moved in too quickly he might lose her again, and this time it would be for good.

Helena, her head resting back against the seat, wondered if Oscar had given so much as a single thought to the way he'd practically overpowered her, both physically and emotionally, that afternoon in the kitchen. His momentary passion had been hot, fiery, ruthlessly demanding yet exquisitely tender all at the same time. The sort of sensations that had been missing from her life for so very, very long. The sort of sensations she'd never expected to feel again. But did he remember how fired up they had both been? And if he did, had it mattered to him since? Today, his attitude had been friendly, businesslike in sorting out her problems for her, but he wasn't here because of her. He was only in

England because of a business necessity. It was a total fluke that she was sitting here with him now.

The May weather couldn't have been more wonderful as they drove swiftly towards their destination. They'd left the motorway a long time ago, and were now making their way through a much prettier region. Sitting on the high seat of the large vehicle, Helena was able to look right out and view the countryside as it rolled past them, most of the trees in full leaf. And every now and then she could see a hilly field dotted with sheep and dozens of tiny lambs. She took a deep breath. This sort of environment just had to be better than the stuffy streets of the city, she thought. She was going to make the most of the next couple of months, she told herself.

Presently Oscar said, 'Would you like to stop for your picnic now? There seem to be suitable places I can pull in.'

Helena suddenly realized how hungry she was feeling. 'Yes—thanks,' she said briefly, cringing inwardly as she thought about her 'picnic'. All she'd done was to empty the fridge of its remaining contents—which were one tomato, a small piece of cucumber, a lemon, a rather sad-looking mushroom and a roll. Plus a chocolate biscuit. Hardly an exciting meal, and not much of it, she thought, because she'd have to ask Oscar to share it. But she had made a good flask of coffee, which she hoped was still reasonably hot. She wondered, rather enviously, what he'd had to eat on the plane...obviously a world away from the rather pathetic things in her holdall.

Within a few minutes Oscar pulled into a lay-by

next to a farm gate, and they both got out of the vehicle, Oscar raising his arms above his head and stretching.

'It is beautiful around here,' he commented, glancing across at Helena, who had already opened the gate and spotted a suitable place just inside to set out the food. She was kneeling down and taking things from her bag and she looked up at him as he joined her.

'When I said "picnic" I think I was exaggerating,' she said lightly. 'This is all the food there was left in the fridge. I hope you weren't expecting anything exceptional.'

'I wasn't expecting anything,' he said, 'because I've already eaten. So it's all for you.'

'Well, I can guarantee the coffee,' Helena said, 'but we'll have to share.' She shot him a rather diffident glance, aware of the easy familiarity of what she'd just said. The words had just slipped off her tongue, and she was rewarded with one of Oscar's dark, lazy half-smiles as he looked down at her.

Helena uncorked the flask and carefully poured some coffee into the plastic top, before handing it to him. And, as their eyes met, an unspoken thought passed between them. Helena forced her gaze away from him. For herself, she couldn't even begin to express her own feelings at this precise moment, only that in these surroundings she felt safe, secure—and almost deliriously happy—to be here with Oscar. A month ago, this present scenario would have been unthinkable. If only she could stop the clock now, she thought...to fix time.

Not feeling at all bothered that she was eating and Oscar wasn't, Helena bit into the tomato carefully, before breaking off a piece of the roll and putting it into her mouth. And, after a moment, he sat down beside her to drink the coffee.

It didn't take long for Helena to eat what she wanted and soon, replacing what was left into her bag, she looked around her, shading her eyes with her hand. 'Oh, look! I can hardly believe it!' she said. 'There are cowslips in this field. I haven't seen any of those for so long!'

'Cowslips?' Oscar was mystified. 'Cowslips?'

Helena jumped to her feet. 'They're a really pretty wild flower that you hardly see any more… I'd love to pick some, but I know how rare they are now. I'm just going to take a closer look.'

Sitting with his legs stretched out in front of him, Oscar leaned back on his elbows watching Helena curiously as she trod carefully between the plants, bending to touch one or two of the flowers tenderly without damaging them. Unlike so many of the worldly women he'd known, it took so little to enchant her, he thought, and so little of her to enchant *him*!

Presently, they got back into the car and set off again, almost immediately coming across a herd of cows lumbering along in the same direction. 'Hmm, this might take some time,' Oscar said mildly, driving carefully behind, giving the herdsman and the two sheepdogs plenty of space.

'I hope Benjamin will let me come with him on his walks with Rosie,' Helena said casually, as they watched the cows being driven into a nearby farm entrance. 'Not having a dog around was one of the things I missed most, living in the city.' She glanced across at

Oscar as she spoke, her eyes taking on a faraway expression as she studied the handsome profile. He was the sort of man that every woman alive would want to be with, she thought. She allowed her eyes to slide downwards for a second, all too aware of the firm, rippling muscles of his thighs beneath his jeans. She swallowed, and stared out of her side window. Dream on, she told herself firmly.

By the time they got to Dorset it was getting quite late. Louise answered Helena's light tap on her door almost at once—obviously relieved that she'd arrived safely—but surprised to see the much larger vehicle there with Oscar sitting at the wheel.

'My car wouldn't start this morning,' Helena explained, 'and luckily for me Oscar was able to come to my rescue.'

'Oh, that was good, then,' Louise said, her shrewd eyes twinkling.

Oscar got out and came over to say hello and Louise opened her door wider. 'Come in...' she began, but Helena shook her head.

'We've got rather a lot to unpack, Louise, thanks,' she said, 'so we'll go on up to the house now.'

'Well, I've left plenty of food—enough for two,' she added, 'and all the bedrooms are ready for occupancy... just as Isobel liked them to be.'

Outside the main entrance to Mulberry Court, Oscar and Helena started unloading, and he glanced down at her.

'Why don't you go and make some tea—I'll do this,' he said.

Helena shot him a grateful look without arguing, and

went to do as he suggested, feeling glad to be home at last. She paused on that thought. *Home?* Yes…glad to be home, she told herself.

In the fridge was one of Louise's famed meat pies. A few minutes in the Aga and that would be delicious, Helena thought happily.

Presently, after he'd had a wash, Oscar joined her. 'I've put a lot of your stuff in your room,' he said, 'but all the books and CDs are in the library.'

Helena smiled quickly. 'Thank you. And while our supper's warming, I'll go and freshen up.'

Upstairs, her cases and bags of clothes and shoes, and the box with her breakables in, were all stacked neatly so that she could reach her bed—which looked so inviting she could collapse into it right now! She'd have plenty of time to unpack after Oscar had gone back, she thought, trying to remember where she'd put her wash bag.

She released her hair from its grip, running her fingers through its long waves. She couldn't find her brush—that would have to do until she shampooed it later, she decided.

When she went back downstairs, Oscar was standing by the window, his hands in his pockets. 'Something smells pretty good,' he said.

'Louise's pies were always wonderful, weren't they?' she said lightly.

After they'd eaten, Helena said, 'When are you due back? When have you booked your return flight?'

'Monday lunch time—but I've a couple of things I need to see to in Dorchester before I return.'

Helena nodded, but said nothing, and after she'd

drunk her glass of white wine from the bottle Louise had left chilling in the fridge, she yawned and got to her feet. 'I suddenly feel desperately in need of a good night's sleep,' she said. She looked down at Oscar. 'Thank you for turning up today,' she said. 'I hope it hasn't inconvenienced you too much.'

He stood up slowly, and Helena's pulse quickened. She hoped this wasn't going to be an action replay of what had happened on that other occasion. Too much had happened already, lately… She could only take so much excitement.

But Oscar moved away, picking up their plates and taking them over to the sink. 'Oh, I never allow myself to be inconvenienced,' he said lazily. 'Anyway, it was in my…our…interests to see that you were safely installed.' He turned to look back at her, a surge of longing hitting his groin. But this was not one of the hot-blooded sisters Allegra, or Callidora, who might have expected him to make love to them tonight, he warned himself. This was Helena, whose heart he had to recapture. And he would succeed, he reassured himself. Timing was everything, and with his usual insight he'd know exactly when the right moment came.

'Goodnight…*Heleena*…' he said softly.

# CHAPTER SIX

MID-AFTERNOON next day, with the windscreen wipers going at full throttle, Oscar made his way back to the house. He hadn't intended being so long in Dorchester, but he'd unexpectedly bumped into John Mayhew and had joined him for a drink at The Bear Hotel. There'd been no reply from Helena when he'd texted her to say he'd be late.

Now, he let himself in at the back door fully expecting to see her in the kitchen, but the house was silent and Oscar's lip tilted briefly. She was probably upstairs still unpacking all her clothes, he thought.

He put the kettle on to make himself a coffee, then wandered over to the window... It was dire weather—the rain had been incessant for hours—and Oscar couldn't help feeling slightly nostalgic for the Greek island paradise that he went to whenever he could. It would be fantastic there now, he thought, the incredible blue-green of the sea competing with the brilliance of a cloudless azure sky. When he was there, time became irrelevant.

But this was England, and he knew that weather like today's was fairly normal—though Oscar had to admit that his youthful memories only seemed to conjure up pictures of long, fine days spent here in the lazy countryside.

Suddenly, he saw Benjamin and Rosie coming down from the grounds to the front of the house, and Oscar smiled faintly. They'd obviously been for a very long walk because both man and dog were soaking wet. When Benjamin saw Oscar standing at the window, he raised his hand and mouthed something, before walking rapidly up to the back door. At once Oscar opened it to let him in, but Benjamin stood back.

'Mr Theotokis, would you be kind enough to let Helena know that I've found this crazy animal?' Benjamin said.

'Oh—what happened?' Oscar enquired.

'We were up at the top,' Benjamin said. 'Rosie was sniffing around, good as gold as usual, when suddenly she took off like a rocket and wouldn't come back when I whistled—which isn't like her. I couldn't believe she'd run right off the property like that and go across the road… Well, a couple of roads it turned out to be in the end.' He sighed, blowing out his cheeks. 'When Helena knew the dog had done a runner she insisted on coming with me to help search. She knew where to start looking… Said the local area is known for its rabbit warrens. Then, when we weren't having any luck, we split up and went off in opposite directions—I went west, and she went east.' Benjamin pushed some wet hair from his forehead. 'I was staggered when I found where Rosie had got to… She'd run for miles! I haven't seen Helena since to tell her but it was really good of her to give me some moral support.'

Oscar shrugged. 'I'm not sure that she's back...' he began.

Benjamin cut in quickly, 'Oh, she must be by now!' he exclaimed. 'And we agreed that when either of us found Rosie, we wouldn't try and find each other, we'd just come on home.'

'So—which area were you covering?' Oscar asked, and when Benjamin told him, he nodded. He knew exactly where they would have been. He knew this part of the countryside almost as well as Helena did, even though it was a long time since he'd been around to do any walking.

Presently, after checking that Helena was nowhere in the house, Oscar made himself a coffee, then opened the Sunday newspaper he'd bought, his eyes glancing at the clock on the wall. He shrugged inwardly. She was sure to be back soon, he thought, noting that she hadn't taken her mobile with her because it was there on the table in front of him.

After a while, and not really taking in what he was reading, Oscar made a decision. He put down the paper and went into the utility room, shrugging on the wax jacket he'd hung on the back of the door. Helena had obviously been out for a long time now... He might as well go and meet her, he thought.

Leaving the house, he started trudging up through the grounds. He didn't really know why he was feeling mildly concerned. Although he knew it wouldn't get dark for a long time yet, the clouds were still ominously grey and heavy with rain. Not an ideal day for a woman to be wandering about by herself.

Oscar increased his stride, soon reaching the main

road, then struck out towards the small wooded area where he remembered they used to take Bella for walks sometimes. In the near distance he could see the tree-lined hill that offered a spectacular view from the top, and he decided to make his way up there. Unsurprisingly, there were no other walkers about, he noted, the only significant sounds being the dripping water from the trees and the thrust of his tread on the soaking undergrowth.

At the top of the hill, he cupped his hands around his mouth and called out. 'Helena!' he shouted. *'Heleena!'*

And then he saw her. She was there at the bottom of the field, sitting on a stone stile by a gateway next to the public footpath. She was leaning forward, intent on something, with her head on her knees. Oscar started running down the field, reaching her in a couple of minutes.

She looked up and saw him, a rueful expression on her face. She was wearing a raincoat, but she had nothing on her head and her hair was falling in streaming waves around her face. Her jeans were rolled up to her knees, and her legs and feet were bare and covered in mud.

'Helena…' he began.

She cut in quickly, 'Has Rosie been found?'

Oscar nodded. 'Yes—Benjamin came back with her more than an hour ago but…why on earth are you…?'

Helena grimaced. 'Oh, it's just that I'd completely forgotten about the bog down there at the bottom,' she said, obviously annoyed with herself. 'I was running along and stumbled right into it—and the rain today has made it like glue.' She shuddered. 'Anyway, I was squelching my way through it and I lost my footing and, unfortunately, one of my trainers—which is still stuck down there somewhere.' She leaned back for a second, looking up at him. 'However hard I tried, I could not get it back, and anyway I don't think I'd want it back now. So… I've been trudging along with just one on, and it's very uncomfortable—and cold,' she added, shivering slightly.

Oscar pulled her to her feet. 'Come on,' he said briefly.

Together they made their way slowly back. Oscar had his arm tightly around her waist and Helena leaned against him gratefully, saying 'ouch' once or twice under her breath because her feet were beginning to feel very sore by now and she'd been stung by all the prickles and more than one really cruel nettle. But the only thing she cared about was that the dog had been found.

'I bet I know where Rosie had made for,' she said, glancing up at Oscar. 'After all, it's her job to find things, and this time of year it's an Aladdin's cave to a Retriever.' She paused. 'Poor Benjamin was getting really worried.'

Oscar made no comment, and presently they arrived back at the house.

'I think I need to go up and have a long, hot bath,' Helena said as they hung their wet coats in the utility room. 'Though would you pass me that towel first?' she asked Oscar. 'I can't walk through the house with my feet in this filthy condition.'

'Sit there for a minute,' Oscar commanded, pulling out a wooden stool.

With his back to her, he filled a small bowl with warm water, then took soap and a clean towel and knelt down in front of Helena. He paused for a second, then looked up at her slowly, a quizzical expression in his eyes, and in spite of this most unpromising romantic scenario, Helena felt a tremor of sexual excitement ripple through her. She knew she was looking dreadful, her hair in soaking wet waves around her mud-spattered face—yet Oscar's penetrating gaze made her feel utterly feminine, utterly desirable. A heated flush stained her cheeks as their eyes met.

Slowly, he began soaping her feet, one at a time, moving his fingers carefully over each toe. Then his strong brown hands began massaging the calves of her legs, behind her knees, moving down to cup her heels in his palms, moving rhythmically, his touch reaching every part of her bare flesh, and with her head dropped back and her eyes half-closed in pure ecstasy, Helena gave a long sigh of uninhibited pleasure. She could not remember a time in her life when anyone had bathed her—even partially, or touched her in the way that Oscar was doing—and it was making her feel guilty to be revelling in the sensuous experience.

'Oh…that feels…so…lovely…' she murmured.

After a few blissful moments she opened her eyes to see him looking at her with that dangerous, penetrating gaze that had always reduced her to helplessness. What he was doing to her was going far beyond the call of duty, she thought—but she didn't want it to stop! Wanted it to go on and on!

Finally, Oscar lifted her feet from the bowl and began to dry them carefully, his dark head bent to the task, his manipulating, sensitive fingers continuing far longer than was necessary because he knew that she was enjoying the warmth of his hands, the erotic pressure of his touch that might easily lead to something far more. He allowed himself a wry inward smile. He had never made love to a woman in such surroundings… but he was all too aware that place was unimportant as long as the chemistry was there. And he knew that he and Helena had enough chemistry between them to last them two lifetimes.

Alerted to the strength of feeling that had developed between them, Helena got up quickly, a familiar, persistent warning bell bringing an end to her passionate reverie. 'Thanks…thanks…that's OK—that's fine,' she said. As she made for the door she turned to look back at him. 'I'll make supper for us in an hour or so,' she said.

Much later, as they sat in the conservatory with their coffee, Oscar said casually, 'I bought you a car this morning, Helena.'

Helena frowned, looking up at him quickly. 'What do you mean?'

'I bought you a car,' he repeated. Before she could say anything, he went on, 'It occurred to me that you're going to need transport for the time you're here, and I've a contact in one of the garages in the town who was able to sort it out quickly for me.' Oscar drank from his cup. 'It's registered in your name and they'll be delivering it tomorrow morning—it's the newest model of the one you've been driving,' he added.

Helena could hardly believe what she'd heard, and she felt mildly irritated. He'd done what? She did not want Oscar buying her expensive things, she thought. She'd already told him she had enough money of her own for now—but it did not include the possibility of purchasing new cars! She'd never owned a brand new car in her life! That huge expense would have to wait until…well, until next year.

'Oscar, I'm not ready to buy a car yet,' she said firmly.

'You haven't bought it—I have,' he said. Then, see-ing the expression on Helena's face, he said coolly, 'We can call it the Mulberry Court car if you prefer, purely for present, temporary use. And I was not expecting any financial input from you,' he added bluntly.

Helena shook her head briefly. Spending big money so casually was nothing to Oscar—which only showed the huge difference between them, she thought. The difference that could never be breached. Then some-thing else struck her—perhaps this was him attempt-ing to 'buy her out' of their inheritance? To persuade her to take the money and run? As she knew he wanted her to.

Feeling slightly guilty at that uncharitable thought, Helena put it out of her mind at once. Buying the car had been generous—and thoughtful—of him, though if it had been left up to her she'd have merely hired one. That would have been sufficient for the short time in-volved.

For a few moments there was an uneasy silence be-tween them, Oscar sensing that Helena wasn't particu-larly happy. Well, she'd had a very long and wet walk today, and had obviously been anxious about the dog… He glanced at his watch, getting up suddenly.

'I've just remembered that I've left something I need in the car,' he said briefly, leaving the room.

Helena got up and went over to the window, her mind still fixed on those moments when Oscar had bathed her feet. Even now, her thighs tingled at the memory. Why had no other man ever been able to raise her to such sensual heights? And with such ease? And was her unsatisfactory experience in other relationships all because of Oscar? Was she always chasing an impossible dream—*their* impossible dream? And would no other dream, no other man do?

Helena frowned at all this introspection. It was foolish to ask herself these questions, she told herself.

Just then the mobile phone on the table rang and, without thinking, she turned to answer it. And, too late, she realized it was Oscar's mobile which she'd automatically picked up.

'Hello?' she said uncertainly, glancing towards the door.

The voice on the other end was female. 'Oh… Oh, hello?… Hello?' Then, 'Who is this, please? I wish to speak to Oscar Theotokis.'

'Um…well, he'll be here in a moment,' Helena said. Then, 'Can I give him a message?'

After a brief pause, the voice said—in a rather heavy, imperious tone, 'Yes…why not?' She continued speaking in English, but with a heavily laced accent. 'Tell him that, most unfortunately, my sister Allegra has lost her baby…again.' Silence, then a long sigh before the woman continued. 'I know that Oscar will want to know that,' she added. 'Tell him, also, that I would like to speak to him soon… This is Callidora speaking.'

Helena swallowed over a dry tongue. 'Look…um… I'm sure he will be back in a moment,' she said, 'if you'll just hang on…'

'No—I have to go. Please make sure he gets this message.' And with that, the phone went dead.

Helena put the mobile back down on the table, wishing with all her heart that she hadn't answered it. It had been an instinctive act on her part to do so, but the call had obviously been a very personal one, and she'd rather not have known about it. She stared down at the instrument as if hoping it might reveal more information. So this woman—Allegra—had lost her baby, the caller had said—and it seemed important that Oscar knew about it…

Helena shook her head briefly and began putting their coffee things on to the tray just as Oscar returned carrying a large file. Without looking at him, she said, 'I just answered your mobile—sorry—I should have let it ring.' She reached for the small cream jug and put it down carefully with the mugs. 'It was someone—a lady—Callidora…and she rang to let you know that her sister has just lost her baby. And also that she would like to speak to you—soon.'

Now Helena did look up at Oscar, horribly conscious of the dark, unfathomable expression in his eyes—and unable to ignore the sinking of her own heart.

'Oh…I see,' was all he said casually, taking the tray from Helena and going out before her to the kitchen. 'Did you tell Callidora that I would be back in Greece tomorrow?' he added.

'I didn't tell her anything,' Helena said.

Presently, up in her bedroom, Helen undressed

slowly and got ready for bed. She had been plunged from a sense of unbelievable pleasure and well-being to feeling acutely depressed. Depressed and insecure.

Because there was so much she knew about Oscar—and so much she didn't know. Not any more. Nor was she ever likely to know.

At around midnight, Oscar came up the stairs to bed. More than anything in the world, he wanted to make love to Helena. Now. And it wasn't just romantic passion that was torturing him. He longed to hold her close to him, to protect her... She had looked so defenceless down in that field earlier in the day, so utterly vulnerable. So hotly desirable. And there had been a few moments, later, as he'd dried her toes, when he'd recognized that special look in her magical eyes that had told him all he needed to know.

Going past his own room, he walked softly towards Helena's door and stood for a moment, listening. The only sound he could hear was her gentle breathing, and very carefully he opened the door just wide enough to look inside.

She was lying on her back on the bed, one slim leg carelessly over the side, her arms raised above her, her hair fanning out loosely on the pillow. She still had her underwear on, the rest of her clothes and the duvet were scattered on the floor beside her.

Unable to resist going closer, Oscar went inside and stood looking down. She was deeply asleep, a pale moon reflecting light on the skin of her slender neck, on the rounded curve of her naked thigh. Her long eyelashes swept her cheeks, her lips were slightly parted, her breasts in the lacy bra rising and falling gently with each breath.

With his blood rushing and almost overcome with need, Oscar swallowed hard, then stooped to pick up the duvet. Very carefully, he placed it over her, gathering the folds up around her neck, tucking them in gently. He paused for only a second before turning to leave.

'*Kalinihta, agapi mou,*' he whispered.

# CHAPTER SEVEN

ON MONDAY morning the new silver-blue car arrived and, although Helena had felt annoyed at Oscar taking what she saw as an unnecessary step in buying it for her, she had to admit to a feeling of pride as she drove it for the first time. And, of course, he had been right. She was obviously going to need some form of transport while she was here, either to go into Dorchester for fresh supplies or, more importantly, to get her to any future job she may have to find. Helena frowned as she remembered her feeling of hopelessness at not being able to drive away on Saturday afternoon and she also remembered how she'd felt when she awoke to find Oscar's quizzical eyes gazing at her through the open window. It was a huge stroke of luck that he'd happened to be in the UK, she thought—had her guardian angel been at work again?

By the end of the week, Helena had settled into Mulberry Court with no problem. Louise popped up to the house fairly frequently, to do the sort of tasks she normally did, and Helena enjoyed helping her some-times—and chatting about the past.

But what was mostly on Helena's mind was listing all the valuable contents of the house. Although she'd been aware of Oscar taking some notes the other day, she wanted to catalogue everything herself—for her own satisfaction—and to start thinking about eventually taking some of it away with her, even though that thought made her shudder. It was here, in this house, where everything truly belonged, not split up and sold off—it would almost feel like vandalism. But she had to be realistic, she realized that. Quite apart from her figurines, which she kept peeping in to look at, there was so much expensive stuff here and it all had to go somewhere. And as for the library with hundreds of Isobel's books, she thought, looking around her now... A lot of them would find their way into her new home—wherever that turned out to be.

She looked pensively out of the window for a moment. She'd have to find that special job in London first, then probably rent somewhere on a short-term let while she looked around for a permanent home. But she wouldn't know what to look for until she knew what her resources might be... Until they sold Mulberry Court next year.

She bit her lip. She did not want to think about the financial aspect of all this, had deliberately shut her mind to it until the day came. Being here, now, was all she needed because, apart from the cottage she'd shared with her father all those years ago, this was the place she would always think of as home. It always made her feel so comfortable, so welcome, so wanted. And she certainly felt no anxiety at the thought of sleeping here by herself, as Oscar had thought she might.

She'd received numerous calls from him since he'd gone back, which was something of a surprise. Now

that he knew she was keeping potential squatters at
bay and that she'd settled in, surely there was no need
for him to keep checking up? But she freely admitted
that she looked forward to hearing from him, hearing
his voice, and yesterday he'd said he was making arrangements to come back to the UK, probably within
a few days. Helena hugged herself as she thought of
that. Although she knew that her renewed feelings for
Oscar were causing her to tread on dangerous ground,
it couldn't do any harm to enjoy being with him again
for just the brief interlude which fate had decreed. It
didn't have to mean anything to her—not anything serious, she assured herself. In fact, she'd make sure it
didn't. She'd grown up in the last ten years, had taken
a few knocks and was quite ready for a few more if that
was what life decided. Until then, it wasn't a crime to
enjoy being in the company of the most handsome man
on God's earth, was it? The only 'crime' would be if
she let herself get carried away. And she would not let
that happen this time. She was going to just live for the
moment.

Helena was in the utility room putting some of her
clothes into the washing machine when Louise came in,
obviously concerned about something and in a somewhat breathless state.

'Helena…I've just had a phone call from Sarah, my
cousin—and it's not good news.'

Helena looked up quickly. 'Oh—what's happened,
Louise?'

'She's just rung me now, from the hospital…she's
suffered a detached retina, poor thing. It happened all

of a sudden, apparently, They operated last night, and she expects to be home on Monday, all being well. But the thing is—she's going to need someone to look after her for a week or so because she won't be able to see for a while. And, quite honestly, I'm the only one available…I'm her only relation, you see. Sarah's very proud. She won't want to leave it up to neighbours, even though they're all very kind.' Louise frowned anxiously.

'So when are you going—and have you found out the train times? I can drive you to the station,' Helena said at once.

They went into the kitchen, and Louise sat at the table for a moment, looking up at Helena. 'There's a train at ten-thirty in the morning,' she said, 'but…I feel really upset at having to go, because it means I won't be with you, Helena… It's so nice having you down here again. It's like old times.' She frowned anxiously. 'And of course I can't say exactly when I'll be back. It'll all depend how I find things at Durham, and how well Sarah is going to recover. Everything takes that bit longer as you get older,' she added. 'But I'm going to really hate missing out being here with you, Helena.'

'Oh, these things happen, Louise,' Helena said kindly. 'And don't worry—I'm not returning to London just yet. You're sure to come home before I do. And, in the meantime, Sarah needs you, so you must go.' Helena went over to put the kettle on. 'I'll bring the car down to the cottage at nine forty-five, shall I. That'll give us plenty of time to get to the station,' she added, thinking that Oscar had been right in buying the car, after all.

'The other thing that's a bit unfortunate is that this weekend Benjamin won't be here, either. He's going to spend some time with his children—which doesn't happen very frequently,' Louise said, watching as Helena put out two mugs for the coffee she was making for them. 'His ex-wife always makes it so difficult for him, and he's such a good man, so reliable and kind,' Louise added. She looked thoughtful for a second.

Helena nodded in agreement. 'Oscar told me all about what happened to him,' she added.

After a moment Louise said, shooting a glance at Helena, 'Seeing Mr Oscar again is quite something, isn't it?' She paused. 'Of course, he didn't visit Isobel that much of late, but she knew the reason for that… She often mentioned his very responsible job, the long hours he has to work. But he was often around in the old days, when you were both youngsters, wasn't he?' she added.

'Yes, he was always here for his holidays,' Helena said casually. 'I haven't seen anything of him since, and of course the only reason for him being about now is because of the will.' She brought the coffee over to the table and sat down, and Louise stirred hers slowly, watching the liquid swirl around in the mug.

'Life's a funny old thing, isn't it, when you think about it,' Louise said. 'You never know how it's going to turn out, or what's going to turn up next.'

Helena could only nod in agreement.

At around midnight on Sunday, something—and she could not identify what it was—made Helena wake up and sit bolt upright in bed, her heart gathering pace.

What *was* it she had heard that had brought her rapidly from a deep sleep to an alert wakefulness?

She stayed quite still for a moment, then slipped from beneath her duvet and went across to look out of the window. Nothing. Only the whispering of a light breeze ruffling the leaves on the trees, the pale moon overhead half-shrouded by cotton wool clouds causing dark shadows to filter in and out of the night. But... something was different... Something had brought Helena swiftly to a state of tense alertness, and she knew she wouldn't get back to sleep until she'd gone to have a look around.

She dragged on her dressing gown, a sudden instinct making her pause to take her mobile from her bag. Then, bare-foot, she left the room and went downstairs, treading silently along the hall. Hesitating, she pulled herself up for a moment. There it was again...and she knew now! It was coughing that she'd heard. Someone was coughing, someone was choking, and there was whispering... Then another smothered wheezy cough.

Although momentarily rooted to the spot, Helena didn't feel frightened—and afterwards she would ask herself why she hadn't been. She went into the kitchen and over to the window and stared out, the house security lights illuminating the scene all around.

Two men were there, wearing dark hoodies, one of them bigger than the other. They were crouching forward, attempting to force the back door to gain entry, totally intent on what they were doing.

By now, Helena's tongue had dried and her pulse was racing, yet despite that she knew she was feeling amazingly calm, almost detached. It was like watching a scene being played out in front of her, she thought fleetingly. Then she saw one of them push the hood away from his face and she frowned, peering to take a closer look. This was not a *man*, she saw at once; it was a young boy with pale unshaven features, and he was in the midst of a very bad asthma attack. Helena recognized it at once because Jason had been a sufferer, too.

Relaxing her tense shoulders and as if in sympathy, Helena drew in her own breath deeply, then stepped forward and released both inside locks, throwing the door open wide.

'Allow me to save you the trouble, gentlemen,' she said pleasantly. 'What is it you want?'

Driving rapidly in the direction of Mulberry Court, Oscar's expression was dark, the thought of what might have happened to Helena sending icy shivers right down his spine. It had certainly been enough to bring him back from Greece at the earliest possible moment.

Three days earlier he'd learned from Helena that Louise had gone to Durham to look after her cousin, and then Helena had added, almost airily, that there'd been night-time intruders at the house. Which, for once in his life, had left Oscar speechless.

He'd pressed her for details, but Helena had refused to elaborate, saying that it had all been dealt with. But that hadn't satisfied Oscar and he couldn't wait to return and find out more—and convince himself that Helena was all right, that nothing bad had happened to her.

Now, it was Wednesday evening as he drew up to

the entrance of Mulberry Court. As he got out of the car, Helena opened the front door to greet him, smiling brightly.

She was wearing a long, swirly black skirt almost down to her toes, teamed with a flimsy peasant-style top, and she'd brushed her hair out loose so that it fell halfway down her back. Oscar stared down at her, his eyes forbiddingly dark. Her small stature made her look so defenceless as she stood framed in the doorway and he gritted his teeth. It hadn't been such a good idea for her to stay here by herself, he thought, even though it had been what she wanted.

'Hi,' she said carelessly. 'Good flight?' With a slightly sinking heart, Helena recognized that familiar brooding look on his face. She knew that she was going to have to face an inquisition about Sunday night. Maybe she *should* have acted differently, she thought. What if, thanks to her, the place had been ransacked, all the valuable contents whisked away, never to be seen again? That possibility would obviously be the most important thing on Oscar's mind when she eventually tried to explain.

With only a brief response to her enquiry, Oscar went up the stairs carrying his large luggage holdall and business equipment. In his room, he washed the dust of the journey from his hands and face, then took a clean shirt from his case. He'd brought enough of everything with him to stay much longer this time—to stay as long as it took—and work would carry on much as usual, thanks to the current high-class technology at his disposal. But, for once, he had much more personal things on his mind… For once, he was not putting the company first.

Presently, down in the kitchen, he watched as Helena prepared the supper she'd said she would be making for them. Reluctantly tearing his gaze away from her, he glanced around him briefly. He was tired, and suddenly the long cushioned sofa at one end of the room seemed particularly inviting.

The scrubbed wooden table was set with two places and there was a jug of water and a bottle of wine. As Helena brought over a large serving dish from the oven, she said lightly, 'Although I've watched Louise do enough cooking here over the years, I obviously had no reason to do much of it myself.' She smiled up at Oscar quickly. 'I hope you approve of gammon cutlets with pineapple and salad…and our own little new potatoes which Benjamin dug for us this morning.'

She put the rest of the meal in front of them, then sat down. 'I've really enjoyed preparing it,' she added.

Oscar pulled out his own chair and sat down. 'It all looks…excellent…Helena,' he said briefly. 'Thank you.'

As she carefully passed the plate to Oscar, it was impossible for Helena to ignore the somewhat uneasy atmosphere in the room as they made desultory conversation. As she helped herself to one or two of the buttery potatoes, she gave him a sidelong glance—and realized that he'd been looking at her. She looked away again. Then, 'I wonder just who will be sitting here next year,' she said. 'They're going to be very lucky, whoever they are.' She paused for a moment, putting down her fork. 'I hope they turn out to be nice people…I mean, people worthy of Mulberry Court. I hate to think of strangers taking over…it's going to feel all wrong—and they'll never love it as we do,' she added.

They ate in silence for a few moments, then Oscar said, without looking at her, 'Now, you're going to tell me *exactly* what happened here the other night, Helena.'

Well, she'd been waiting for the interrogation, she thought, so she'd better get it over with. She finished her meal, then stood up and went over to make the coffee.

'It was nothing—not really—' she began over her shoulder.

Before she could go on he interrupted harshly, 'It was not "nothing", *Heleena!* It was something…' and, trembling slightly, Helena heard the tantalizing, marked inflexion of his mother tongue, the sound that always made her weak at the knees. 'I cannot bring myself to believe that you handled it yourself, that you didn't call the police when you knew intruders were trying to gain entry to Mulberry Court! What on earth were you thinking?' He almost spat out the words.

Steadying her hand as she finished making the coffee, Helena said calmly, 'Well, where would you like me to begin, Oscar?'

'At the beginning—naturally,' he said dryly.

There was silence for a few moments, then, pouring the coffee into two mugs, she brought the tray over to the table and sat down.

'That night, something made me wake up. I can't remember the time, but it was very late—or very early—and I knew I had to go down and find out what it was.'

She looked across at him defiantly. 'I wasn't frightened. I was—well—curious, that's all.'

Oscar's eyes were locked on to hers, but he said nothing as she continued.

'When I peeped out of the kitchen window I saw two...two men, I thought...and they were trying to fit a key into the door lock. They were whispering, and one of them was coughing and gasping for breath—and that's what had woken me up. It was a horrible sound,' she added, and as Oscar was about to speak she went on quickly. 'I had to do something so I opened the door, because I suddenly realized that these were not men at all, they were *kids*...a couple of kids...and when they came inside I could see that one of them was in a seriously bad way.'

Oscar's eyebrows shot up. 'You actually...*invited*... them *in*? he asked incredulously.

'Of course I did—' Helena began, and he interrupted.

*'Ya to onoma tou Theiou!'* he exclaimed, lapsing into a spontaneous and very rare expletive. 'You should have called the police straight away!'

'What a waste of public money *that* would have turned out to be!' Helena retorted. 'Anyway, I might have done if I'd seen a couple of gangsters wielding baseball bats but they weren't even trying to break down the door, or cause any damage... They just had a random handful of keys, hoping one of them would fit. And such was their "street wisdom" it didn't seem to occur to them that there might be bolts on the inside,' she added, smiling faintly.

'I don't know what you find so amusing,' Oscar said

bluntly. 'They might have been kids, as you say, but they were tall enough for you not to realize that at first and there were two of them and one of you. They could have overpowered you and vandalised the place.' He shook his head as if he could not believe what Helena was telling him. Wasn't part of her reason for staying here to look after Mulberry Court? Surely that didn't include welcoming in random burglars!

'Why on earth didn't you think to ring Benjamin?' he demanded. 'He would have come straight up, whatever time it was.'

'Because,' Helena said, 'Benjamin was away visiting his children.'

At this piece of news, Oscar glowered visibly. So, Helena had been here, totally alone, with no one near enough to be of assistance. His mouth set in a determined line. He'd make sure that she was never in that position again, he told himself.

'Anyway—' Helena took another sip of her coffee '—I made them tell me what they thought they were doing. Apparently, they'd told their mother they were having a sleepover at a friend's house, but what they'd really wanted was to sleep out rough to see what it was like, I suppose—it's "cool". But when it began to get cold, Harry, the younger one—he's only twelve—succumbed to one of his rare asthma attacks and they both got frightened.'

'Why didn't they just go home?' Oscar demanded.

'They couldn't do that! They said their mother would kill them when she found out what they'd been up to!'

'But what made them come *here*? I suppose it couldn't have had anything to do with the fact that they knew the place was empty—or they thought it was,' Oscar suggested scornfully. 'Where they could break in uninterrupted.'

'It was not like that at all,' Helena said, knowing that her colour was rising with every word Oscar was saying. 'Mulberry Court is well-known to the boys,' she went on. 'They'd been here carol singing and trick-or-treating...and apparently Isobel would invite them in every time—and their friends as well.' Helena paused, adding quietly, 'They said they knew Mrs Theotokis had died but that she would have let them in if she'd been here.'

There was silence for a few moments, then Helena said, 'Isobel always took people on trust. That's why everyone loved her.'

Taking people on trust is all very well—up to a point, Oscar thought tightly. But he decided to let that pass.

'So, after you'd made your...assessment...of the situation,' Oscar said, his mouth still set in an obstinate line, 'what happened after that?'

'I made them cosy for the rest of the night, and...'

'You did *what*? You mean—they *slept* here?' Oscar demanded.

'Yes—eventually—after I'd calmed Harry down and made sure his breathing had improved,' she said. 'Then I made them some hot chocolate.' Helena paused. 'They were nice lads,' she added thoughtfully.

'So, where did they actually sleep?' Oscar asked, realizing that this was a battle he was never going to win.

'Don't worry—not in your bed, or mine,' Helena

said. 'I brought down a couple of duvets and made Harry comfy on the sofa over there, and then I put cushions from the conservatory on the floor next to him for Caleb.' She met Oscar's gaze levelly. 'They were asleep in less than five minutes, and I had to wake them up in the morning,' she added.

'But how can you be sure they didn't steal something?' Oscar demanded, still not willing to admit defeat.

Helena sighed with exasperation. 'Oscar, when they were awake I was with them all the time—apart from the few moments while I went to fetch the duvets.' She looked at him quickly. That was what had worried Oscar, she thought. That some of their valuable belongings might have disappeared. 'I promise you,' she said tightly, 'not a single teaspoon is missing.'

For a few moments they looked at each other in silent combat.

'And at what time did they vacate the premises?' Oscar asked.

'I had to wake them at eight o'clock, and after I'd sent them along to the wet room for a wash, I made them tea and toast.' Helena shrugged. 'I did give them a gentle lecture before sending them on their way.' She smiled, remembering something. 'And as they left, they both looked at me seriously and said, "Thank you for having us." Wasn't that sweet?' Helena said.

Oscar gazed at her, his thoughts in turmoil. Of course Helena was right—as it happened, she had not been in any danger, this time. But it would have been so different if the intruders had been different people…

He didn't want to think of what could have happened to her...

'And what about you... Did you get any sleep at all during that night?' he said at last.

Helena shook her head briefly. 'No, I was wide awake—and, anyway, I thought it best not to go to sleep, so I made myself comfortable in the sitting room. I had the TV on very quietly,' she added.

'Better not to disturb the guests,' Oscar said, trying not to sound too cynical.

'Quite. It's what Isobel would have expected,' Helena said neatly.

Suddenly, Oscar leaned forward and filled both their glasses with wine. 'I don't know how long you expect to stay here for your short...sabbatical...Helena, but I've actually made arrangements to stay longer myself this time.' When Helena went to say something, he went on quickly, 'The fact that Louise is not going to be around for some while does change things.'

'I'll be perfectly OK here without Louise to hold my hand, Oscar!' Helena exclaimed. 'And Benjamin's always—well, usually—around. Surely you haven't the time to waste on me!'

She looked at him defiantly...before the more obvious point struck her. He wasn't thinking of *her* welfare—he was thinking about Mulberry Court. And he was clearly of the opinion that she couldn't be trusted to take care of it without him there.

'I won't be wasting any time,' Oscar said calmly. 'I shall be working each day in the study.'

As well as making a rather more personal plan, he thought, which was to get Helena away from here. Just for a few days. Away from Mulberry Court, where there were too many memories, too much emotional baggage. Too much 'stuff' getting in his way.

He knew there was a lot of ground to be made up, and he knew how he was going to do that best. And soon.

By making love to Helena under the seductive influence of an azure Mediterranean sky.

# CHAPTER EIGHT

MUCH later that night as he was preparing for bed, Oscar kept going over and over everything Helena had told him. He still found it hard to believe that she would have opened the door to those men—boys—it didn't matter which. She would have been no match for them. And it had had to take place on the very rare occasion when no one had been at the cottages. When there would have been absolutely no one to come to her aid. He didn't want to go on thinking of the possibilities. Of what might have been.

He stood thoughtfully under the shower for a few minutes, then, with a white towel slung around his tanned shoulders, he padded naked and barefoot over to the bed, rubbing briskly at his wet hair with the corner of the huge towel. He was going to have to convince Helena that a few days away in hot sunshine might compare favourably with the rather damp conditions which Dorset was having at the moment. He'd pick his moment to suggest it. But it would happen. He'd make sure it would happen.

He was about to flop down on the bed when a sound outside made him stop and turn to listen. Someone was talking—well, whispering—someone was out there…

Grabbing the towel and tying it around his waist, Oscar reached his door in a few strides and opened it to see Helena, wearing a short, flimsy nightdress, her hair in total disarray, move slowly past. Her eyes were shut tightly, her lips forming inaudible words. Treading as if her feet were hardly touching the ground, she reached the top of the staircase. Realizing at once what was happening, Oscar went over to her silently, automatically slipping his arm around her protectively.

Unaware that anyone was beside her, Helena took each step down, one at a time, like a child learning to walk, and now, with his head close to hers, Oscar could make out what she was whispering.

'My figurines…I want to see if they've taken my figurines…' Her voice was breathy, fragile as, with her hand on the banister, she continued her dream-state walk. 'Isobel said they were mine, that's all I wanted… I never wanted anything else at all. And now the boys might have taken them…they might have taken them away…I must go and see…I must try to find them, to get them back.'

Desperately trying not to frighten her into wakefulness, Oscar said very gently, 'It's all right…the figurines are still in the library, Helena, where they've always been…no one has taken them, I promise you.'

They reached the bottom of the stairs and, still with her eyes closed, Helena said, her voice quivering, 'Are you sure they're safe? The boys didn't steal them, did they…?'

'No, they didn't. They're quite safe, Helena.'

Helena smiled a sweet, childlike smile. 'Of course… I knew Isobel would look after them for me.'

She turned around slowly. 'I'm glad the boys didn't take them,' she said, her head lolling down on her chest.

Quietly, carefully, with Oscar half-carrying her, the two made the return journey up the stairs and into Helena's bedroom. Oscar helped her get into bed and covered her up, waiting for her to stir or say something else. But by now she was in a deep sleep, her breathing easy, her expression one of pure contentment as she lay there, and to Oscar she looked like a pale goddess in the half-light.

Feeling as if he, himself, had been in some kind of dream, he stood watching her for several minutes, loving the enchanting sight of her, not wanting to leave her. Then, bending, he kissed her forehead lightly and left the room.

Next morning, it was gone nine o'clock before Helena awoke and she sat up, her shoulders drooping. She was feeling as tired as if she hadn't slept a wink, she thought dismally, her head feeling distinctly woolly, giving her a sense of being detached from her brain. She knew that she'd been dreaming all night—and it was all to do with that telephone call from 'Callidora', that message about the lost baby.

She climbed out of bed and went into the bathroom, and the mirror told its own story as she stared at her reflection. Her eyes looked huge in a pale face which showed evidence of silent tears being shed as she'd been sleeping...

Shaking herself properly awake, Helena switched the shower on to hot, then, as she let the water stream over her hair and body, she couldn't resist trying to catch some of the fast disappearing moments of her night's restless sleep. It was like trying to pick up quicksilver in her fingers, she thought, as she struggled to reclaim the mental picture that was uppermost, the dream she was desperate not to lose. And then, quite clearly, it came back to her. The moment that she'd watched herself walking up the aisle on her father's arm.

Oscar had been standing at the altar. He'd turned to greet her as she'd approached, and her heart had almost burst with love as their eyes had met. Her dainty straight white cotton dress was trimmed with a delicate lace edging, her hair piled on top and held in place by a single white rose, matching the small spray she was carrying and which she'd picked from the garden that morning.

But then, with a horrible sickening twist, a woman appeared from nowhere. And she was carrying a baby—a baby which Oscar took and held close to him…

Annoyed with herself for feeling so upset by recalling the dream—the stupid, pointless dream—Helena got out of the shower and dried herself, doubly certain, now, of something she'd always known. Her lifelong love for Oscar had no future. And Mulberry Court didn't belong to her, despite the terms of the will. From the very beginning, her world and Oscar's had been so far apart they might just as well have been born on different planets. And so much time had passed since they'd been so close—so much time he would obviously have spent in the company of many, many women.

She finished getting dressed and reached for her hairbrush. She could hardly bear to wait for the sale of the house now, she thought, dragging her hair back and pushing it haphazardly into some sort of order. Her connection with Mulberry Court would eventually reach a conclusion, and when it did she would rethink her career and start all over again.

And as for the money she'd receive from Isobel's estate, which had always felt wrong and undeserved, well, she'd put that safely away with what her father had left her, she decided.

She hadn't heard a sound from Oscar that morning, and when she went down into the kitchen there was a note on the table. *Gone to Dorchester. Back later. O.*

Helena shrugged, and put the kettle on to make herself some tea. And as soon as she'd had breakfast, she thought, she'd find Benjamin and perhaps they could go for a walk with the dog.

Helena was just about to leave the house when the doorbell rang, and she raised her eyes. That couldn't be Benjamin because he always tapped on the back door, and Oscar had his own key...

She went quickly along the hall and opened the door. A young, very pretty dark-haired woman stood there, two small boys at her side.

'Mrs Theotokis?' she asked uncertainly, and before Helena could reply, she said, 'I'm sorry to bother you... but is he...is Mr Theotokis at home?' The accent was foreign, cultured.

Helena stood back, feeling awkward for a second. 'Um, no...I'm afraid he's not,' she said. 'But can I help?'

The woman shook her head briefly. 'No, I don't think so, thank you.' She paused. 'I want to speak to Mr Theotokis myself...face to face...so I'd be grateful if you could let me know if and when he might be available.' And, seeing the confused expression on Helena's face, she added, 'It won't take long, but the children would like to see him. And it's...it's very important that they do.'

Helena's gaze rested on the boys for a moment. They were such beautiful children, clear-eyed, dark-skinned and with lustrous black hair. Who was this woman, and who were these children? she asked herself. She found her voice at last.

'I'm not sure when...when Mr Theotokis will be back, but can I give him a message?' she asked.

The woman thought for a moment, then, 'No, this is something far too personal, I'm afraid,' she said. 'And not something that can be said by proxy. But don't worry, I'll make sure that I catch up with him at some point.' She reached into her handbag and took out a large envelope. 'In the meantime, would you be kind enough to give him this?' She hesitated. 'We've been here on an extended holiday, but we're flying back home this afternoon so time is short, I'm afraid.' She held out her hand to shake Helena's. 'Well, goodbye— and I'm sorry to have bothered you.'

And with that she turned to go. With her frown deepening, Helena watched them walk away towards a waiting taxi at the end of the drive, the children casting backward glances at her as they went.

Later, in the library, Helena opened the windows wide, letting the spring air bring in a delicate scent of new growth to tease her nostrils, and she took a deep breath. Then a sudden shaft of sunlight picked out the alcove where her shepherd and shepherdess stood, where they had been standing for as long as Helena could remember. She went over to look down at them again.

The creator of those exquisite porcelain figures had breathed life, real life, into them, she thought, had given them feelings which could be interpreted by anyone taking the time to just stand and stare for a few moments. The caring, manly stance of the shepherd, and the gentle tilt of his head, indicated the purest form of true love for the lady he was gazing down at so adoringly—and the expression on the dainty features of his shepherdess was so touching it made a lump form in Helena's throat. She swallowed. Why hadn't she noticed all that before? she asked herself. Had it been there all this time, or was she just feeling extra-sensitive today?

Drawing her attention away from the love scene she had unwittingly stumbled upon, Helena looked up to see Isobel's eyes searching for hers and she went across to stand beneath the portrait for a moment. Apart from her figurines, she thought, she would ask Oscar if she could have the portrait too, so that wherever Helena's next home turned out to be, Isobel would have pride of place there.

Much later, Oscar returned. Helena was in the conservatory reading her book. He glanced down at her. She was wearing a simple cream cotton dress and strappy sandals, her shoulder-skimming hair tied loosely. He cleared his throat.

'I happened to meet John Mayhew in town this morning,' he said.

Helena didn't look up. 'Oh?'

'He told me he's been approached about the sale of Mulberry Court. Apparently Amethyst Trust Hotels want to buy it, so that they can convert it. They want to build a spa, treatment rooms, a conference centre and swimming pool.' Oscar went across to the window, looking out. He paused before going on. 'They feel it would be a perfect site for such a development, with the unusually extensive grounds and garden, all of which would be completely swallowed up, of course. In fact, if they have their way, Mulberry Court as it is now would be wiped off the map for ever,' he added, keeping his voice deliberately cool.

Now Helena did look up, a frown pleating her forehead. 'Well, I hope John Mayhew told them that the house is not up for sale...not yet, anyway,' she said.

'Oh, they know that,' Oscar said. 'But these people are all about forward planning. They wouldn't care how long it took, just so long as they got it in the end. Apparently, the local Planning Department have already been informally approached and have given Amethyst sufficient optimism to think that such a project could go through. Assuming, of course, the all-important matter of first acquiring the land,' he added.

Helena snapped her book shut and stood up. 'Well, *assuming* that I...we...have the sole responsibility of selling Mulberry Court to the *right* owner,' she said, 'you can tell John Mayhew that Amethyst whoever-they-are can get lost. I would never, never agree to sell to such people!'

Oscar couldn't help smiling at Helena's obvious aggravation at what he'd just told her. And he'd known what her reaction would be. He put out his hand to halt her progress as she went to go past him. 'We don't need to worry about any of that yet,' he said soothingly, 'but John was quite right to keep us informed.'

'I suppose so,' Helena said reluctantly. Then, 'Oh...' She began, sneezing into her hand, and Oscar immediately reached into his pocket and passed her a handkerchief. Helena took it from him. 'Oh, dear, that's the third time I've done that...I think I'm getting a cold,' she sniffed, dabbing furiously. 'My throat felt suspiciously sore when I woke up this morning.'

'Hardly a surprise,' Oscar said mildly, 'considering the wet weather you've been experiencing here lately...' He stood up. 'And that's why there's something else I need to tell you. I'm making arrangements for us to have a short holiday,' he said. 'You need a dose of real sunshine, Helena.'

Helena looked up at him. 'What do you mean... What sort of holiday?' she mumbled through the large handkerchief, which was almost covering her face.

'To Greece...or to my island getaway, I should say,' Oscar said.

'But...what about leaving Mulberry Court empty? Aren't you worried about someone gaining entry?' Helena asked.

'Oh, the house will look after itself for the few days I have in mind,' Oscar said evenly. 'And this time we'll make sure that Benjamin's around, in any case.'

Helena stared at him, biting her lip. Although she'd always longed to visit Oscar's homeland—and he'd always promised her that one day she would—now she wasn't sure she wanted to, at least not with him. Wouldn't it be helping to prolong something which could only end in more heartache? Relaxing in the sun, bathing in a warm sea…having nothing to think about except enjoying long, lazy moments—a heady, dangerous cocktail. 'I'll have to think about it,' she said. 'I have things to do here, and I'm not really sure whether…whether I want to go.'

Oscar went before her towards the door, then looked back, his dark eyebrows slightly raised. 'Oh, I'm sure it's the right thing to do.' He smiled. 'I'll book the flight for the day after tomorrow—that'll give you time to get ready,' he said smoothly.

Helena looked up at him steadily. Why was he so certain she'd agree? She sniffed again. 'I'll make us some supper in a minute,' she said. She paused before turning to go upstairs. 'Oh, by the way, someone called earlier and left something for you,' she said.

Oscar glanced back, surprised. 'Oh? Who was it?'

Helena stared up at him, her face expressionless. 'It was a woman—she had two small boys with her. And she was very insistent that she spoke to you…that she and her sons…saw you, in person. She wouldn't tell me what it was all about.' Helena paused. 'The letter she left is on the kitchen table. I'm sure it will explain everything,' she added, treading firmly up the stairs.

# CHAPTER NINE

For a long time after she'd gone upstairs, Helena sat staring out of the window at the familiar scene all around her, hating the thought of what it may look like if developers ever got their hands on Mulberry Court. She put her hand to her mouth as she imagined what it might become—a massive hotel…a huge commercial extension…and, worse, possibly a total demolition of the house, the entire property completely changed for ever. She shuddered as she imagined it.

And it was all very well for her to announce that *she* would never be party to selling to such people, she thought realistically, but even if a young family were to buy it—which Isobel had hoped might be the case— that didn't mean that eventually they, too, wouldn't sell to prospectors. Especially if the price was right. Helena knew that money was a powerful weapon, especially in the wrong hands. And the almost casual way in which Oscar had imparted the news convinced her that he didn't feel the same about the house as she did. He would look for the highest bidder, of course he would—he was a businessman. Well, he couldn't sell without *her* agreement, Helena thought decisively, and he was going to have to wait a long time for that!

She blew into Oscar's handkerchief again; she *was* getting a cold, she thought, wiping her eyes. But it wasn't just the cold that was irritating her tear ducts. She had several other reasons for feeling a bit low and, apart from the solicitor's news, they all concerned Oscar. Helena knew she was being unreasonable. So what if he did have numerous women in tow? Hardly a surprise and no more than she would have expected and, anyway, what did it matter to her? What if Allegra—whoever she was—had lost her baby?

And as for the woman and those children—they could be anybody...a family he'd known for ages, just trying to catch up before they went back home—wherever home was. In any case, none of this was any of her business, she told herself again angrily. She and Oscar were just old friends, nothing more, whose ways had parted a long time ago, and unexpectedly brought together again by the rather whimsical act of an elderly lady. And that time he'd kissed her, and any sensuous feelings which had happened between them in the past few weeks were totally unimportant...they didn't *mean* anything—to him. Oscar liked women—in every sense—and she, Helena, happened to be the woman he happened to be with at the moment. 'Allegra' or 'Callidora'—or anyone else—would have done just as well.

Telling herself this was all right up to a point, Helena started to slowly get ready for bed, but the unalterable and painful fact was that Oscar still had an intractable emotional hold over her, an unassailable ability to make her ecstatically happy, to revel in being anywhere near him and to admit again and again that she had never stopped loving him. Yet she had to accept the reality of their situation. This time next year Mulberry Court would no longer be theirs, she would be back in London with, presumably, enough money to buy herself a home of her own, and hopefully holding down a job which would keep her mind fully occupied, and away from pointless thoughts of the only man she had ever loved. And far, far away from imagining which woman he was spending his days with. His nights with...

All this introspection had made Helena temporarily forget Oscar's proclamation that they were going away for a short break. She sniffed. You could hardly call it a suggestion, she thought; he hadn't asked her whether she'd like to go or not—just that they were going, the day after tomorrow.

Helena had done very little travelling in her twenty-eight years, but had learned enough to whet the appetite. And it was after giving the matter a lot of thought she'd decided she would agree to go with Oscar, because it could be her only chance to see Greece—to see it with him. Something she'd once thought she might do one day. But this was not going to be a dream holiday, she assured herself—it was to be merely a mini-break, which busy people allowed themselves now and then. It would be a unique experience for her. And one which would never be repeated.

'We're going to a tiny island,' he'd informed her over supper. 'You'll love it. It's very beautiful but rather isolated, so you'll only need to pack a small amount of light stuff, and sensible footwear—and plenty of sun-block.'

On Saturday morning they arrived at the airport and within twenty minutes they had been swiftly transported across the tarmac to Oscar's private jet. The speed with which it happened almost took Helena's breath away. The few times she'd flown anywhere, the waiting around to join various endless queues had been one of her abiding memories of airports. But today their arrangements were prompt and seamless and soon they were climbing the few steps into the aircraft. As she was shown into the cabin—which resembled a small opulent sitting room—Helena wondered whether she was going to wake up in a minute. Was this really happening? she asked herself as she almost fell back into the luxurious depth of one of the armchairs.

Oscar sat down opposite her, stretching his arms above his head lazily. He was wearing dark trousers and a dark cotton shirt open at the neck, and he smiled lazily across at Helena, his perfect teeth blindingly white against the polished bronze of his tanned skin.

'I've ordered us some food once we are in the air,' he said briefly. 'Is that OK?'

Helena could only smile in response. She had nothing to complain about—so far! She knew she was excited—and she was going to put the sale of the house and her own future at the very back of her mind...just for these couple of days.

The one uniformed cabin attendant brought them their meal, served with iced water, and he spoke in rapid Greek to Oscar, who replied in the same way. As the steward backed away, it was quite obvious from the man's deferential attitude that Oscar was held in very high regard. Well, why wouldn't he be? It would be

Oscar's signature that appeared on the all-important pay cheques of his vast number of employees.

After the man had gone they began their meal, and Oscar leaned forward to fill their glasses with more water. And, presently, Helena put down her fork and sat back.

'I've never tasted stuffed vine leaves quite like those,' she murmured. 'Thank you, it was a very nice meal.'

Presently, their lunch things were removed and after a few minutes Oscar could see that Helena's eyelids were beginning to droop. 'How are you feeling?' he enquired briefly. She was looking pale, and winsomely desirable, dressed in a long rust-coloured cotton skirt and a soft cream top which exposed her slender neck and shoulders.

'Much better,' Helena said, sitting forward at once, but he gestured for her to relax.

'Have a sleep for an hour or so,' he said easily. 'When we land, there'll be a car to take us to the quay. And a private ferry will get us to the island. And then I'll show you one of the best places in the whole world.'

By mid-afternoon they were aboard the small private ferry which would take them to their destination. Aristi, the boat owner, greeted Oscar very enthusiastically, shaking him by the hand as he welcomed them on board, and casting a dark, appreciative glance in Helena's direction.

It was a very hot day and Oscar looked down at Helena as they stood together at the prow of the small vessel, letting the cool draught fan their faces. 'Aristi informs me that this weather is going to continue for some weeks,' he said. 'It's a shame we only have a couple of days, but that'll be long enough for me to show you around.' He pushed his sunglasses on to the top of his head for a moment. 'On the whole, it's quite a barren landscape, with just enough fertile land to support a small area of olive trees and vines, but it's not a popular place with tourists because there's very little on offer other than the natural beauty and solitude of the place. And the local population is small,' he added.

'So, what do people do with themselves?' Helena wanted to know.

'Oh, they keep goats, and work the land where they can—and there's a small harbour which provides a useful living for some,' Oscar replied. 'He looked down at her. 'Civilization roughly comprises a small hamlet of about a dozen houses—there are a couple of bars, and a taverna—which is where I always stay. The locals go over to the mainland for their other various needs,' he added.

Helena looked at him pensively. In spite of all the places that someone as wealthy as Oscar could go to recharge his batteries from time to time, the remote island she was about to see was where he liked best. And of course it was close enough to Athens—and work—for him to get back easily enough. It warmed her heart to think that this rich, vastly important man enjoyed the simple pleasures of life.

They arrived at a small jetty and Aristi helped them off the boat, shaking Oscar's hand vigorously before setting off again back to the mainland, shouting, *'Ade ha'sou! Kali tihi!'* as he went.

Oscar glanced down at Helena. 'He was hoping we'd have a nice day—and wishing us good luck,' he explained and he smiled inwardly. He was fairly certain he wasn't going to need any luck.

Oscar was carrying their two holdalls and they started walking up and away from the jetty, Helena wearing her large sun hat.

'The taverna is only about a mile away,' he said, glancing down at Helena's feet. 'Are you OK to walk in those sandals?'

'Perfectly, thanks,' she said, though thinking that maybe she should have worn her deck shoes. The ground was dusty and rather stony, and after only a few minutes some tiny bits of gravel began filtering in between her toes. But she'd grit her teeth, she thought. She wasn't going to complain this early on in their 'holiday'.

The picture Oscar had painted of the island had led Helena to think that it was far more remote than it turned out to be, because within twenty minutes they came to a small cluster of white-painted, cube-shaped houses, whose blue-shuttered windows were partly obscured by pots of flame-red geraniums, suggesting a kind of carnival atmosphere. In almost every small patch of garden were one or two tethered goats. And all around them were flourishing bushes of bougainvillea, and the tangible, overpowering perfume of rosemary and other sweet-scented herbs.

'This is "civilization",' Oscar said briefly.

'Oh,' Helena breathed. 'What a *pretty* scene; it's like a picture book!'

Oscar looked down at her, pleased at her reaction.

Helena smiled up at him, knowing that she was going to love being here, despite the intense heat, which she could only tolerate for so long. 'It's very quiet,' she said, lowering her voice so as not to disturb the pervading silence, and Oscar nodded.

'It's still siesta time,' he said. 'Everyone sleeps during the afternoon, but I know Alekos will be about, because he's expecting us.' He darted a quick glance at Helena. 'Are you OK to keep walking? We'll be there in just a few minutes.'

'I'm fine,' Helena replied.

Presently, they came to the taverna, which, Helena could see, was a somewhat larger version of the other houses on the island, but with an open frontage sporting decking on which were two small tables and wooden chairs shaded by blue-striped canopies which moved gently in the rather sparse breeze. There were balconies all around the first floor, bedecked with showers of more red geraniums, and under the shade of an adjacent olive tree a silent donkey stood, its head bowed, and it didn't even look up as the two approached.

'Alekos has had that ancient animal for years,' Oscar said. 'I don't think it does much carrying any more—trucks are used now, of course. But in the old days, donkeys did all the work.'

Oscar ushered Helena in before him, and she breathed a small sigh of relief to be in the shade of the building. Hearing their footsteps, a small, excitable, black-eyed, black-haired middle-aged man came forward, uttering, to Helena, unintelligible words of welcome as he embraced Oscar, banging him furiously on the back, his deeply olive complexion creased in genuine smiles of delight.

*'Oscarrr!'* the man exclaimed. *'Ya su! Pos ise?'*

'I'm good, thanks, Alekos,' Oscar said, releasing the man's affectionate hold, and looking down at Helena. 'This is Helena, Alekos, and she does not speak our language…'

The man immediately took Helena's hand and kissed it effusively. 'Of course…I am sorry! We shall continue in English! Come…come…drinks, water…?'

They all went into the sitting room and Helena took off her hat and ran her fingers through her dampened hair. What she'd like now, she thought, was a long, cool shower.

'Where is Adrienne?' Oscar asked Alekos, and the older man grinned.

'My wife is in Athens! With our daughter! Because we have a new grandson, Petros—God be praised!' Alekos exclaimed. 'Adrienne will be returning in three days—but you are going before then?' the older man asked.

'Afraid so,' Oscar said. 'But many, many congratulations, Alekos! A child! What a blessing!' he exclaimed.

*'Neh!'* Alekos agreed. 'And a boy! God be praised!' he repeated.

After other pleasantries had been exchanged and the three had sat in the darkened interior refreshing themselves with their drinks, Alekos led them up the stairs to a sparsely furnished room in which there was a massive bed spread with a pure white cover, a thick bolster and pillows at the head. The floors were wooden, with no carpeting of any kind, there were two small cabinets with drawers, and two chairs. The shutters at the windows were tightly shut to keep out the heat, giving the room a cool, secretive atmosphere. And to the side was a minute room with shower and toilet.

After Alekos had departed, Helena sat gingerly on the edge of the bed and looked up at Oscar. She realized that she hadn't given any thought to where they might be staying—she'd just followed Oscar's plans, with no questions asked. But now she realized she was feeling stupidly shy at the position she was in... They were going to be sharing a bed. How was she going to deal with that? she asked herself, feeling frantic at the thought. Although they had been close, very close, a long time ago, they had never actually slept together, not in the accepted sense of that phrase. And things were different now; he had moved on—and away. She swallowed hard as their eyes met.

Then, as if reading her thoughts, Oscar said, 'Europeans go in for wide beds,' he said casually. 'Useful—and necessary—in hot climates.'

And, with that, he kicked off his shoes and flopped down on the other side of the bed, well away from Helena. He yawned, not looking at her. 'After we've had a rest and a shower, I'll take you exploring. Alekos will be making us one of his superb suppers. Which we won't be eating until much later in the evening when everything's cooled down.'

Oscar closed his eyes, waiting for Helena to say something, but instead he heard her take off her sandals and lie down quietly beside him, positioning herself almost on the edge of her side of the bed. He smiled inwardly. He'd waited this long; he could wait a bit longer, he thought… Wait for that special moment…

It was seven o'clock before they both surfaced, Oscar first, and for several minutes he lay on his side, propped up on his elbow, just drinking in Helena's appearance. Her skirt was pulled up around her thighs and her loose top had fallen slightly, exposing the rounded curve of her breasts in the lacy bra. She'd pulled the clip from her hair, which hung loosely around her shoulders, and her face was pale in sleep—pale and perfect, he thought, longing to touch her. He shifted slightly, and the movement made Helena wake with a start. She sat up quickly, drawing her skirt down and looking across at him.

'How long have we been asleep?' she asked. 'I can't believe I dropped off so easily!'

'That's what the Greek climate does to you,' Oscar said, getting up and swinging his legs off the bed. He glanced back. 'I'll have a shower first, allow you to wake up properly. Then I'll show you around my is-land. It'll be getting cool now.'

Later, both having changed into light shorts and fresh tops—and with Helena wearing her deck shoes, they set off.

'You can walk the whole island in a couple of hours or so,' Oscar said briefly. 'But tonight we'll head down to the little cove I like best. It's usually nice and breezy down there.'

As they made their way across the rough ground together, Helena took a deep breath. Not just because of where they were, and of the tangible sense of peace and tranquillity, but because she and Oscar were alone, just the two of them again, just strolling along as they used to do, talking only when they felt like it, absorbing their togetherness. Helena was not going to think of anything else, not allow her anxieties about her life to spoil these precious moments which would never come again. At this point in time her heart felt like a singing bird.

Just then, her foot caught on something and she staggered slightly, lurching forward. But not before Oscar had caught her, holding her to him briefly.

'Careful,' he murmured. Then, 'It gets easier in a minute.' But he didn't let go of her, clasping her hand in his tightly as they walked on, with Oscar pointing out certain things that interested him.

As they started to make their way down towards the sea, they came across a tiny white-washed domed chapel, and Helena glanced up at Oscar.

'Could we go inside…just for a second?' she asked, thinking that she would like to say one or two things to her guardian angel.

Oscar made no comment, but led the way towards the door, which was partially open. As they went inside, Helena almost choked with emotion as she looked around. The place was cool, dark, mysterious, with just three small rows of chairs leading to an altar on which was a single tall candle, a simple cross and a gilded icon. And below was a small prayer table on which were a few lit candles flickering softly.

After she'd taken in her surroundings, Helena went forward slowly and stood gazing up for a moment. Then, turning to Oscar who had come up behind her, she said softly, 'Did you bring any money with you? I would like to…I would like to light a candle…'

Immediately, Oscar withdrew a note from his pocket, slipping it into the donation box, and Helena lit a candle and placed it alongside the others. Then she moved over to the nearest chair and knelt down, closing her eyes. She knew she'd have to stay there for a moment until she'd regained her composure because the whole atmosphere was making tears well up behind her eyelids, and she did not want to make a fool of herself in front of Oscar, who she didn't imagine had her spiritual sensitivity.

But Oscar had moved right away from her, allowing her privacy, and when she got up and turned back to him he reached out his hand and took hers again, not saying anything. He led her back out into the softly darkening night and she looked up at him gratefully.

'Thanks,' she said. 'At that moment, I had an overwhelming need to ask for something.'

He smiled down at her, releasing her hand and putting his arm around her shoulders instead. 'What were you asking for? Or am I not allowed to ask?' he said.

'Well, seeing that you paid for my candle, you are entitled to know that,' Helena said, feeling so utterly, utterly happy and contented she could tell him anything.

'I was asking that Mulberry Court is always looked after properly, and that it never gets into the hands of the wrong people, that it will never become a monstrous, money-making place that would have horrified Isobel,' she said slowly. 'And that whoever eventually owns the house…and the wonderful land surrounding it…will give it the love and cherishing that it's always been used to.'

Oscar made no comment, yet Helena was somehow aware that he understood her feelings; the occasional pressure of his hand on her bare shoulder as he tucked her in closer said things that needed no words…not just then.

By the time they got to the little beach, the light was finally beginning to fade. They found a small sandy hillock and Oscar sat first, pulling Helena down beside him, and as they looked up into the night sky the visible universe appeared before them, a myriad tiny stars twinkling in their thousands, as if thrown there carelessly by an overindulgent god.

Sitting up, with her arms wrapped around her knees, Helena said, 'Even in this light, the sea still looks a beautiful colour, doesn't it…I noticed it when we were coming across this afternoon—shades of azure and turquoise and emerald, all mixed up.' She glanced down at Oscar, who'd been gazing up at her. 'I can't say I've ever noticed colours in the water like that anywhere else before.'

He smiled at her, his dark-fringed eyes gleaming in the dusk. 'We have our very own god Apollo to thank for that,' he murmured. 'He continues to send us a permanent supply of an extra-special light to produce such fluorescence.' Oscar paused. 'I'm glad you noticed,' he added.

Looking away, Helena put her head on one side thoughtfully. Was he teasing her because of what she'd said in the chapel? Did he really give any credence to the idea of other-worldly beings? Perhaps he, too, had

a guardian angel, some unseen presence that he needed
to get in touch with now and then. She smiled inwardly.
That the all-important, almost obscenely successful
Oscar Theotokis might need anything, or anyone, other
than his own self-belief, was a most unlikely thought.

They sat there for several minutes, basking in the
warmth of the night. Then Oscar's meltingly sexy tone
interrupted Helena's dreamy thinking.

*'Heleena,'* he murmured quietly.

Drawing her down to lie beside him on the soft sand,
he turned towards her on his side, lowering his head to
close his mouth over hers, and Helena, her heart leaping in response to his touch, knew that she was lost,
utterly lost. She was here in this divine place with the
most desirable man in the world, and nothing, ever
again, was going to compare with this brief interlude
in her life.

She closed her eyes, loving the feel of his lips parting hers, the gentle thrust of his tongue, the feel of his
hands entwining her hair as he bent over her. She kissed
him back with increasing fervour, lost in the urgency
of her need, not caring that these were to be temporary,
passing moments that would never come again…

*'Heleena,'* he said again softly, gazing down into her
now wide eyes. Then he began undressing her, touching each part of her with his lips as he went, her pale
forehead, the tip of her nose, the tender skin at the base
of her throat, the round smoothness of her naked body,
knowing that he was heightening her unashamed passion, bringing it to the stratospheric level of his own…

'You make me so happy, *Heleena,*' he murmured,

gazing down at her. 'You always, always made me so happy...'

And all Helena could do was to whisper his name, over and over again. *'Oscar...Oscar...'* He was so gorgeous, she thought, feeling almost dazed in ecstasy at the feel of him, at the sight of him, his dark, suntanned skin shining faintly with perspiration, his hair glistening black in the soft light. *My Oscar...*

Gently, tenderly, he went on making slow, passionate love to her, knowing that neither of them wanted it to end quickly. As she felt his vigorous, naked body against hers Helena felt shafts of indescribable pleasure ripple through her and she moved restlessly beneath him, clinging to him with increasing intensity, her breathlessness becoming painful, and she kept on whispering his name again and again...

And then, finally, he was inside her, and their worlds exploded in a dramatic firework display of wave upon wave of heated emotion until exhausted, sated, they lay back side by side, holding hands, saying nothing to disturb their sublime contentment.

And they remained there, silent as statues, until they saw Venus sink slowly in the west.

# CHAPTER TEN

LATER, with their arms around each other's waists, they strolled back to the taverna, neither of them wanting to spoil their ecstatic moment on the beach by soiling the memory with words.

Helena glanced up at Oscar, admiring for the millionth time the chiselled contours of his face, the broad forehead, the firm mouth which had claimed hers with such intensity that she could still feel her lips tingling.

'Alekos seemed very happy at having a grandson,' she said presently.

'Well, of course he is,' Oscar said. 'Families are an essential part of the Greek culture, and having a boy child is considered extremely fortunate. For obvious reasons,' he added dryly.

He said no more, and Helena shot him a look, realizing that Oscar's own family must be very thankful that he was there to shoulder the burden of their company. But after him...then who? she thought.

Their rather late meal of thinly sliced boiled octopus in olive oil on a bed of glistrada leaves wouldn't have been Helena's first choice, but she was surprised at how much she enjoyed it. Alekos was clearly very experienced at presenting tasty dishes for his visitors, and the man's delight when he collected their empty plates was palpable.

Presently, after sharing more than one bottle of local wine with Alekos to christen the new baby's head, Helena and Oscar made their way upstairs. And when Helena cast her eyes once more on that snowy-white bed, she had no sense of trepidation, only a warm rush of pleasure at the thought of lying there with Oscar. Of being close. Of feeling his warmth meld with hers.

And in the small hours of the morning, he came to her again, embracing her tenderly, inviting her to make another journey of love within his arms. And this time it was even more wonderful than before because now they knew each other, and the familiarity of the moments only enhanced the sensual act taking place.

Then, finally, cradled in each other's arms, the surging tides of passion gave way to blissful, wonderful peace, and at last the lovers slept.

The rest of their break passed in a blur to Helena, and soon they were once more flying back towards London.

Sitting opposite her in the aircraft, Oscar gazed across at Helena, wondering what was going through her mind, what lay behind the expression in those beautiful, sometimes sad and soulful eyes.

The few days had passed exactly as he'd planned—and he knew that Helena had enjoyed it. Had enjoyed *them*. But that still didn't tell him what he really wanted to know, where exactly their paths might lead, how exactly this last chapter was going to be written. He shifted in his seat and leaned forward to stare out of the window.

And, for herself, Helena was feeling more than slightly confused at her present situation with Oscar. Their short holiday had been beyond wonderful, she thought. Their lovemaking had been fantastic, unbelievable and had sent her into paroxysms of joy she would never be able to easily describe.

And yet, and yet…Oscar had not told her he loved her. The three words she wanted to hear him say, the three words that every woman needed to hear. She knew that he'd wanted her—in the erotic sense. Oh yes, he'd made that plain enough. As much as she had wanted him. But all he had murmured over and over again was that she made him happy…that was all. She—made—him—happy. Was that enough? And what did it really mean? Did he imply that *they* could be happy again together? Or was it that their mutual pleasure had given him just a passing happiness?

She frowned as her thoughts tormented her. Was it merely the sort of happiness that went with satisfied lust? Something which he could obtain quite easily with others? And doubtless very frequently did? Or was it more significant? She bit her lip. She would probably never know the answers to all that, she thought.

They had both been rather quiet that morning, perhaps not relishing the thought of picking up the strands of normal life again. Helena looked across at Oscar, noting the familiar determined set of his jaw. His mind was probably already fixated on the work which would be waiting for him when they returned to Mulberry Court, she thought. Their holiday romance was at an end—and wasn't that to be expected? All holiday flings came to nothing, everyone knew that. They were merely passing flights of temporal fantasy. So?...So? Well, just live with it, she told herself.

She wished—not for the first time—that she could spend a few hours with her friend Anna and pour out her heart. Anna was one of those people who seemed able to read the lives and problems of others and come up with definitive answers—or, at any rate, some sound advice. But although the two girls had had several conversations on the phone since Helena had come to Dorset, Helena could never bring herself to talk about Oscar—had deliberately been evasive when questioned about the other person involved in the will. And, anyway, although Anna and Helena had been close over the years, Helena had never revealed details of her youthful love affair to another living soul because it would have been too painful. And pointless. Pointless going over something which had ended, and which it would have been far better never to have begun.

Much later, Oscar and Helena arrived back at Mulberry Court and, having eaten during their journey, no more food was considered necessary. All Helena wanted to do was to shower and get some sleep. With her foot on the bottom stair, she looked back at Oscar, who'd said he would be doing work in the study before going to bed himself.

'Goodnight, Oscar,' she said to his departing back. 'And...um...thank you...thank you for my...holiday.' She paused. 'I loved your island,' she added softly.

He turned briefly and gazed up at her, his heart almost bursting with love for her, his fertile mind doing somersaults, longing to tell her, longing to know...

'I knew you would like it there as much as I do,' he

said. And then, impulsively, he added, 'By the way, I want you to know…um…I don't want you to lose any sleep about the future of Mulberry Court.'

Helena stared back at him. 'I'll try not to…' she began, and he interrupted.

'No, what I mean is that I'm not going to sell this place—to strangers, I mean.' He cleared his throat. 'I intend keeping it, keeping it in the Theotokis family, where it belongs. And I intend…I shall be bringing my wife here one day—if I can persuade her to see my point of view,' he added obliquely.

Frozen to the spot as she stared up at him, Helena felt as if she was going to pass out. His *wife*? What wife? she asked herself incredulously. He'd never mentioned a wife before, and in fact he'd implied that he would probably never marry anyone! She forced herself to appear unperturbed by what he'd just said.

'Oh, well…' she swallowed '…it's a great relief that you intend saving Mulberry Court from a terrible fate.' She paused. 'I hope your wife will appreciate the place as much as we…as much as I…have always done,' she added.

Oscar gazed down, his eyes gleaming blackly. 'Oh, I know her well enough to be absolutely certain that she will,' he said slowly. 'And I know she'll love living here for as much of the year as is possible, allowing for work commitments. She'll have to understand that we'll need to be away fairly regularly,' he added.

'Oh, I'm sure she'll fall in with all your requirements, Oscar,' Helena said tightly.

He shrugged. 'I hope so,' he said, 'but women can be…unpredictable…at times.'

Helena could think of several ways to respond to that remark, but thought better of it. Instead, she turned and went resolutely up the stairs.

''Night,' she said casually over her shoulder, before going into her room and shutting the door firmly.

For a full five minutes she stood there, her blood racing through her veins. If Oscar had taken a gun and shot her through the heart, she couldn't feel more shocked and empty. How could he even *mention* a wife to her after what had taken place between them under the stars only a few days ago? What *was* it with men, that they could switch passion on and off like that? And what was it with Oscar Theotokis that he could treat women like he did…and that they came back for more? As she had done! Perhaps if—and when—he introduced them, she should tell Oscar's lady love just what she'd be taking on!

Helena sat down on her bed with a thump. One thing was certain—no Greek woman was going to like being in England for very long, she thought fiercely; they wouldn't survive the variable temperatures of the local climate. There wasn't usually any need to slap on the factor five thousand *here*! And, whoever she was, she'd soon start complaining when it rained for two weeks without stopping!

Then Helena's shoulders drooped. Who else would appreciate this very special place as she did? she asked herself. Who else would know the warm, personal welcome that filled every room in the house, who else would ever bother to roam every corner of the grounds, find out where the wild flowers peeped out in early spring, or want to help with fruit picking in the autumn? Or want to take a book and have a lazy read inside the long, sheltering branches of the willow tree? It would be a complete waste to bring another woman here, she thought, especially one not used to the simple pleasures in life. She would just not fit in. And she'd make Oscar's life a misery, always wanting to get back where the sun perpetually shone.

As she started to unpack her holdall listlessly, Helena knew that none of that mattered. This was all about Oscar. Nothing to do with the ownership of a property. And the unpalatable truth was that she was jealous—jealous as hell to think of anyone else being his wife even though he'd never given her any reason to think he'd want her, Helena, to fill that role. He'd never told her that, or even hinted at it. Oscar didn't want her, had never wanted her—not in a lasting, bonding sense.

She gripped her hands together tightly. Oh, why, why, *why* had Isobel thrown them together again? she asked herself desperately.

And downstairs Oscar admitted to feeling bad, feeling uncomfortable at what he'd said to Helena. It had been disingenuous, to put it mildly, but at the last second something had made him hesitate before going on to say what was really in his mind and heart.

His jaw tightened. With their past history, he knew he was standing on uneven emotional ground with Helena—and he had to be careful not to take a false step. He knew that she desired him, but could she risk trusting him? Would she ever take another chance with him, and was it fair of him to expect it? His eyes narrowed. All was fair in love and war, and he'd do what-ever it took to convince her. And wait for that golden moment when he would make it impossible for Helena to refuse him.

Next day, Helena woke up feeling surprisingly in charge of her emotions. Even though Oscar's mind-boggling announcement last night had taken the wind right out of her sails, at least he would see that no wretched devel-opment took place here, she thought. Mulberry Court was going to be safe. And, anyway, he'd wanted to buy her out all along, so he'd be getting his wish. No sur-prises there. Oscar was used to getting his own way. He had the powerful personality—and the money—to do it.

And she should also be grateful that he'd left her in no doubt that when choosing a wife he wasn't looking in her direction! Because any man who could transport a woman to such dizzy heights of emotion—and then act as if it had meant nothing—wasn't worth the time of day! Not in *her* book! Oscar didn't know the meaning of true love—unconditional, selfless love. Passion—of course—naturally! But love, true love, which meant permanent bonding? Forget it!

Helena marched over to the chest of drawers for some fresh clothes. Whoever Oscar's future unknown wife was out there, she thought…well, she had *her* sym-pathy!

It was gone nine o'clock before Helena went down into the kitchen to make herself some breakfast. As she passed the study, she could hear Oscar. He was ob-viously speaking on the telephone and his voice was raised, sounding urgent. Helena made a face to herself. It had been amazing that he'd managed to actually have almost three days away without someone contacting him, she thought.

She put the kettle on to make some tea and took bread from the freezer to make toast. Oscar could join her when it suited him, she thought, laying two places at the table and putting grounds into the cafetière for his coffee, forcing herself to hum a little tune. She'd made up her mind to act perfectly normally when she came face to face with him today, as if she hadn't given another thought to what he'd said last night. And, after all, what had changed? Nothing, she told herself. She was back to square one, having a simple break away from London for a few weeks, except that there was nothing simple about it. It would have been if Oscar wasn't part of the equation...if they'd never met up again, if he hadn't whisked her off to that sunlit island...

Suddenly, her mobile rang. It was Anna, and hearing her friend's voice made Helena's heart lift instantly. After the two girls had exchanged greetings, Anna said, 'You remember that position I told you about here... the vacancy I knew was coming up? Well, it has— much sooner than I'd thought—they want it filled by the beginning of August, and they're going to be interviewing shortly, but you'll have to get your application in on time.' Anna stopped for breath before going on, 'This sort of opportunity doesn't often come up in our place, so I hope you'll go for it, Helena—it's just your thing, I know it is! And you'd fit in a treat! And wouldn't it be fantastic to be seeing more of each other again? I miss you, Helena! It seems ages since we had some fun together. I'll send all the details to Mulberry Court tonight, shall I, and then you can think it over. OK? But don't leave it late, will you…?' And, as an afterthought, 'You must be feeling right back to your old self by now, lapping up all that peace and quiet, not to mention being totally free from the deadly male species for a change!' It had been Anna who had helped mop up Helena's tears after the failed relationship with Mark. 'And don't forget, you can always stay with us until you find your dream home!' Anna said cheerfully.

Helena smiled broadly. It was so good to hear her friend's voice, especially this morning.

The two girls spent a few minutes while Anna filled in more details about the job and just catching up, then they finished the call and Helena snapped her mobile shut thoughtfully. That was just what she needed. Not just to hear Anna's voice, but to make her realize that she should think seriously about her future. It was time to turn her back on Mulberry Court and return to real life. Being here, she was hiding her head in the sand.

She was just making her tea when Oscar appeared, and she glanced up. 'Hi,' she said brightly. 'Do you want your coffee now?'

He came across and stood next to her and Helena thought, please don't touch me. I don't want you to ever touch me again. She took a step to the side, avoiding any contact, and took their drinks over to the table.

'I've just had a very interesting call from Anna—my friend in London,' she said, glancing up at him briefly. 'She told me about a very exciting opportunity coming up in her firm. She's going to send me all the details so that I can apply.' Helena sat down and reached for the rack of toast. 'It does sound as if it might suit me,' she went on, spreading some butter on her slice of toast, 'and if I was lucky enough to get it, I wouldn't start until August so I'd still have a few weeks here. So that would be good, wouldn't it?' She took a generous bite from the toast and scrunched away, looking up at him, realizing that he hadn't spoken a word.

'I have to go back to Greece as soon as possible, now, this morning,' he said, his expression darkly serious.

'Well, I hope you can stop long enough to have your coffee,' Helena said, rather tritely.

He stared down at her. 'I've just been told they've brought my father back to Greece,' he said quietly. 'I'm afraid he's dying.'

# CHAPTER ELEVEN

A WEEK later Louise returned and Helena was especially thankful to have some company. To hear about someone else's problems was always a relief, she thought, as one morning she made her way down to the cottages.

Oscar had left almost immediately after receiving the call from Greece, only staying long enough to have a quick coffee, refusing any food. It was obvious that the news had hit him unbelievably hard, and Helena was filled with sympathy as she'd looked up at his drawn features. She was never going to forget what her reaction had been on hearing about her own father's death, how she'd felt so devastated, so empty. She knew that losing one's parents was a natural sequence of human events, but that didn't make it any more acceptable when it happened.

She had found it easy to offer just one or two words of sympathy, squeezing Oscar's arm tightly, and he'd covered her hand with his own briefly. With his voice thick with worry, he'd said he would be in touch with her as soon as possible. And, rather surprisingly, given the particular circumstances, as he'd left he had asked her not to apply for the London job until he returned, saying it could complicate matters. And although

Helena hadn't really understood the point, she wasn't going to question it…not then. Family matters were a far more important concern than jobs—or even the selling of houses. And that was obviously the 'complication' he was alluding to, she thought. His buying Mulberry Court from her and all the formalities that would have to be dealt with. And he knew that, now, she would readily fall in with his plan because it meant no one else would get their grasping hands on the place.

All the information about the job had arrived in the post two days later and, leafing through it, Helena had to agree with Anna that it did seem to fit her credentials perfectly, almost tailor-made for her, in fact. But there was no need to return the forms just yet, she'd thought, putting them back into the envelope. Not until she'd spoken to Oscar. She'd had only one rather tense call from him, telling her very little, and she remembered what he'd said about Greeks being very family-oriented and emotionally close. His parents were Oscar's only family, as far as she knew, and it was his father's name which had always cropped up in conversations. In a way, Helena wished she was there with him to give some support, but he'd have no need of her. There'd be plenty of other people—other women— to give him support. Not to mention his future wife!

Now, Helena tapped lightly on the door of Louise's cottage and Benjamin, with Rosie at his heels and a mug of coffee in his hand, opened it to let Helena come in. Louise came across from the kitchen with some drinks on a tray, her face creased in a broad smile.

'It's so good to be home again,' she said, putting down the tray and giving Helena a big hug. 'Now, I know we've only had a few words on the phone so far, but I want to know everything that's been happening!' She handed Helena a mug of coffee.

Helena said quickly, 'You start first, Louise—how's your cousin now?'

Benjamin cleared his throat, looking at each of them in turn. 'Well, Rosie and I must be off—so I'll leave you two to it,' he said amiably. He glanced across at Louise. 'Thanks for the coffee, Louise—the best one I've had for weeks!'

'Flatterer,' Louise said as she handed Helena a plate of biscuits. 'And by the way, I'm making a steak and kidney pudding for supper, Benjamin. I know it's your favourite, so we'll eat at eight, if that's OK.' She looked across at Helena. 'There'll be plenty for three if you'd like to join us, Helena,' she said, adding, 'It's wonderful to be using my own cooker again. Didn't realize how much I'd miss it!'

After Benjamin had gone, and Helena had insisted on knowing every detail about Sarah's problems, Louise said, 'Now, I want to know how *you've* been getting on.' She shot a look at Helena. 'Benjamin told me that Oscar's been about quite a lot…'

'Yes…he has been, on and off,' Helena replied guardedly. She smiled. 'I think he wants to keep a very close eye on his property, but at the moment he's with his father, who's not at all well, I understand,' she added, deciding not to be more specific.

'Mmm,' Louise murmured equivocally. She paused, then, casually, 'Benjamin and I were chatting the other night, and we came up with the idea that wouldn't it be wonderful if you and Mr Oscar were to, you know, keep the house and…were to get married one day…'

Helena interrupted this flight of fancy. 'Louise! There's about as much chance of that happening as time moving backwards!' she exclaimed. 'Oscar would never want to marry me, I know that for a fact.'

'I don't see why not,' Louise said. 'It's obvious that he…likes you…Helena. Always did. Just think of the hours you both spent here together…'

She didn't go on, but Louise remembered those times clearly—what a handsome couple the youthful pair had made, how they'd revelled in each other's company… and it was no different now, not from the looks she'd seen Oscar give Helena…

Helena shrugged. 'We've both grown up, Louise,' she said firmly. 'And anyway, if Oscar ever marries, it won't be to an Englishwoman. He'll probably have to marry a suitable Greek woman.'

Louise pursed her lips. 'Well, Isobel's husband obviously had his own ideas about that,' she said. 'Now, those two were a devoted couple. He worshipped the ground Isobel walked on.'

'They were a different generation, Louise, and Oscar is obviously different from Paul Theotokis,' Helena said lightly, not wishing to continue with this conversation. She wasn't going to say a word about the wife Oscar had alluded to, nor that he intended becoming the sole owner of Mulberry Court. In any case, that was still some time off because no sale could go through until one year had elapsed—which was still some time away. Best to leave things unsaid, for now, she thought. But she couldn't help feeling touched at what Louise obviously hoped for, though Helena hadn't realized that she and Oscar had obviously been discussed at length by the two in the cottages. And of course their dream scenario would be wonderful for them, she thought. The perfect answer to their own personal future.

For the next few days, Helena decided to suspend all thoughts about Oscar, or the house, or the London job, until he came back to England. She still had another couple of weeks before the application form needed to be sent, so she decided to spend a lot of the time being busy cataloguing all the books in the library, even though she knew this wasn't really her problem any more. She made notes of the ones she would like to take away for herself, thinking that it would be useful for Oscar to know exactly what was left on those shelves. Kneeling back on her heels, she added another set of volumes to the list in her hand. And the moisture she was wiping from her eyes had little to do with the occasional dust that drifted about, she knew that. It was sad regret that made her keep taking a tissue from her pocket.

One day, Helena went upstairs to her room, taking her mug of tea with her. She put it on the bedside table, then sat looking around her again for a moment. All the rooms in Mulberry Court were individually distinguished by the furniture and fittings that Isobel had brought back from her travels, and Helena's room— the best one, in her opinion—boasted several items of beautiful hand-crafted Indian workmanship. She stared thoughtfully at her reflection in the ornate mirror opposite, and at its matching chest of drawers. Both items had apparently been the handiwork of a young teenager—the son of the owner of a struggling out-of-town enterprise in Delhi—and, staring at it now, Helena knew that she wanted this special furniture in her own home one day. Well, it wouldn't suit Oscar's style, she thought. He wouldn't want it.

Suddenly, remembering something, Helena smiled faintly and stood up and went over to kneel in front of the chest of drawers. Apart from the one in which she'd put some clean tops, they were empty of any contents but, at Helena's touch, the wider drawer at the bottom slid open smoothly. She let her fingers trace the fine inside seam along its length until she felt the tiny nub which, when compressed, allowed the opening of a compartment designed as a place of safety for treasures.

'I thought it was such fun!' Isobel had said when she'd first shown it to Helena. 'Such amazing crafts-manship by someone so young, with a delightfully cun-ning twist! I had never seen anything like it before, and I think everyone should have somewhere special that no one else knows about! And this is yours, this is for you, Helena,' she'd declared emphatically.

Now, with the firm movement required, Helena was able to draw out the small compartment and, gasping audibly, she felt her fingers close on something inside. Bending further forward, she took out two envelopes and stared at them for a moment, completely mystified.

With her mouth drying, she recognized the first one immediately. It was something she had found in her father's desk after he had died and, without question, Helena had obeyed the simple hand-written instruction on the front.

*'To be returned, unopened, to Mrs Isobel Theotokis.'*

Now, with the blood beginning to gather pace through her arteries, Helena picked up the second envelope. It read:

*'For the sole attention of Miss Helena Kingston.'*

Holding both items in her hands, which were by now shaking, Helena wondered if she was having another of her dreams, whether she was finally losing her grip on reality. She stayed quite still for several minutes, then got up slowly and went over to sit down on the cushioned seat under the window.

Then she opened each envelope carefully and spread the contents out in front of her.

Finally, the worst had happened and, ten days later, Oscar was due to return to Mulberry Court. Helena's feelings were in a state of total confusion as she waited to see his car pull up outside.

From their one or two phone conversations, Helena had learned that Giorgios Theotokis had passed away quietly with Oscar there, holding his hand. From the tone of his voice, and the brevity of what he'd said, Helena knew that it had—naturally—been a traumatic event for Oscar. But she also knew that he would deal with it—and the aftermath—quickly and effectively, in his usual businesslike way. He was no defeatist, and he would recover, probably quicker than she had done after her own bereavement.

But, in spite of death, life went on, Helena reminded herself. And *her* life was somewhat hanging in the balance. She still had no job, and no home of her own that she could move into. In fact, the only thing that she re-

ally owned at the moment was an elderly car waiting
to be picked up at that London garage.

And that other thing she owned. A broken, jealous
heart…

Then a sudden smile tilted the corners of her mouth.
Despite everything else, she had to acknowledge a
warm ripple of contentment running through her every
now and again. It was possible, she realized, to feel
happiness—real happiness—on someone else's behalf,
even in retrospect. Happiness by proxy! Even the dark-
est clouds sometimes had a silver lining, she thought.

At six o'clock on the Friday evening that Oscar was
due back, Helena stood idly in the conservatory, gazing out of the window. He had phoned her on his way
from the airport to say that there was heavy traffic and
that he might be delayed.

She had been surprised that he was able to return to
the UK so soon after the funeral—she'd have thought
there'd have still been a great deal to do. But when she'd
made the comment to Oscar, he'd said that there were
one or two essential points he had to clarify regarding
Mulberry Court, and that he wanted to get them sorted
out as quickly as possible.

In the fridge were some thick, moist slices of home-
cooked gammon, and a generous wedge of duck paté to
go with a loaf of the bread she'd bought for their supper, and presently she went into the kitchen to prepare
a green salad to go with it all. In the new car—which
Helena freely admitted she was going to hate parting with—she'd driven into Dorchester that morning
to buy the provisions—among which were some deli-

cious black cherries, which now she rinsed under the tap before putting them in a ceramic bowl.

It had been a lovely fine day, and the evening was turning out to be just as perfect, with the sun still warm and a light breeze ruffling the leaves and branches. Glancing at her watch for the hundredth time, Helena decided that she wasn't going to waste another moment inside; her days here were numbered, and it could be another hour or more before Oscar returned.

She tore a piece of paper from the notepad in her bag and scribbled the words '6.45—gone for a short walk'. Then she propped it up against one of the wine glasses on the table and went outside.

She was wearing her simple blue shift dress and strappy sandals, her hair in one long plait down her back and, as soon as she set off, Helena's heart surged once more in pleasure just to be here, walking the familiar territory. As she trod lightly across the dry grass, her mind kept going back to the short time on that island... Well, it had been in the forefront of her thoughts ever since they'd returned. How could it not have been? It had been an unforgettable few days and she never would, never could, forget it. How could Oscar have brought her down to earth so cruelly—on the very night they'd come back? It had been heartless of him to even hint at another woman after he'd possessed her so fully! Even if he did know that announcing he was going to keep Mulberry Court in the family would please her! As if that made everything all right! Her heart, and this house, were two very different things, she thought, suddenly feeling defiant again at what he'd said.

She shook herself angrily. She was not going to ruin

this lovely evening by going over and over all that, she thought. It would be a total waste of her emotional energy, and she'd wasted enough of that already.

As she wandered up the gently sloping terrain, she wondered if Benjamin and Rosie would be around somewhere, but so far there'd been no sign of them. Helena smiled to herself; this had been the perfect place for Benjamin, Helena thought, as Isobel had known it would be. And when he and Louise were eventually told that their futures were secure—because Oscar and his wife would obviously be keeping them on—they would be over the moon. Mulberry Court would still be owned—and partly lived in—by the Theotokis family.

As she strolled on, her mind a kaleidoscope of shifting thoughts, Helena found herself at the very top of the grounds which would then lead her down the winding path towards the willow tree. She realized that for some unknown reason she hadn't gone there at all since being here all these weeks. It hadn't been a deliberate thing, more a subconscious wish to leave certain memories alone, she thought briefly. To peer inside the lowering branches might seem like opening a tomb…

So what was dragging her feet towards the tree? she asked herself now as, presently, there it was, its graceful branches reaching the ground, almost still in the light breeze. With an overpowering sense of resignation, Helena knew she was going to go in and sit on that flat tree stump just one more time. *Confront the problem*—she could hear her father's voice—*confronting a problem is halfway to solving it.*

Well, Helena knew she wasn't going to solve this particular problem—the problem of loving someone who loved someone else—but here goes, she thought, as she parted the branches of the tree and entered into the sweet, damp darkness…

It was about half an hour later that she heard his voice and, with her eyes still closed, Helena smiled. She wasn't asleep, she told herself, only daydreaming as she'd been sitting there surrounded by all the gentle, friendly ghosts of her past. She could hear them whispering, telling secrets, laughing…

'Heleena…' The voice, only slightly louder now—but she was not going to open her eyes. This was a mesmerising event…one which would never happen again. Hold on to the daydream, she told herself. Hold on to it…

He had been gazing down at her for some time, drinking in her appearance, She looked so childlike, so naïve, making the years between somehow melt away…

Then, 'I knew this is where I would find you.'

Suddenly, jerked from her semi-consciousness, Helena's eyes shot open and she stared up into Oscar's deep, penetrating gaze. For a full five seconds she didn't know whether she was awake, asleep or somewhere in between, but then he moved towards her, holding out his hands to raise her up, gathering her into his arms, crushing her to him, making her gasp. She *was* awake! This was real!

Saying no more, Oscar's lips found her mouth, her neck, the smooth skin of her bare shoulders—then her mouth once more, deeply, longingly, as if he were quenching his thirst with a draught of pure nectar. 'Heleena,' was all he murmured again.

And, clinging to him, Helena knew she wasn't going to let him go. It was the final curtain on this particular act in her life—this must last her for ever! With her arms raised and her hands entwined in the thickness of his hair, she leaned into him, her head dropping backwards, her trembling lips parting to receive his manly, seductive touch, and the feel of him, the smell of him, made her world revolve in crazy circles…round and round, making her feel so dizzy that if he hadn't been holding her closely she would have sunk to her knees on the ground.

Then, suddenly, abruptly, Helena's principles returned and reluctantly she pulled herself away and stared up at him in total confusion and dismay. What *was* this? she asked herself. What was he making her do? What was she allowing him to do?

'Oscar—' she said shakily '—this…this isn't right… is it?'

Still holding her, he murmured, 'It feels exactly right to me, Helena.'

'But—Allegra?'

He frowned down at her. 'Allegra?'

'Well…I'm assuming that she's the wife you'll be bringing here in the not too distant future,' Helena began, and he interrupted her.

'Allegra Papadopoulos—and her sister Callidora— are old family friends,' he said. 'Nothing more. Allegra is like the kid sister I never had.'

'But…her baby?' Helena said. 'The baby she lost…?'

'Helena, Allegra's baby is absolutely nothing to do with me,' Oscar asserted firmly. He paused. 'Allegra is a rather…unusual…woman. She has no wish to be married, but is determined to produce a child.' He shrugged. 'In my view, every child does better with two parents, if possible. But Allegra's always been terribly headstrong. She'll probably get her way in the end.'

Helena swallowed, for some reason feeling glad that Allegra would not be the wife Oscar intended bringing here, but—did it matter which woman became his wife?

There was silence for a few moments after that, while Helena tried to make sense of this situation. Then, thinking that perhaps his need for her at this moment was more to do with his raw grief following his father's death, she said, 'I hope all the arrangements in Greece went ahead without too many problems, Oscar...' After all, she thought, people usually liked to talk about life-changing events in their lives. He let her go slightly and looked down into her eyes.

'There are other, rather more important things, that are my concern now,' he said.

Helena steeled herself. 'About the house, you mean—and bringing your wife here?' she began but, before she could say another word, he had dragged her back towards him roughly, their faces so close that she could feel his rapid breath fanning her cheek.

'Yes, it is about my wife—or my prospective wife,' he said evenly. 'And I'm hoping you can help me out with that.'

*She* could help him out! How? And why?

'You'll have to give me a clue as to how I can possibly be of assistance,' she said, hearing her voice tremble as she uttered the words.

'I did give you a clue the night we came back from Greece,' he said, 'but unfortunately you didn't pick up on my perhaps clumsy hint.'

'Clue? What clue?' Helena asked, totally mystified. He was talking in riddles!

Then, after the longest moment of her life, Helena heard Oscar say the words she'd thought were lost to her for ever.

'It is *you* that I love, *Heleena*,' he said quietly. '*You* are the wife I was talking about...you are the only woman I would ever want to marry... Didn't you realize...?'

Almost swooning with amazement, Helena looked up at him. How was she supposed to have realized it? 'Well, that wasn't exactly what you implied on that night,' she said. 'You must think I am so stupid!'

Holding her so closely that they might have been one person, he whispered, 'You are not stupid, *Heleena*.... you are the sweet, intelligent, innocent girl that I have always known, have always loved. You are the girl who has made me unable to accept anyone else, to commit to anyone else. You are the woman I have been waiting for.' He rested his mouth on top of her head for a moment. 'Before we met again, I'd convinced myself that I would never marry—because no one else would ever do. And now...' he held her away from him gently '...I have to make you see, make you understand why I was forced to walk away from you—from us—all that time ago. And make you say that you will marry me... marry me soon...*kopella mou*...'

# CHAPTER TWELVE

Hand in hand and saying very little, they made their way back to the house, Helena feeling almost drunk, delirious with happiness. She knew that her colourful imagination went to extreme lengths at times, but today went beyond anything her dreamy mind could come up with. This was paradise. Somewhere, quietly in the background, her guardian angel had been at work.

As they let themselves into the silent house, Oscar led Helena into the conservatory, closing the door behind them. They didn't bother to switch on the lamps; the silver beams from a pale moon was enough to infiltrate the corners, to light up the shadows of the room.

Feeling as if her knees were not going to be able to hold her up for much longer, Helena sat down on the long sofa and looked up at Oscar. He had gone across to gaze out of the window and now he half-turned towards her, the strong profile, the determined jaw testament to his powerful bearing, his superiority in any situation he found himself in. Helena shivered with sensuous pleasure. This was the man who'd always been the love of her life, and he had just told her that he wanted to marry her! And that he *loved* her!

But first he must tell her. She *had* to know.

'Why did you abandon me all that time ago, Oscar? Why didn't you tell me what I had done wrong?' she whispered. 'Why did you stop loving me?'

Now he turned towards her, his expression ominous in its intensity. 'I have never stopped loving you! And you had done *nothing* wrong, *Heleena*! You could, would never do anything wrong!' He ran a hand through his hair restlessly. Then, choosing his words...

'It all happened during the time of our last vacation here...just before you were going off to university,' he said slowly. 'Two dreadful, unimaginable things occurred at the same time and I was called back home urgently.' He paused before going on. 'Our company was within a hair's breadth of total disaster, thanks to unforeseeable circumstances in the industry as a whole, the first such thing to happen in our long history and a total shock, I can tell you. We had to move fast because it was something which had to be dealt with quickly, and it was necessary for me to be there, to understand, almost at once to assume responsibility—to take my place at the head of the team.'

Helena listened without saying anything, realizing what a bombshell the prospect of failure must have been for the mighty Theotokis empire.

After a moment, Oscar went on, 'But much, much worse, at exactly that same time my poor father was diagnosed with a debilitating disease from which he had no hope of recovery.' Oscar swallowed. 'Only the prospect of slowly declining health. And my father was a very proud man. Before his illness he worked every single day of his life, he was an unstoppable, driving force and the prospect of becoming wheelchair-bound was something he could barely face, could barely tolerate.' Oscar shut his eyes against the memory of that hideous time, before going on. 'And he was emphatic that his condition should not be widely known; he didn't want the news to become public property, it would not have been good for the company. He didn't want people to know—and to pity him. To be pitied would have been the final straw.' Oscar shook his head slowly, the pain of that time still hurting him deeply. 'Of course, certain members of the company had to be told, but by various means and for a considerable time it was kept largely a secret until, eventually, that became impossible.'

Oscar turned to look down at Helena, and she could see from the agony in his eyes how much he had loved and respected his father, how much he had cared for the older man's predicament, and for the name of their illustrious company.

'So, there was no alternative; I had to put the rest of my life on hold and do my family duty,' Oscar went on heavily. 'I had so much to learn from my father—and to learn quickly while he still had the strength to instruct and advise me.'

Helena had listened to every word, knowing what it was costing Oscar to go over that painful time. But... 'Couldn't you have told me, Oscar? You know I would have understood,' she said. 'And I would have waited for you, however long it took. Didn't you know that?'

'How could I ask such a thing of an eighteen-year-old girl just about to go out into the world for the first time?' Oscar demanded. 'You would be meeting other people, other men; you deserved to have a life of your own without emotional responsibilities.' He hesitated. 'I knew my path was going to be long and onerous… How could I have held you back? Besides, I was under a vow of secrecy about my father's illness. I could tell no one, not even someone I knew I could trust.' Oscar heaved a long sigh. 'I gave my word, and I could not break that,' he said.

After a moment, Helena said, 'I found it so hard, Oscar, so terribly hard…I just couldn't understand…'

He interrupted her. 'And it was so hard for me, too!' he said harshly. 'Don't you think I was full of regret? Don't you think I felt bad? That not only was I losing you, but I couldn't tell you why!' Oscar's expression contorted at his own words. Then, 'I thought of you so much, *Heleena*…I thought of you all the time…I imagined you married to someone else, and that thought tormented me.' He sighed deeply. 'Until, finally, the pressures I was under forced me to think of nothing else but the task I was faced with.' He paused for a long moment before adding, with a trace of cynicism, 'And I can recommend relentless work, relentless routine, as a very effective antidote to the human need for love.'

Slowly, Helena got to her feet and went over to slide her arms around Oscar's neck, resting her head on his shoulder, and he immediately enfolded her in his arms. But of course she would have waited for him, she thought. Well, without realizing it, hadn't she been doing just that?

He gazed down at her, then kissed her closed eyelids tenderly.

'Must I go down on one knee to hear you say that

you will be my wife, *Heleena*?' he murmured, and she smiled.

'Oscar, you should have known the answer to that—and all you needed to do was to tell me that you still loved me,' she said.

Then, in the enveloping silence of the room, their lips met in a long, deeply sensuous kiss that took them back to those halcyon days, days which were not gone and forgotten…days which were to return.

Presently, gently pulling away, Helena said, 'I've got something I want to tell you, Oscar…something lovely…something amazing.' He raised one dark eyebrow as she continued. 'A few days ago, I found some letters—well, actually they found me.' She swallowed. 'What I mean is—I was meant to find them,' she added, 'and they were written from just after I'd left home to go to university, until the last week before my father's death.'

Helena struggled with her emotions for a moment, unable to continue, and Oscar frowned slightly.

'Go on,' he murmured.

'They were letters between Isobel and my father, Oscar, and they were left in very tidy date order. The first one was from Isobel, thanking him for some extra work she'd asked him to do, and then there was his reply to her. And this correspondence appears to have continued regularly until four years ago.' Now Helena couldn't stop her tears from sliding gently down her face. 'They are the most beautiful letters I have ever read of a slowly emerging love story between two people who surprise themselves by discovering that—later on in their lives, and quite unexpectedly—they have deep feelings for each other. And it obviously gave them pleasure to say all this by writing to each other about it.' Helena wiped her cheek with the back of her hand. 'And it's clear that, eventually, they...they did become lovers.' Helena dropped her voice, as if telling a secret.

If he was astounded at this news, Oscar gave no sign. But—why should he, why should anyone be surprised? His great-aunt had always been a beautiful and gracious woman, and Daniel Kingston an attractive and charming man who, despite having worked all his life on the land, had always had the manner of a rather gallant gentleman. Yes, they would have made perfect partners. And it should never be forgotten that intimate feelings were not the preserve of the young, Oscar thought. Love was for everyone, if you could find it.

'Where did you find the letters?' he asked softly.

Helena smiled briefly. 'In my room there is a chest of drawers which has a secret compartment. Only Isobel and I knew about that,' she said. 'And that's why I know that she wanted me to see the letters, she wanted to share them with me. She knew I'd find them one day.' Helena closed her eyes for a second. Then, 'I feel... ecstatic...that my wonderful dad found love a second time in his life, Oscar, and with a lady who'd meant so much to me, too.' She paused. 'I feel as if I'm having too much happiness all at once,' she said slowly.

It was quite late by the time they eventually decided to have supper and presently, in the kitchen, Oscar watched while Helena took the delicious food from the fridge, then carefully poured oil and vinegar and honey into a bowl to prepare a dressing for their salad. He loved watching the way she used her slim fingers, the way her pale forehead creased into the merest semblance of a frown as she bent over the task, the way her dark eyelashes fanned the curve of her cheek…

They ate the meal in comparative silence, both relishing the distinctive love-enhanced atmosphere in the room, the sense of emotional security that bound them. And every now and again their eyes would meet and a silent message would pass between them—a message which had hung, unspoken, for so long.

But Oscar knew that there were things he must say to Helena—to make sure that she understood that by marrying him, her life was never going to be the same again.

He took a deep breath, and looked across at her. 'Are you fully aware of how marrying me is going to change your life, Helena?' he asked. 'Are you…are you sure you are ready for it? Are you sure you can bear it?'

Helena looked at him steadily, a faint smile on her lips. 'When people commit to a relationship,' she said slowly, 'it usually does mean a complete change to their lives, doesn't it? Isn't that what both parties expect… and want?'

'Of course,' Oscar said, 'and it's certainly what I want! But I realize how far you've come from your childhood here, how hard you've worked to achieve the independence you've earned. Are you prepared to give that up?' His face was serious for a moment. 'Because, you see, I cannot give up *my* career. I will never be able to just walk away from my responsibilities, and it will mean that you, too, will be affected.' He reached across and covered Helena's hand with his own, holding her tightly, before going on.

'I have to be in Greece and travel elsewhere abroad at regular intervals—and you will need to be with me sometimes. I will need to introduce you as my wife, I mean, it'll be important for us to be together. Not all the time, of course,' he added quickly, 'and Mulberry Court would always be our English base—but we cannot be here as often as perhaps you would like, Helena,' he said. 'Some compromise will be needed.'

Helena's eyes swam with tenderness. Precious though Mulberry Court was, it could never be as precious as flesh and blood, she thought. Could never be compared with being in the company of someone you deeply, truly loved.

'But Oscar, wasn't that what Isobel did—all her life?' Helena asked. 'She made it work. She travelled with Paul and was often abroad with him—but still managed to keep a firm foothold here as well.' Helena smiled. 'It's going to be history repeating itself, isn't it—and what better example do we have to follow?' She paused. 'And if you're worrying about my career being cut short—well, I can help *you*, can't I? I'd really love to find out how you make the company work, what it entails…the secret of its success.'

Thoroughly enthused by this thought, Helena went on, 'I mean it, Oscar. It would be a complete change of scene for me—and I'd enjoy the challenge.' She smiled at him pertly. 'I do very well at interviews. I'm sure you would find me a suitable candidate for the post of your PA.'

Oscar looked across at her flushed features longingly. Then, 'There is something else that perhaps we should talk about,' he began, and Helena raised her eyebrows. What else could there be?

Oscar came straight to the point. 'I want us to have children...I mean I would *love* us to have children. Several children, to be a real, noisy family.' He paused. 'I've never heard you express an opinion on parenthood, but...'

'You mean...I would be expected to produce heirs for the family firm, to carry on the name?' Helena began, and he interrupted fiercely.

'Hell, *no!*' Oscar exclaimed, leaning closer and taking both of her hands in his. 'I want us to have children for *us*, to see them grow up happily—and for much of the time here, at Mulberry Court. To give them brothers and sisters, something that I never had.' He shrugged. 'And who knows? If we are lucky enough to produce children and one of them chooses to follow in the family footsteps—well, that'll be fine. But it won't be a pre-condition of being a Theotokis,' he added firmly. He paused, smiling briefly. 'And, anyway, I seem to remember that Isobel stated a wish that a couple with children might buy the house. So...we would be carrying out her instructions, wouldn't we?' he said.

Suddenly, the ensuing silence was broken by Helena's mobile ringing and, raising her eyes at Oscar, she picked it up to answer it. It was Louise and, after a few moments of brief conversation, Helena ended the call and stood up.

'Louise apologizes profusely for the lateness of the call,' Helena said, 'but wonders whether we would like to go down to the cottages for a celebratory nightcap.' She shrugged. 'I didn't realize it, but today is Benjamin's birthday,' she added.

It was past midnight before Oscar and Helena left the cottage and started strolling back to the house. It was a perfect evening, enriched by the early summer scents of honeysuckle, hawthorn and cow parsley. As Helena gazed upwards briefly, the stars in the night sky twinkled and shone seductively, matching the glow in her eyes. Oscar encircled Helena's waist tightly.

'Well,' he said, looking down at her, 'did you have any inkling about that?'

Helena smiled. 'Sort of,' she said, not really surprised at Benjamin's request that Mulberry Court might look after itself for a few days at the beginning of next month while he took Louise to London to show her the sights. And with a further request that he might bring his young children back for a short holiday in Dorset.

'Louise has heard me banging on about Andrew and Daisy for long enough; I think she deserves to see them for herself,' Benjamin had said, adding, 'I don't get many chances to bring them away for a holiday, and Mulberry Court is such a perfect place for children.'

Helena glanced up at Oscar. 'It's impossible not to see how close, more than close, Benjamin and Louise have become,' Helena said. 'And I think it's lovely for them, don't you?' She smiled quickly. 'Louise adores children, I do know that, and she's going to love having Benjamin's here for a holiday.' And after a moment Helena added, 'Wouldn't it be great if Louise and Benjamin got together, and really became a couple?'

'It would be perfect all round,' Oscar agreed. He

paused. 'Do you think that might have been one of Isobel's little plans?' he asked. 'She was always an incurable romantic.'

Helena smiled. 'I shouldn't be at all surprised,' she said. She looked away for a second, thinking what a very long, eventful day it had turned out to be. 'I notice that neither of us bothered to mention anything about the new owners who were going to be residing frequently at Mulberry Court,' she said. Oscar squeezed her waist more tightly.

'Tonight didn't seem the appropriate occasion,' he said. 'After all, we had spoken at length of my father's demise, and Louise had been so touchingly sympathetic, and, after that, we were enlightened about her and Benjamin's wish to spend time together, away from here, and about his children coming to stay...' Oscar paused... 'Of course, for obvious reasons, they are going to be thrilled and excited when we do tell them, but I thought our own personal announcement could wait.' He smiled down into Helena's upturned face. 'Because I want to savour it...to hold on to it for just us...for a little while longer,' he added.

They let themselves into the silent house and, as they passed the door to the library, Oscar instinctively led Helena inside and looked up at the portrait of his great-aunt.

'Aunt Isobel,' he said softly, 'what plots have you been hatching?'

Helena wandered over to the alcove which held her figurines, and glanced up at Oscar. 'You know, Oscar, the only things I ever imagined I would possess are these two beautiful lovers,' she said quietly. 'To be left so much else of value never even crossed my mind.'

Oscar was well aware of that. Helena was the most generous, unworldly woman he had ever met. And her night-time mumblings as she'd sleepwalked that night proved her own words.

Suddenly, something made Helena pause in her thoughts—something she'd been meaning to ask Oscar and had kept forgetting to do, and which she was past caring about now. But still… Without looking at him, she said, 'Who was the lady who turned up the other day—the lady with the children, Oscar?'

'Oh—that,' he said non-committally. He frowned briefly, as if trying to remember something, then went over to one of the shelves and took down the envelope he'd left on top of the books. Without a word, he handed it to Helena and, after hesitating for a second, she opened it slowly.

Inside was a handwritten letter and two brightly coloured childish pictures decorated with hearts and flowers and a big *'Thank You'* emblazoned on the front of them. The more formal one read:

*Dear Mr Theotokis*
*What words are there, in any language, to ex-*
*press one's gratitude for the gift of life? You*
*may remember a dreadful road accident which*
*happened a few months ago to me and my fam-*
*ily while we were in the area on holiday. I later*
*learned that you were the person who rescued us*
*from almost certain death. Subsequently, we were*
*in hospital for a number of weeks, but thank-*

*fully, are fully recovered now. I have tried to con-
tact you before this, but was told you live mainly
abroad. We are able to return home to Italy now,
but I do hope there is an opportunity for the children to meet you one day, to thank you properly
for your swift and selfless action which saved our
lives. But for now—I thank you, Mr Theotokis. I
thank you from the bottom of my heart, and God
bless you.*

It was signed *'from Maria, Antonio and Paolo
Giolitti'.*

Helena looked up with tears in her eyes but, before
she could speak, Oscar said, 'Do you remember the
night I was held up on my way to the Horseshoe Innn?
That first weekend?'

Of course she remembered, and Helena felt a pang
of true remorse. She'd thought his surly attitude that
night had been because he was annoyed at being held
up on his journey. Instead of that, something much,
much more important had happened.

'So—tell me about it,' she said quietly.

Oscar shrugged. 'It was pure chance that I was first
on the scene,' he said casually. 'I saw them trapped in
the back of the car, which had landed on its side...so
I ran across and managed to get them out...the doors
were jammed so I had to smash the window.'

Helena shuddered as she pictured the scene, hating
herself for her ungenerous thoughts at the time. And
when the woman and children had turned up here at
the house, she'd thought the very worst of him then,

too. How wrong could you be? she thought. Jumping to conclusions was a dangerous thing to do.

Carefully, Helena tucked the letters back into the large envelope and replaced it on the bookshelf. 'I had...wondered...whether those beautiful boys might have been yours, Oscar,' she admitted quietly.

He smiled down at her. 'I don't have any children,' he said, adding darkly, 'Not yet.'

They made their way upstairs together and, without hesitation, Oscar guided Helena into his bedroom and closed the door firmly. Without putting on the lights, he took her hand and they wandered across to gaze out of the window, the peace of the beautiful surroundings matching the peace in both their hearts—the peace of knowing that something longed for had happened, had come true at last.

Then he put his arms around her in a close embrace and Helena leaned her head into his neck, loving the feel of him, loving the familiar, sensuous smell of his warm skin. She turned her head slowly to gaze up at Oscar, nestling into him, her soft curves melding with the masculine strength of his frame. She raised her hand, tracing the contours of his face, touching his lips gently with her forefinger, which he immediately took between his teeth. Then, 'Do we have to...I mean is it necessary for us to be married in Greece?' she asked tentatively. 'It's just that I would really love to...'

He interrupted her, his dark eyes burning deeply into hers. 'We shall be married wherever you like, Helena. Just so long as it's soon.'

'Then I would like it to be here, in the garden at Mulberry Court...with just a few of us. Of course we would go to Greece afterwards for an appropriate ceremony, do whatever protocol demands—that would only be fair…' Her words came quickly, and Oscar hushed her gently.

'That's a minor detail,' he assured her, 'which will be dealt with as necessary.' He paused. 'And I, too, would like the ceremony to be held here, with just the people we love—past and present—to hear us make our vows.'

And in her dreamy mind's eye Helena could already see it. She would be wearing a simple white cotton dress, trimmed with lace, and there would be a single white rose in her hair and a spray of similar flowers in her hand. And the modest expense would be settled with her father's legacy. The money she had been keeping for something very, very special.

For several moments they remained there locked together, without speaking, and Helena could only marvel at the surging tide of happiness that rippled through her entire body, painting her cheeks with a rosy warmth, sending a delightful tingle right down her spine to her toes. She shuddered slightly, pleasurably, and Oscar looked down at her, his expression telling her everything she'd ever wanted to know. Then he lowered his head to kiss her, pulling her gently even closer, and Helena clasped her arms around his neck and closed her eyes, her lips very slightly parted to receive his kiss. A kiss so soft yet so passionate, so all consuming.

Then, with his perfect timing, Oscar led her over to the bed and they both sat down, and Helena leant forward to slip off her sandals, conscious that he was unzipping her dress, releasing her bra…

He laid her down gently and took his place beside her, and Helena turned her head to gaze into his eyes, those black, impenetrable eyes which had haunted her memory for so long.

'As to the matter you mentioned a little while ago, Oscar,' she murmured, 'I think—perhaps two of each—if you're happy with that?'

He smiled at her darkly. 'Perfect…to start with,' he agreed. 'And since there's no time like the present, *kopella mou*—tonight, we shall make a beginning.'

\* \* \* \* \*

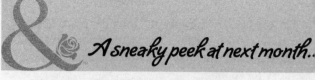

*A sneaky peek at next month...*

# MODERN™

**INTERNATIONAL AFFAIRS, SEDUCTION & PASSION GUARANTEED**

## My wish list for next month's titles...

In stores from 16th March 2012:

- ❏ A Deal at the Altar – Lynne Graham
- ❏ Gianni's Pride – Kim Lawrence
- ❏ The Legend of de Marco – Abby Green
- ❏ Deserving of His Diamonds? – Melanie Milburne

In stores from 6th April 2012:

- ❏ Return of the Moralis Wife – Jacqueline Baird
- ❏ Undone by His Touch – Annie West
- ❏ Stepping out of the Shadows – Robyn Donald
- ❏ Girl Behind the Scandalous Reputation – Michelle Cond
- ❏ Redemption of a Hollywood Starlet – Kimberly Lang

Available at WHSmith, Tesco, Asda, Eason, Amazon and Apple

### Just can't wait?

**Visit us Online**

You can buy our books online a month before they hit the shops! **www.millsandboon.co.u**

031

# Special Offers

very month we put together collections and
nger reads written by your favourite authors.

ere are some of next month's highlights—
d don't miss our fabulous discount online!

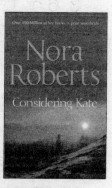

sale 16th March

On sale 16th March

On sale 6th April

## Save 20%
### on all Special Releases

ind out more at
ww.millsandboon.co.uk/specialreleases

Visit us
Online

0312/ST/MB364

## The World of Mills & Boon®

There's a Mills & Boon® series that's perfec
for you. We publish ten series and with new
titles every month, you never have to wait
long for your favourite to come along.

*Blaze.*  Scorching hot,
sexy reads

By Request  Relive the romance wit
the best of the best

*Cherish*  Romance to melt the
heart every time

*Desire*  Passionate and drama
love stories

# *Have Your Say*

## *You've just finished your book.*
## *So what did you think?*

We'd love to hear your thoughts on our 'Have your say' online panel
**www.millsandboon.co.uk/haveyours**

- Easy to use
- Short questionnaire
- Chance to win Mills & Boon® goodies

# SIX NOT-SO-EASY PIECES

Richard P. Feynman was one of this century's most brilliant theoretical physicists and original thinkers. Born in Far Rockaway, New York, in 1918, he studied at the Massachusetts Institute of Technology, where he graduated with a BS in 1939. He went on to Princeton and received his Ph.D. in 1942. During the war years he worked at the Los Alamos Scientific Laboratory. He became Professor of Theoretical Physics at Cornell University, where he worked with Hans Bethe. He all but rebuilt the theory of quantum electrodynamics and it was for this work that he shared the Nobel Prize in 1965. His simplified rules of calculation became standard tools of theoretical analysis in both quantum electrodynamics and high-energy physics. Feynman was a visiting professor at the California Institute of Technology in 1950, where he later accepted a permanent faculty appointment, and became Richard Chace Tolman Professor of Theoretical Physics in 1959. He had an extraordinary ability to communicate his science to audiences at all levels, and was a well-known and popular lecturer. Richard Feynman died in 1988 after a long illness. Freeman Dyson, of the Institute for Advanced Study in Princeton, New Jersey, called him 'the most original mind of his generation', while in its obituary the *New York Times* described him as 'arguably the most brilliant, iconoclastic and influential of the postwar generation of theoretical physicists'.

A number of collections and adaptations of his lectures have been published, including *The Feynman Lectures on Physics*, *QED* (Penguin, 1990), *The Character of Physical Law* (Penguin, 1992), *Six Easy Pieces* (Penguin, 1998), *The Meaning of It All* (Penguin, 1999), *Six Not-So-Easy Pieces* (Allen Lane, 1998; Penguin, 1999), *The Feynman Lectures on Gravitation* (Penguin, 1999) and *The Feynman Lectures on Computation* (Penguin, 1999). His memoirs, *Surely You're Joking, Mr Feynman*, were published in 1985.

# SIX
# NOT-SO-EASY
# PIECES

*Einstein's
Relativity, Symmetry,
and Space-Time*

# RICHARD P.
# FEYNMAN

*Originally prepared for publication by
Robert B. Leighton and Matthew Sands*

New Introduction by Roger Penrose

PENGUIN BOOKS

PENGUIN BOOKS

Published by the Penguin Group
Penguin Books Ltd, 27 Wrights Lane, London W8 5TZ, England
Penguin Putnam Inc., 375 Hudson Street, New York, New York 10014, USA
Penguin Books Australia Ltd, Ringwood, Victoria, Australia
Penguin Books Canada Ltd, 10 Alcorn Avenue, Toronto, Ontario, Canada M4V 3B2
Penguin Books (NZ) Ltd, Private Bag 102902, NSMC, Auckland, New Zealand

Penguin Books Ltd, Registered Offices: Harmondsworth, Middlesex, England

This selection first published in the USA by Addison-Wesley 1997
First published in Great Britain by Allen Lane The Penguin Press 1998
Published in Penguin Books 1999
3 5 7 9 10 8 6 4 2

Printed in England by Clays Ltd, St Ives plc

# Contents

# Introduction

To understand why Richard Feynman was such a great teacher, it is important to appreciate his remarkable stature as a scientist. He was indeed one of the outstanding figures of twentieth-century theoretical physics. His contributions to that subject are central to the whole development of the particular way in which quantum theory is used in current cutting-edge research and thus to our present-day pictures of the world. The Feynman path integrals, Feynman diagrams, and Feynman rules are among the very basic tools of the modern theoretical physicist—tools that are necessary for the application of the rules of quantum theory to physical fields (e.g., the quantum theory of electrons, protons, and photons), and which form an essential part of the procedures whereby one makes these rules consistent with the requirements of Einstein's Special Relativity theory. Although none of these ideas is easy to appreciate, Feynman's particular approach always had a deep clarity about it, sweeping away unnecessary complications in what had gone before. There was a close link between his special ability to make progress in research and his particular qualities as a teacher. He had a unique talent that enabled him to cut through the complications that often obscure the essentials of a physical issue and to see clearly into the deep underlying physical principles.

Yet, in the popular conception of Feynman, he is known more for his antics and buffoonery, for his practical jokes, his irreverence

*Introduction*

towards authority, his bongo-drum performing, his relationships
with women, both deep and shallow, his attendance at strip clubs,
his attempts, late in life, to reach the obscure country of Tuva in
central Asia, and many other schemes. Undoubtedly, he must have
been extraordinarily clever, as his lightning quickness at calculation, his exploits involving safe-cracking, outwitting security services, deciphering ancient Mayan texts—not to mention his
eventual Nobel Prize—clearly demonstrate. Yet none of this quite
conveys the status that he unquestionably has amongst physicists
and other scientists, as one of the deepest and most original thinkers
of this century.

The distinguished physicist and writer Freeman Dyson, an early
collaborator of Feynman's at a time when he was developing his
most important ideas, wrote in a letter to his parents in England in
the spring of 1948, when Dyson was a graduate student at Cornell
University, "Feynman is the young American professor, half genius
and half buffoon, who keeps all physicists and their children
amused with his effervescent vitality. He has, however, as I have
recently learned, a great deal more to him than that. . . ." Much
later, in 1988, he would write: "A truer description would have said
that Feynman was all genius and all buffoon. The deep thinking and
the joyful clowning were not separate parts of a split personality. . . .
He was thinking and clowning simultaneously."* Indeed, in his
lectures, his wit was spontaneous, and often outrageous. Through it
he held his audiences' attention, but never in a way that would
distract from the purpose of the lecture, which was the conveying of
genuine and deep physical understanding. Through laughter, his
audiences could relax and be at ease, rather than feel daunted by
what might otherwise be somewhat intimidating mathematical
expressions and physical concepts that are tantalizingly difficult to
grasp. Yet, although he enjoyed being center stage and was
undoubtedly a showman, this was not the purpose of his exposi-

* The Dyson quotations are to be found in his book *From Eros to Gaia* (Pantheon
Books, New York, 1992) pages 325 and 314, respectively.

## Introduction

tions. That purpose was to convey some basic understanding of underlying physical ideas and of the essential mathematical tools that are needed in order to express these ideas properly.

Whereas laughter played a key part of his success in holding an audience's attention, more important to the conveying of understanding was the immediacy of his approach. Indeed, he had an extraordinarily direct no-nonsense style. He scorned airy-fairy philosophizing where it had little physical content. Even his attitude to mathematics was somewhat similar. He had little use for pedantic mathematical niceties, but he had a distinctive mastery of the mathematics that he needed, and could present it in a powerfully transparent way. He was beholden to no one, and would never take on trust what others might maintain to be true without himself coming to an independent judgment. Accordingly, his approach was often strikingly original whether in his research or teaching. And when Feynman's way differed significantly from what had gone before, it would be a reasonably sure bet that Feynman's approach would be the more fruitful one to follow.

Feynman's preferred method of communication was verbal. He did not easily, nor often, commit himself to the printed word. In his scientific papers, the special "Feynman" qualities would certainly come through, though in a somewhat muted form. It was in his lectures that his talents were given full reign. His exceedingly popular "Feynman Lectures" were basically edited transcripts (by Robert B. Leighton and Matthew Sands) of lectures that Feynman gave, and the compelling nature of the text is evident to anyone who reads it. The SIX NOT-SO-EASY PIECES that are presented here are taken from those accounts. Yet, even here, the printed words alone leave something significantly missing. To sense the full excitement that Feynman's lectures exude, I believe that it is important to hear his actual voice. The directness of Feynman's approach, the irreverence, and the humor then become things that we can immediately share in. Fortunately, there are recordings of all the lectures presented in this book, which give us this opportunity—and I strongly recommend, if the opportunity is there, that at least some of these audio versions are listened to first. Once we have heard Feynman's forceful, enthralling, and witty commentary, in the tones of this streetwise New Yorker, we do not forget how he sounds, and it gives us an image to latch on to when we read his words. But whether we actually read the chapters or not, we can share something of the evident thrill that he himself feels as he explores—and continually re-explores—the extraordinary laws that govern the workings of our universe.

The present series of six lectures was carefully chosen to be of a level a little above the six that formed the earlier set of Feynman lectures entitled *Six Easy Pieces* (Addison-Wesley Longman 1995, Penguin 1998). Moreover, they go well together and constitute a superb and compelling account of one of the most important general areas of modern theoretical physics.

This area is *relativity,* which first burst forth into human awareness in the early years of this century. The name of Einstein figures preeminently in the public conception of this field. It was, indeed, Albert Einstein who, in 1905, first clearly enunciated the profound principles which underlie this new realm of physical endeavor. But there were others before him, most notably Hendrik Antoon Lorentz and Henri Poincaré, who had already appreciated most of the basics of the (then) new physics. Moreover, the great scientists Galileo Galilei and Isaac Newton, centuries before Einstein, had already pointed out that in the dynamical theories that they themselves were developing, the physics as perceived by an observer in uniform motion would be identical with that perceived by an observer at rest. The key problem with this had arisen only later, with James Clerk Maxwell's discovery, as published in 1865, of the equations that govern the electric and magnetic fields, and which also control the propagation of light. The implication seemed to be that the relativity principle of Galileo and Newton could no longer hold true; for the speed of light must, by Maxwell's equations, have a definite speed of propagation. Accordingly, an observer at rest is distinguished from those in motion by the fact that only to an observer at rest does the light speed appear to be the same in all

## Introduction

directions. The relativity principle of Lorentz, Poincaré, and Einstein differs from that of Galileo and Newton, but it has this same implication: the physics as perceived by an observer in uniform motion is indeed identical with that perceived by an observer at rest.

Yet, in the new relativity, Maxwell's equations *are* consistent with this principle, and the speed of light is measured to have a definite fixed value in every direction, no matter in what direction or with what speed the observer might be moving. How is this magic achieved so that these apparently hopelessly incompatible requirements are reconciled? I shall leave it to Feynman to explain—in his own inimitable fashion.

Relativity is perhaps the first place where the physical power of the mathematical idea of *symmetry* begins to be felt. Symmetry is a familiar idea, but it is less familiar to people how such an idea can be applied in accordance with a set of mathematical expressions. But it is just such a thing that is needed in order to implement the principles of special relativity in a system of equations. In order to be consistent with the relativity principle, whereby physics "looks the same" to an observer in uniform motion as to an observer at rest, there must be a "symmetry transformation" which translates one observer's measured quantities into those of the other. It is a symmetry because the physical laws appear the same to each observer, and "symmetry" after all, asserts that something has the same appearance from two distinct points of view. Feynman's approach to abstract matters of this nature is very down to earth, and he is able to convey the ideas in a way that is accessible to people with no particular mathematical experience or aptitude for abstract thinking.

Whereas relativity pointed the way to additional symmetries that had not been perceived before, some of the more modern developments in physics have shown that certain symmetries, previously thought to be universal, are in fact subtly violated. It came as one of the most profound shocks to the physical community in 1957, as the work of Lee, Yang, and Wu showed, that in certain basic physical

## Introduction

processes, the laws satisfied by a physical system are not the same as those satisfied by the mirror reflection of that system. In fact, Feynman had a hand in the development of the physical theory which is able to accommodate this asymmetry. His account here is, accordingly, a dramatic one, as deeper and deeper mysteries of nature gradually unfold.

As physics develops, there are mathematical formalisms that develop with it, and which are needed in order to express the new physical laws. When the mathematical tools are skillfully tuned to their appropriate tasks, they can make the physics seem much simpler than otherwise. The ideas of vector calculus are a case in point. The vector calculus of three dimensions was originally developed to handle the physics of ordinary space, and it provides an invaluable piece of machinery for the expression of physical laws, such as those of Newton, where there is no physically preferred direction in space. To put this another way, the physical laws have a *symmetry* under ordinary rotations in space. Feynman brings home the power of the vector notation and the underlying ideas for expressing such laws.

Relativity theory, however, tells us that *time* should also be brought under the compass of these symmetry transformations, so a *four*-dimensional vector calculus is needed. This calculus is also introduced to us here by Feynman, as it provides the way of understanding how not only time and space must be considered as different aspects of the same four-dimensional structure, but the same is true of energy and momentum in the relativistic scheme.

The idea that the history of the universe should be viewed, physically, as a *four*-dimensional space-time, rather than as a three-dimensional space evolving with time is indeed fundamental to modern physics. It is an idea whose significance is not easy to grasp. Indeed, Einstein himself was not sympathetic to this idea when he first encountered it. The idea of space-time was not, in fact, Einstein's, although, in the popular imagination it is frequently attributed to him. It was the Russian/German geometer Hermann Minkowski, who had been a teacher of Einstein's at the Zurich

*Introduction*

Polytechnic, who first put forward the idea of four-dimensional space-time in 1908, a few years after Poincaré and Einstein had formulated special relativity theory. In a famous lecture, Minkowski asserted: "Henceforth space by itself, and time by itself, are doomed to fade away into mere shadows, and only a kind of unity between the two will preserve an independent reality."*

Feynman's most influential scientific discoveries, the ones that I have referred to above, stemmed from his own *space-time* approach to quantum mechanics. There is thus no question about the importance of space-time to Feynman's work and to modern physics generally. It is not surprising, therefore, that Feynman is forceful in his promotion of space-time ideas, stressing their physical significance. Relativity is not airy-fairy philosophy, nor is space-time mere mathematical formalism. It is a foundational ingredient of the very universe in which we live.

When Einstein became accustomed to the idea of space-time, he took it completely into his way of thinking. It became an essential part of his extension of special relativity—the relativity theory I have been referring to above that Lorentz, Poincaré, and Einstein introduced—to what is known as *general* relativity. In Einstein's general relativity, the space-time becomes *curved,* and it is able to incorporate the phenomenon of *gravity* into this curvature. Clearly, this is a difficult idea to grasp, and in Feynman's final lecture in this collection, he makes no attempt to describe the full mathematical machinery that is needed for the complete formulation of Einstein's theory. Yet he gives a powerfully dramatic description, with insightful use of intriguing analogies, in order to get the essential ideas across.

In all his lectures, Feynman made particular efforts to preserve accuracy in his descriptions, almost always qualifying what he says when there was any danger that his simplifications or analogies

---

* The Minkowski quote is from the Dover reprint of seminal publications on relativity *The Principle of Relativity* by Einstein, Lorentz, Weyl, and Minkowski (originally Methuen and Co., 1923).

## Introduction

might be misleading or lead to erroneous conclusions. I felt, how-ever, that his simplified account of the Einstein field equation of general relativity did need a qualification that he did not quite give. For in Einstein's theory, the "active" mass which is the source of gravity is not simply the same as the energy (according to Einstein's $E=mc^2$); instead, this source is the energy density *plus the sum of the pressures,* and it this that is the source of gravity's inward accelera-tions. With this additional qualification, Feynman's account is superb, and provides an excellent introduction to this most beauti-ful and self-contained of physical theories.

While Feynman's lectures are unashamedly aimed at those who have aspirations to become physicists—whether professionally or in spirit only—they are undoubtedly accessible also to those with no such aspirations. Feynman strongly believed (and I agree with him) in the importance of conveying an understanding of our universe—according to the perceived basic principles of modern physics—far more widely than can be achieved merely by the teaching provided in physics courses. Even late in his life, when taking part in the investigations of the *Challenger* disaster, he took great pains to show, on national television, that the source of the disaster was something that could be appreciated at an ordinary level, and he performed a simple but convincing experiment on camera showing the brittleness of the shuttle's O-rings in cold conditions.

He was a showman, certainly, sometimes even a clown; but his overriding purpose was always serious. And what more serious purpose can there be than the understanding of the nature of our universe at its deepest levels? At conveying this understanding, Richard Feynman was supreme.

December 1996                                          ROGER PENROSE

# Special Preface
## (from *Lectures on Physics*)

Toward the end of his life, Richard Feynman's fame had transcended the confines of the scientific community. His exploits as a member of the commission investigating the space shuttle Challenger disaster gave him widespread exposure; similarly, a bestselling book about his picaresque adventures made him a folk hero almost of the proportions of Albert Einstein. But back in 1961, even before his Nobel Prize increased his visibility to the general public, Feynman was more than merely famous among members of the scientific community—he was legendary. Undoubtedly, the extraordinary power of his teaching helped spread and enrich the legend of Richard Feynman.

He was a truly great teacher, perhaps the greatest of his era and ours. For Feynman, the lecture hall was a theater, and the lecturer a performer, responsible for providing drama and fireworks as well as facts and figures. He would prowl about the front of a classroom, arms waving, "the impossible combination of theoretical physicist and circus barker, all body motion and sound effects," wrote *The New York Times*. Whether he addressed an audience of students, colleagues, or the general public, for those lucky enough to see Feynman lecture in person, the experience was usually unconventional and always unforgettable, like the man himself.

He was the master of high drama, adept at riveting the attention of every lecture-hall audience. Many years ago, he taught a course in Advanced Quantum Mechanics, a large class comprised of a few registered graduate students and most of the Caltech physics faculty. During one lecture, Feynman started explaining how to represent certain complicated integrals diagrammatically: time on this axis, space on that axis, wiggly line for this straight line, etc. Having described what is known to the world of physics as a Feynman diagram, he turned around to face the class, grinning wickedly. "And this is called *THE* diagram!" Feynman had reached the denouement, and the lecture hall erupted with spontaneous applause.

For many years after the lectures that make up this book were given, Feynman was an occasional guest lecturer for Caltech's freshman physics course. Naturally, his appearances had to be kept secret so there would be room left in the hall for the registered students. At one such lecture the subject was curved-space time, and Feynman was characteristically brilliant. But the unforgettable moment came at the beginning of the lecture. The supernova of 1987 has just been discovered, and Feynman was very excited about it. He said, "Tycho Brahe had his supernova, and Kepler had his. Then there weren't any for 400 years. But now I have mine." The class fell silent, and Feynman continued on. "There are $10^{11}$ stars in the galaxy. That used to be a *huge* number. But it's only a hundred billion. It's less than the national deficit! We used to call them astronomical numbers. Now we should call them economical numbers." The class dissolved in laughter, and Feynman, having captured his audience, went on with his lecture.

Showmanship aside, Feynman's pedagogical technique was simple. A summation of his teaching philosophy was found among his papers in the Caltech archives, in a note he had scribbled to himself while in Brazil in 1952:

"First figure out why you want the students to learn the subject and what you want them to know, and the method will result more or less by common sense."

What came to Feynman by "common sense" were often brilliant twists that perfectly captured the essence of his point. Once, during

*Special Preface*

a public lecture, he was trying to explain why one must not verify an idea using the same data that suggested the idea in the first place. Seeming to wander off the subject, Feynman began talking about license plates. "You know, the most amazing thing happened to me tonight. I was coming here, on the way to the lecture, and I came in through the parking lot. And you won't believe what happened. I saw a car with the license plate ARW 357. Can you imagine? Of all the millions of license plates in the state, what was the chance that I would see that particular one tonight? Amazing!" A point that even many scientists fail to grasp was made clear through Feynman's remarkable "common sense."

In 35 years at Caltech (from 1952 to 1987), Feynman was listed as teacher of record for 34 courses. Twenty-five of them were advanced graduate courses, strictly limited to graduate students, unless undergraduates asked permission to take them (they often did, and permission was nearly always granted). The rest were mainly introductory graduate courses. Only once did Feynman teach courses purely for undergraduates, and that was the celebrated occasion in the academic years 1961 to 1962 and 1962 to 1963, with a brief reprise in 1964, when he gave the lectures that were to become *The Feynman Lectures on Physics*.

At the time there was a consensus at Caltech that freshman and sophomore students were getting turned off rather than spurred on by their two years of compulsory physics. To remedy the situation, Feynman was asked to design a series of lectures to be given to the students over the course of two years, first to freshmen, and then to the same class as sophomores. When he agreed, it was immediately decided that the lectures should be transcribed for publication. That job turned out to be far more difficult than anyone had imagined. Turning out publishable books required a tremendous amount of work on the part of his colleagues, as well as Feynman himself, who did the final editing of every chapter.

And the nuts and bolts of running a course had to be addressed. This task was greatly complicated by the fact that Feynman had only a vague outline of what he wanted to cover. This meant that no

## Special Preface

one knew what Feynman would say until he stood in front of a lecture hall filled with students and said it. The Caltech professors who assisted him would then scramble as best they could to handle mundane details, such as making up homework problems.

Why did Feynman devote more than two years to revolutionizing the way beginning physics was taught? One can only speculate, but there were probably three basic reasons. One is that he loved to have an audience, and this gave him a bigger theater than he usually had in graduate courses. The second was that he genuinely cared about students, and he simply thought that teaching freshmen was an important thing to do. The third and perhaps most important reason was the sheer challenge of reformulating physics, as he understood it, so that it could be presented to young students. This was his specialty, and was the standard by which he measured whether something was really understood. Feynman was once asked by a Caltech faculty member to explain why spin 1/2 particles obey Fermi-Dirac statistics. He gauged his audience perfectly and said, "I'll prepare a freshman lecture on it." But a few days later he returned and said, "You know, I couldn't do it. I couldn't reduce it to the freshman level. That means we really don't understand it."

This specialty of reducing deep ideas to simple, understandable terms is evident throughout *The Feynman Lectures on Physics*, but nowhere more so than in his treatment of quantum mechanics. To aficionados, what he has done is clear. He has presented, to beginning students, the path integral method, the technique of his own devising that allowed him to solve some of the most profound problems in physics. His own work using path integrals, among other achievements, led to the 1965 Nobel Prize that he shared with Julian Schwinger and Sin-Itero Tomanaga.

Through the distant veil of memory, many of the students and faculty attending the lectures have said that having two years of physics with Feynman was the experience of a lifetime. But that's not how it seemed at the time. Many of the students dreaded the class, and as the course wore on, attendance by the registered students started dropping alarmingly. But at the same time, more and more faculty and graduate students started attending. The room stayed full, and Feynman may never have known he was losing some of his intended audience. But even in Feynman's view, his pedagogical endeavor did not succeed. He wrote in the 1963 preface to the *Lectures*: "I don't think I did very well by the students." Rereading the books, one sometimes seems to catch Feynman looking over his shoulder, not at his young audience, but directly at his colleagues, saying, "Look at that! Look how I finessed that point! Wasn't that clever?" But even when he thought he was explaining things lucidly to freshmen or sophomores, it was not really they who were able to benefit most from what he was doing. It was his peers—scientists, physicists, and professors—who would be the main beneficiaries of his magnificent achievement, which was nothing less than to see physics through the fresh and dynamic perspective of Richard Feynman.

Feynman was more than a great teacher. His gift was that he was an extraordinary teacher of teachers. If the purpose in giving *The Feynman Lectures on Physics* was to prepare a roomful of under-graduate students to solve examination problems in physics, he cannot be said to have succeeded particularly well. Moreover, if the intent was for the books to serve as introductory college textbooks, he cannot be said to have achieved his goal. Nevertheless, the books have been translated into ten foreign languages and are available in four bilingual editions. Feynman himself believed that his most important contribution to physics would not be QED, or the theory of superfluid helium, or polarons, or partons. His foremost contri-bution would be the three red books of *The Feynman Lectures on Physics*. That belief justifies this commemorative issue of these celebrated books.

DAVID L. GOODSTEIN
GERRY NEUGEBAUER
California Institute of Technology

*April 1989*

# Feynman's Preface
## (from *Lectures on Physics*)

These are the lectures in physics that I gave last year and the year before to the freshman and sophomore classes at Caltech. The lectures are, of course, not verbatim—they have been edited, sometimes extensively and sometimes less so. The lectures form only part of the complete course. The whole group of 180 students gathered in a big lecture room twice a week to hear these lectures and then they broke up into small groups of 15 to 20 students in recitation sections under the guidance of a teaching assistant. In addition, there was a laboratory session once a week.

The special problem we tried to get at with these lectures was to maintain the interest of the very enthusiastic and rather smart students coming out of the high schools and into Caltech. They have heard a lot about how interesting and exciting physics is—the theory of relativity, quantum mechanics, and other modern ideas. By the end of two years of our previous course, many would be very discouraged because there were really very few grand, new, modern ideas presented to them. They were made to study inclined planes, electrostatics, and so forth, and after two years it was quite stultifying. The problem was whether or not we could make a course which would save the more advanced and excited student by maintaining his enthusiasm.

The lectures here are not in any way meant to be a survey course, but are very serious. I thought to address them to the most intelligent in the class and to make sure, if possible, that even the most intelligent student was unable to completely encompass everything that was in the lectures—by putting in suggestions of applications of the ideas and concepts in various directions outside the main line of attack. For this reason, though, I tried very hard to make all the statements as accurate as possible, to point out in every case where the equations and ideas fitted into the body of physics, and how—when they learned more—things would be modified. I also felt that for such students it is important to indicate what it is that they should—if they are sufficiently clever—be able to understand by deduction from what has been said before, and what is being put in as something new. When new ideas came in, I would try either to deduce them if they were deducible, or to explain that it *was* a new idea which hadn't any basis in terms of things they had already learned and what was not supposed to be provable—but was just added in.

At the start of these lectures, I assumed that the students knew something when they came out of high school—such things as geometrical optics, simple chemistry ideas, and so on. I also didn't see that there was any reason to make the lectures in a definite order, in the sense that I would not be allowed to mention something until I was ready to discuss it in detail. There was a great deal of mention of things to come, without complete discussions. These more complete discussions would come later when the preparation became more advanced. Examples are the discussions of inductance, and of energy levels, which are at first brought in in a very qualitative way and are later developed more completely.

At the same time that I was aiming at the more active student, I also wanted to take care of the fellow for whom the extra fireworks and side applications are merely disquieting and who cannot be expected to learn most of the material in the lecture at all. For such a student, I wanted there to be at least a central core or backbone of material which he *could* get. Even if he didn't understand everything in a lecture, I hoped he wouldn't get nervous. I didn't expect him to understand everything, but only the central and most direct features. It takes, of course, a certain intelligence on his part to see which are the central theorems and central ideas, and which are the more advanced side issues and applications which he may understand only in later years.

In giving these lectures there was one serious difficulty: in the way the course was given, there wasn't any feedback from the students to the lecturer to indicate how well the lectures were going over. This is indeed a very serious difficulty, and I don't know how good the lectures really are. The whole thing was essentially an experiment. And if I did it again I wouldn't do it the same way—I hope I *don't* have to do it again! I think, though, that things worked out—so far as the physics is concerned—quite satisfactorily in the first year.

In the second year I was not so satisfied. In the first part of the course, dealing with electricity and magnetism, I couldn't think of any really unique or different way of doing it—of any way that would be particularly more exciting than the usual way of presenting it. So I don't think I did very much in the lectures on electricity and magnetism. At the end of the second year I had originally intended to go on, after the electricity and magnetism, by giving some more lectures on the properties of materials, but mainly to take up things like fundamental modes, solutions of the diffusion equation, vibrating systems, orthogonal functions, . . . developing the first stages of what are usually called "the mathematical methods of physics." In retrospect, I think that if I were doing it again I would go back to that original idea. But since it was not planned that I would be giving these lectures again, it was suggested that it might be a good idea to try to give an introduction to the quantum mechanics—what you will find in Volume III.

It is perfectly clear that students who will major in physics can wait until their third year for quantum mechanics. On the other hand, the argument was made that many of the students in our course study physics as a background for their primary interest in other fields. And the usual way of dealing with quantum mechanics makes that subject almost unavailable for the great majority of students because they have to take so long to learn it. Yet, in its real applications—especially in its more complex applications, such as in electrical engineering and chemistry—the full machinery of the differential equation approach is not actually used. So I tried to describe the principles of quantum mechanics in a way which wouldn't require that one first know the mathematics of partial differential equations. Even for a physicist I think that is an interesting thing to try to do—to present quantum mechanics in this reverse fashion—for several reasons which may be apparent in the lectures themselves. However, I think that the experiment in the quantum mechanics part was not completely successful—in large part because I really did not have enough time at the end (I should, for instance, have had three or four more lectures in order to deal more completely with such matters as energy bands and the spatial dependence of amplitudes). Also, I had never presented the subject this way before, so the lack of feedback was particularly serious. I now believe the quantum mechanics should be given at a later time. Maybe I'll have a chance to do it again someday. Then I'll do it right.

The reason there are no lectures on how to solve problems is because there were recitation sections. Although I did put in three lectures in the first year on how to solve problems, they are not included here. Also there was a lecture on inertial guidance which certainly belongs after the lecture on rotating systems, but which was, unfortunately, omitted. The fifth and sixth lectures are actually due to Matthew Sands, as I was out of town.

The question, of course, is how well this experiment has succeeded. My own point of view—which, however, does not seem to be shared by most of the people who worked with the students—is pessimistic. I don't think I did very well by the students. When I look at the way the majority of the students handled the problems on the examinations, I think that the system is a failure. Of course, my friends point out to me that there were one or two dozen students who—very surprisingly—understood almost everything in all of the lectures, and who were quite active in working with the material and worrying about the many points in an excited and interested way. These people have now, I believe, a first-rate back-

## Feynman's Preface

ground in physics—and they are, after all, the ones I was trying to get at. But then, "The power of instruction is seldom of much efficacy except in those happy dispositions where it is almost superfluous." (Gibbon)

Still, I didn't want to leave any student completely behind, as perhaps I did. I think one way we could help the students more would be by putting more hard work into developing a set of problems which would elucidate some of the ideas in the lectures. Problems give a good opportunity to fill out the material of the lectures and make more realistic, more complete, and more settled in the mind the ideas that have been exposed.

I think, however, that there isn't any solution to this problem of education other than to realize that the best teaching can be done only when there is a direct individual relationship between a student and a good teacher—a situation in which the student discusses the ideas, thinks about the things, and talks about the things. It's impossible to learn very much by simply sitting in a lecture, or even by simply doing problems that are assigned. But in our modern times we have so many students to teach that we have to try to find some substitute for the ideal. Perhaps my lectures can make some contribution. Perhaps in some small place where there are individual teachers and students, they may get some inspiration or some ideas from the lectures. Perhaps they will have fun thinking them through—or going on to develop some of the ideas further.

*June 1963*                                   RICHARD P. FEYNMAN

# One

# VECTORS

## *1-1 Symmetry in physics*

In this chapter we introduce a subject that is technically known in physics as *symmetry in physical law*. The word "symmetry" is used here with a special meaning, and therefore needs to be defined. When is a thing symmetrical—how can we define it? When we have a picture that is symmetrical, one side is somehow the same as the other side. Professor Hermann Weyl has given this definition of symmetry: a thing is symmetrical if one can subject it to a certain operation and it appears exactly the same after the operation. For instance, if we look at a vase that is left-and-right symmetrical, then turn it 180° around the vertical axis, it looks the same. We shall adopt the definition of symmetry in Weyl's more general form, and in that form we shall discuss symmetry of physical laws.

Suppose we build a complex machine in a certain place, with a lot of complicated interactions, and balls bouncing around with forces between them, and so on. Now suppose we build exactly the same kind of equipment at some other place, matching part by part, with the same dimensions and the same orientation, everything the same only displaced laterally by some distance. Then, if we start the two machines in the same initial circumstances, in exact correspondence, we ask: will one machine behave exactly the same as the other? Will it follow all the motions in exact parallelism? Of course the answer may well be *no*, because if we choose the wrong place for our machine it might be inside a wall and interferences from the wall would make the machine not work.

All of our ideas in physics require a certain amount of common sense in their application; they are not purely mathematical or abstract ideas. We have to understand what we mean when we say that the phenomena are the same when we move the apparatus to a new position. We mean that we move everything that we believe is relevant; if the phenomenon is not the same, we suggest that something relevant has not been moved, and we proceed to look for it. If we never find it, then we claim that the laws of physics do not have this symmetry. On the other hand, we may find it—we expect to find it—if the laws of physics do have this symmetry; looking around, we may discover, for instance, that the wall is pushing on the apparatus. The basic question is, if we define things well enough, if all the essential forces are included inside the apparatus, if all the relevant parts are moved from one place to another, will the laws be the same? Will the machinery work the same way?

It is clear that what we want to do is to move all the equipment and *essential* influences, but not *everything* in the world—planets, stars, and all—for if we do that, we have the same phenomenon again for the trivial reason that we are right back where we started. No, we cannot move *everything*. But it turns out in practice that with a certain amount of intelligence about what to move, the machinery will work. In other words, if we do not go inside a wall, if we know the origin of the outside forces, and arrange that those are moved too, then the machinery *will* work the same in one location as in another.

## 1-2 Translations

We shall limit our analysis to just mechanics, for which we now have sufficient knowledge. In previous chapters we have seen that the laws of mechanics can be summarized by a set of three equations for each particle:

$$m(d^2x/dt^2) = F_x, \quad m(d^2y/dt^2) = F_y, \quad m(d^2z/dt^2) = F_z. \qquad (1.1)$$

## Vectors

Now this means that there exists a way to *measure x, y,* and *z* on three perpendicular axes, and the forces along those directions, such that these laws are true. These must be measured from some origin, but *where do we put the origin?* All that Newton would tell us at first is that there *is* some place that we can measure from, perhaps the center of the universe, such that these laws are correct. But we can show immediately that we can never find the center, because if we use some other origin it would make no difference. In other words, suppose that there are two people—Joe, who has an origin in one place, and Moe, who has a parallel system whose origin is somewhere else (Figure 1-1). Now when Joe measures the location of the point in space, he finds it at *x, y,* and *z* (we shall usually leave *z* out because it is too confusing to draw in a picture). Moe, on the other hand, when measuring the same point, will obtain a different *x* (in order to distinguish it, we will call it *x'*), and in principle a different *y,* although in our example they are numerically equal. So we have

$$x' = x - a, \quad y' = y, \quad z' = z. \tag{1.2}$$

Now in order to complete our analysis we must know what Moe would obtain for the forces. The force is supposed to act along some line, and by the force in the *x*-direction we mean the part of the total which is in the *x*-direction, which is the magnitude of the force times this cosine of its angle with the *x*-axis. Now we see that

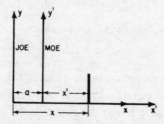

*Figure 1-1.* Two parallel coordinate systems.

Moe would use exactly the same projection as Joe would use, so we have a set of equations

$$F_{x'} = F_x, \quad F_{y'} = F_y, \quad F_{z'} = F_z. \tag{1.3}$$

These would be the relationships between quantities as seen by Joe and Moe.

The question is, if Joe knows Newton's laws, and if Moe tries to write down Newton's laws, will they also be correct for him? Does it make any difference from which origin we measure the points? In other words, assuming that equations (1.1) are true, and the Eqs. (1.2) and (1.3) give the relationship of the measurements, is it or is it not true that

$$
\begin{align}
&\text{(a)} \quad m(d^2x'/dt^2) = F_{x'}, \\
&\text{(b)} \quad m(d^2y'/dt^2) = F_{y'}, \tag{1.4}\\
&\text{(c)} \quad m(d^2z'/dt^2) = F_{z'}?
\end{align}
$$

In order to test these equations we shall differentiate the formula for $x'$ twice. First of all

$$\frac{dx'}{dt} = \frac{d}{dt}(x - a) = \frac{dx}{dt} - \frac{da}{dt}.$$

Now we shall assume that Moe's origin is fixed (not moving) relative to Joe's; therefore $a$ is a constant and $da/dt = 0$, so we find that

$$dx'/dt = dx/dt'$$

and therefore

$$d^2x'/dt^2 = d^2x/dt^2;$$

therefore we know that Eq. (1.4a) becomes

$$m(d^2x/dt^2) = F_{x'}.$$

(We also suppose that the masses measured by Joe and Moe are equal.) Thus the acceleration times the mass is the same as the other fellow's. We have also found the formula for $F_{x'}$, for, substituting from Eq. (1.1), we find that

$$F_{x'} = F_x.$$

## Vectors

Therefore the laws as seen by Moe appear the same; he can write Newton's laws too, with different coordinates, and they will still be right. That means that there is no unique way to define the origin of the world, because the laws will appear the same, from whatever position they are observed.

This is also true: if there is a piece of equipment in one place with a certain kind of machinery in it, the same equipment in another place will behave in the same way. Why? Because one machine, when analyzed by Moe, has exactly the same equations as the other one, analyzed by Joe. Since the *equations* are the same, the *phenomena* appear the same. So the proof that an apparatus in a new position behaves the same as it did in the old position is the same as the proof that the equations when displaced in space reproduce themselves. Therefore we say that *the laws of physics are symmetrical for translational displacements*, symmetrical in the sense that the laws do not change when we make a translation of our coordinates. Of course it is quite obvious intuitively that this is true, but it is interesting and entertaining to discuss the mathematics of it.

### 1-3 Rotations

The above is the first of a series of ever more complicated propositions concerning the symmetry of a physical law. The next proposition is that it should make no difference in which *direction* we choose the axes. In other words, if we build a piece of equipment in some place and watch it operate, and nearby we build the same kind of apparatus but put it up on an angle, will it operate in the same way? Obviously it will not if it is a grandfather clock, for example! If a pendulum clock stands upright, it works fine, but if it is tilted the pendulum falls against the side of the case and nothing happens. The theorem is then false in the case of the pendulum clock, unless we include the earth, which is pulling on the pendulum. Therefore we can make a prediction about pendulum clocks if we believe in the symmetry of physical law for rotation: something else is involved in the operation of a pendulum clock besides the machinery of the clock, something outside it that we should look for. We may also predict that pendulum clocks will not work the same way when located in different places relative to this mysterious source of asymmetry, perhaps the earth. Indeed, we know that a pendulum clock up in an artificial satellite, for example, would not tick either, because there is no effective force, and on Mars it would go at a different rate. Pendulum clocks *do* involve something more than just the machinery inside, they involve something on the outside. Once we recognize this factor, we see that we must turn the earth along with the apparatus. Of course we do not have to worry about that, it is easy to do; one simply waits a moment or two and the earth turns; then the pendulum clock ticks again in the new position the same as it did before. While we are rotating in space our angles are always changing, absolutely; this change does not seem to bother us very much, for in the new position we seem to be in the same condition as in the old. This has a certain tendency to confuse one, because it is true that in the new turned position the laws are the same as in the unturned position, but it is *not* true that *as we turn* a thing it follows the same laws as it does when we are not turning it. If we perform sufficiently delicate experiments, we can tell that the earth *is rotating*, but not that it *had rotated*. In other words, we cannot locate its angular position, but we can tell that it is changing.

Now we may discuss the effects of angular orientation upon physical laws. Let us find out whether the same game with Joe and Moe works again. This time, to avoid needless complication, we shall suppose that Joe and Moe use the same origin (we have already shown that the axes can be moved by translation to another place). Assume that Moe's axes have rotated relative to Joe's by an angle $\theta$. The two coordinate systems are shown in Figure 1-2, which is restricted to two dimensions. Consider any point $P$ having coordinates $(x, y)$ in Joe's system and $(x', y')$ in Moe's system. We shall begin, as in the previous case, by expressing the coordinates $x'$ and $y'$ in terms of $x$, $y$, and $\theta$. To do so, we first drop perpendiculars from $P$ to all four axes and draw $AB$ perpendicular to $PQ$. Inspection of the figure shows that $x'$ can be written as the sum of two

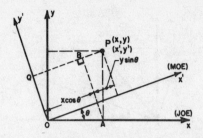

*Figure 1-2.* Two coordinate systems having different angular orientations.

lengths along the $x'$-axis, and $y'$ as the difference of two lengths along $AB$. All these lengths are expressed in terms of $x$, $y$, and $\theta$ in equations (1.5), to which we have added an equation for the third dimension.

$$
\begin{aligned}
x' &= x \cos \theta + y \sin \theta, \\
y' &= y \cos \theta - x \sin \theta, \\
z' &= z.
\end{aligned}
\tag{1.5}
$$

The next step is to analyze the relationship of forces as seen by the two observers, following the same general method as before. Let us assume that a force $F$, which has already been analyzed as having components $F_x$ and $F_y$ (as seen by Joe), is acting on a particle of mass $m$, located at point $P$ in Figure 1-2. For simplicity, let us move both sets of axes so that the origin is at $P$, as shown in Figure 1-3. Moe sees the components of $F$ along his axes as $F_{x'}$ and $F_{y'}$. $F_x$ has components along both the $x'$- and $y'$-axes, and $F_y$ likewise has components along both these axes. To express $F_{x'}$ in terms of $F_x$ and $F_y$, we sum these components along the $x'$-axis, and in a like manner we can express $F_{y'}$ in terms of $F_x$ and $F_y$. The results are

$$
\begin{aligned}
F_{x'} &= F_x \cos \theta + F_y \sin \theta, \\
F_{y'} &= F_y \cos \theta - F_x \sin \theta, \\
F_{z'} &= F_z.
\end{aligned}
\tag{1.6}
$$

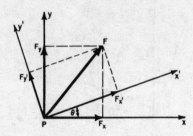

*Figure 1-3.* Components of a force in the two systems.

It is interesting to note an accident of sorts, which is of extreme importance: the formulas (1.5) and (1.6), for coordinates of $P$ and components of $F$, respectively, *are of identical form.*

As before, Newton's laws are assumed to be true in Joe's system, and are expressed by equations (1.1). The question, again, is whether Moe can apply Newton's laws—will the results be correct for his system of rotated axes? In other words, if we assume that Eqs. (1.5) and (1.6) give the relationship of the measurements, is it true or not true that

$$m(d^2x'/dt^2) = F_{x'},$$
$$m(d^2y'/dt^2) = F_{y'},$$
$$m(d^2z'/dt^2) = F_{z'}?$$

(1.7)

To test these equations, we calculate the left and right sides independently, and compare the results. To calculate the left sides, we multiply equations (1.5) by $m$, and differentiate twice with respect to time, assuming the angle $\theta$ to be constant. This gives

$$m(d^2x'/dt^2) = m(d^2x/dt^2)\cos\theta + m(d^2y/dt^2)\sin\theta,$$
$$m(d^2y'/dt^2) = m(d^2y/dt^2)\cos\theta - m(d^2x/dt^2)\sin\theta,$$
$$m(d^2z'/dt^2) = m(d^2z/dt^2).$$

(1.8)

We calculate the right sides of equations (1.7) by substituting equations (1.1) into equations (1.6). This gives

## Vectors

$$F_{x'} = m(d^2x/dt^2) \cos \theta + m(d^2y/dt^2) \sin \theta,$$
$$F_{y'} = m(d^2y/dt^2) \cos \theta - m(d^2x/dt^2) \sin \theta, \qquad (1.9)$$
$$F_{z'} = m(d^2z/dt^2).$$

Behold! The right sides of Eqs. (1.8) and (1.9) are identical, so we conclude that if Newton's laws are correct on one set of axes, they are also valid on any other set of axes. This result, which has now been established for both translation and rotation of axes, has certain consequences: first, no one can claim his particular axes are unique, but of course they can be more *convenient* for certain particular problems. For example, it is handy to have gravity along one axis, but this is not physically necessary. Second, it means that any piece of equipment which is completely self-contained, with all the force-generating equipment completely inside the apparatus, would work the same when turned at an angle.

## 1-4 Vectors

Not only Newton's laws, but also the other laws of physics, so far as we know today, have the two properties which we call invariance (or symmetry) under translation of axes and rotation of axes. These properties are so important that a mathematical technique has been developed to take advantage of them in writing and using physical laws.

The foregoing analysis involved considerable tedious mathematical work. To reduce the details to a minimum in the analysis of such questions, a very powerful mathematical machinery has been devised. This system, called *vector analysis*, supplies the title of this chapter; strictly speaking, however, this is a chapter on the symmetry of physical laws. By the methods of the preceding analysis we were able to do everything required for obtaining the results that we sought, but in practice we should like to do things more easily and rapidly, so we employ the vector technique.

We begin by noting some characteristics of two kinds of quantities that are important in physics. (Actually there are more than two, but let us start out with two.) One of them, like the number of potatoes in a sack, we call an ordinary quantity, or an undirected quantity, or a *scalar*. Temperature is an example of such a quantity. Other quantities that are important in physics do have direction, for instance velocity: we have to keep track of which way a body is going, not just its speed. Momentum and force also have direction, as does displacement: when someone steps from one place to another in space, we can keep track of how far he went, but if we wish also to know *where* he went, we have to specify a direction.

All quantities that have a direction, like a step in space, are called *vectors*.

A vector is three numbers. In order to represent a step in space, say from the origin to some particular point $P$ whose location is $(x, y, z)$, we really need three numbers, but we are going to invent a single mathematical symbol, **r**, which is unlike any other mathematical symbols we have so far used.* It is *not* a single number, it represents *three* numbers: $x$, $y$, and $z$. It means three numbers, but not really only *those* three numbers, because if we were to use a different coordinate system, the three numbers would be changed to $x'$, $y'$, and $z'$. However, we want to keep our mathematics simple and so we are going to use the *same mark* to represent the three numbers $(x, y, z)$ and the three numbers $(x', y', z')$. That is, we use the same mark to represent the first set of three numbers for one coordinate system, but the second set of three numbers if we are using the other coordinate system. This has the advantage that when we change the coordinate system, we do not have to change the letters of our equations. If we write an equation in terms of $x$, $y$, $z$, and then use another system, we have to change to $x'$, $y'$, $z'$, but we shall just write **r**, with the convention that it represents $(x, y, z)$ if we use one set of axes, or $(x', y', z')$ if we use another set of axes, and so on. The three numbers which describe the quantity in a given coordinate system are called the *components* of the vector in the

* In type, vectors are represented by boldface; in handwritten form an arrow is used: $\vec{r}$.

direction of the coordinate axes of that system. That is, we use the same symbol for the three letters that correspond to the *same object, as seen from different axes*. The very fact that we can say "the same object" implies a physical intuition about the reality of a step in space, that is independent of the components in terms of which we measure it. So the symbol **r** will represent the same thing no matter how we turn the axes.

Now suppose there is another directed physical quantity, any other quantity, which also has three numbers associated with it, like force, and these three numbers change to three other numbers by a certain mathematical rule, if we change the axes. It must be the same rule that changes $(x, y, z)$ into $(x', y', z')$. In other words, any physical quantity associated with three numbers which transform as do the components of a step in space is a vector. An equation like

$$\mathbf{F} = \mathbf{r}$$

would thus be true in *any* coordinate system if it were true in one. This equation, of course, stands for the three equations

$$F_x = x, \quad F_y = y, \quad F_z = z,$$

or, alternatively, for

$$F_{x'} = x', \quad F_{y'} = y', \quad F_{z'} = z'.$$

The fact that a physical relationship can be expressed as a vector equation assures us the relationship is unchanged by a mere rotation of the coordinate system. That is the reason why vectors are so useful in physics.

Now let us examine some of the properties of vectors. As examples of vectors we may mention velocity, momentum, force, and acceleration. For many purposes it is convenient to represent a vector quantity by an arrow that indicates the direction in which it is acting. Why can we represent force, say, by an arrow? Because it has the same mathematical transformation properties as a "step in space." We thus represent it in a diagram as if it were a step, using a scale such that one unit of force, or one newton, corresponds to a

## 12

### SIX NOT-SO-EASY PIECES

certain convenient length. Once we have done this, all forces can be represented as lengths, because an equation like

$$\mathbf{F} = k\mathbf{r},$$

where $k$ is some constant, is a perfectly legitimate equation. Thus we can always represent forces by lines, which is very convenient, because once we have drawn the line we no longer need the axes. Of course, we can quickly calculate the three components as they change upon turning the axes, because that is just a geometric problem.

## 1-5 Vector algebra

Now we must describe the laws, or rules, for combining vectors in various ways. The first such combination is the *addition* of two vectors: suppose that **a** is a vector which in some particular coordinate system has the three components $(a_x, a_y, a_z)$, and that **b** is another vector which has the three components $(b_x, b_y, b_z)$. Now let us invent three new numbers $(a_x + b_x, a_y + b_y, a_z + b_z)$. Do these form a vector? "Well," we might say, "they are three numbers, and every three numbers form a vector." No, *not* every three numbers form a vector! In order for it to be a vector, not only must there be three numbers, but these must be associated with a coordinate system in such a way that if we turn the coordinate system, the three numbers "revolve" on each other, get "mixed up" in each other, by the precise laws we have already described. So the question is, if we now rotate the coordinate system so that $(a_x, a_y, a_z)$ become $(a_{x'}, a_{y'}, a_{z'})$ and $(b_x, b_y, b_z)$ become $(b_{x'}, b_{y'}, b_{z'})$, what do $(a_x + b_x, a_y + b_y, a_z + b_z)$ become? Do they become $(a_{x'} + b_{x'}, a_{y'} + b_{y'}, a_{z'} + b_{z'})$ or not? The answer is, of course, yes, because the prototype transformations of Eq. (1.5) constitute what we call a *linear* transformation. If we apply those transformations to $a_x$ and $b_x$ to get $a_{x'} + b_{x'}$, we find that the transformed $a_x + b_x$ is indeed the same as $a_{x'} + b_{x'}$. When **a** and **b** are "added together" in this sense, they will form a vector which we may call **c**. We would write this as

*Vectors*

$$c = a + b.$$

Now **c** has the interesting property

$$c = b + a,$$

as we can immediately see from its components. Thus also,

$$a + (b + c) = (a + b) + c.$$

We can add vectors in any order.

What is the geometric significance of **a** + **b**? Suppose that **a** and **b** were represented by lines on a piece of paper, what would **c** look like? This is shown in Figure 1-4. We see that we can add the components of **b** to those of **a** most conveniently if we place the rectangle representing the components of **b** next to that representing the components of **a** in the manner indicated. Since **b** just "fits" into its rectangle, as does **a** into its rectangle, this is the same as putting the "tail" of **b** on the "head" of **a**, the arrow from the "tail" of **a** to the "head" of **b** being the vector **c**. Of course, if we added **a** to **b** the other way around, we would put the "tail" of **a** on the "head" of **b**, and by the geometrical properties of parallelograms we would get the same result for **c**. Note that vectors can be added in this way without reference to any coordinate axes.

Suppose we multiply a vector by a number $\alpha$, what does this mean? We *define* it to mean a new vector whose components are

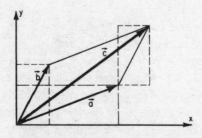

*Figure 1-4.* The addition of vectors.

$\alpha a_x$, $\alpha a_y$, and $\alpha a_z$. We leave it as a problem for the student to prove that it *is* a vector.

Now let us consider vector subtraction. We may define subtraction in the same way as addition, but instead of adding, we subtract the components. Or we might define subtraction by defining a negative vector, $-\mathbf{b} = -1\mathbf{b}$, and then we would add the components. It comes to the same thing. The result is shown in Figure 1-5. This figure shows $\mathbf{d} = \mathbf{a} - \mathbf{b} = \mathbf{a} + (-\mathbf{b})$; we also note that the difference $\mathbf{a} - \mathbf{b}$ can be found very easily from $\mathbf{a}$ and $\mathbf{b}$ by using the equivalent relation $\mathbf{a} = \mathbf{b} + \mathbf{d}$. Thus the difference is even easier to find than the sum: we just draw the vector from $\mathbf{b}$ to $\mathbf{a}$, to get $\mathbf{a} - \mathbf{b}$!

Next we discuss velocity. Why is velocity a vector? If position is given by the three coordinates $(x, y, z)$, what is the velocity? The velocity is given by $dx/dt$, $dy/dt$, and $dz/dt$. Is that a vector, or not? We can find out by differentiating the expressions in Eq. (1.5) to find out whether $dx'/dt$ *transforms* in the right way. We see that the components $dx/dt$ and $dy/dt$ *do* transform according to the same law as $x$ and $y$, and therefore the time derivative is a vector. So the velocity *is* a vector. We can write the velocity in an interesting way as

$$\mathbf{v} = d\mathbf{r}/dt.$$

What the velocity is, and why it is a vector, can also be understood more pictorially: How far does a particle move in a short time $\Delta t$?

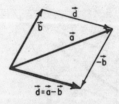

*Figure 1-5.* The subtraction of vectors.

## Vectors

Answer: $\Delta\mathbf{r}$, so if a particle is "here" at one instant and "there" at another instant, then the vector difference of the positions $\Delta\mathbf{r} = \mathbf{r}_2 - \mathbf{r}_1$, which is in the direction of motion shown in Figure 1-6, divided by the time interval $\Delta t = t_2 - t_1$, is the "average velocity" vector.

In other words, by vector velocity we mean the limit, as $\Delta t$ goes to 0, of the difference between the radius vectors at the time $t + \Delta t$ and the time $t$, divided by $\Delta t$:

$$\mathbf{v} = \lim_{\Delta t \to 0} (\Delta\mathbf{r}/\Delta t) = d\mathbf{r}/dt. \qquad (1.10)$$

Thus velocity is a vector because it is the difference of two vectors. It is also the right definition of velocity because its components are $dx/dt$, $dy/dt$, and $dz/dt$. In fact, we see from this argument that if we differentiate *any* vector with respect to time we produce a new vector. So we have several ways of producing new vectors: (1) multiply by a constant, (2) differentiate with respect to time, (3) add or subtract two vectors.

## 1-6 Newton's laws in vector notation

In order to write Newton's laws in vector form, we have to go just one step further, and define the acceleration vector. This is the time derivative of the velocity vector, and it is easy to demonstrate that its

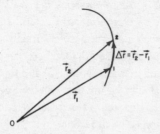

*Figure 1-6.* The displacement of a particle in a short time interval $\Delta t = t_2 - t_1$.

components are the second derivatives of $x$, $y$, and $z$ with respect to $t$:

$$\mathbf{a} = \frac{d\mathbf{v}}{dt} = \left(\frac{d}{dt}\right)\left(\frac{d\mathbf{r}}{dt}\right) = \frac{d^2\mathbf{r}}{dt^2}, \tag{1.11}$$

$$a_x = \frac{dv_x}{dt} = \frac{d^2x}{dt^2}, \quad a_y = \frac{dv_y}{dt} = \frac{d^2y}{dt^2}, \quad a_z = \frac{dv_z}{dt} = \frac{d^2z}{dt^2}. \tag{1.12}$$

With this definition, then, Newton's laws can be written in this way:

$$m\mathbf{a} = \mathbf{F} \tag{1.13}$$

or

$$m(d^2\mathbf{r}/dt^2) = \mathbf{F}. \tag{1.14}$$

Now the problem of proving the invariance of Newton's laws under rotation of coordinates is this: prove that $\mathbf{a}$ is a vector; this we have just done. Prove that $\mathbf{F}$ is a vector; we *suppose* it is. So if force is a vector, then, since we know acceleration is a vector, Eq. (1.13) will look the same in any coordinate system. Writing it in a form which does not explicitly contain $x$'s, $y$'s, and $z$'s has the advantage that from now on we need not write *three* laws every time we write Newton's equations or other laws of physics. We write what looks like *one* law, but really, of course, it is the three laws for any particular set of axes, because any vector equation involves the statement that *each of the components is equal*.

The fact that the acceleration is the rate of change of the vector velocity helps us to calculate the acceleration in some rather complicated circumstances. Suppose, for instance, that a particle is moving on some complicated curve (Figure 1-7) and that, at a given instant $t$, it had a certain velocity $\mathbf{v}_1$, but that when we go to another instant $t_2$ a little later, it has a different velocity $\mathbf{v}_2$. What is the acceleration? Answer: Acceleration is the difference in the velocity divided by the small time interval, so we need the difference of the two velocities. How do we get the difference of the velocities? To subtract two vectors, we put the vector across the ends of $\mathbf{v}_2$ and $\mathbf{v}_1$; that is, we

## Vectors

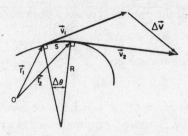

*Figure 1-7.* A curved trajectory.

draw $\Delta$ as the difference of the two vectors, right? *No!* That only works when the *tails* of the vectors are in the same place! It has no meaning if we move the vector somewhere else and then draw a line across, so watch out! We have to draw a new diagram to subtract the vectors. In Figure 1-8, $\mathbf{v}_1$ and $\mathbf{v}_2$ are both drawn parallel and equal to their counterparts in Figure 1-7, and now we can discuss the acceleration. Of course the acceleration is simply $\Delta\mathbf{v}/\Delta t$. It is interesting to note that we can compose the velocity difference out of two parts; we can think of acceleration as having *two components*, $\Delta\mathbf{v}_{\parallel}$ in the direction tangent to the path and $\Delta\mathbf{v}_{\perp}$ at right angles to the path, as indicated in Figure 1-8. The acceleration tangent to the path is, of course, just the change in the *length* of the vector, i.e., the change in the *speed v*:

$$a_{\parallel} = dv/dt. \tag{1.15}$$

The other component of acceleration, at right angles to the curve, is easy to calculate, using Figures 1-7 and 1-8. In the short time $\Delta t$ let the change in angle between $\mathbf{v}_1$ and $\mathbf{v}_2$ be the small angle $\Delta\theta$. If

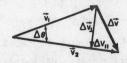

*Figure 1-8.* Diagram for calculating the acceleration.

the magnitude of the velocity is called $v$, then of course

$$\Delta v_\perp = v \,\Delta \theta$$

and the acceleration $a$ will be

$$a_\perp = v \,(\Delta\theta/\Delta t).$$

Now we need to know $\Delta\theta/\Delta t$, which can be found this way: If, at the given moment, the curve is approximated as a circle of a certain radius $R$, then in a time $\Delta t$ the distance $s$ is, of course, $v\,\Delta t$, where $v$ is the speed.

$$\Delta\theta = v(\Delta t/R), \quad \text{or} \quad \Delta\theta/\Delta t = v/R.$$

Therefore, we find

$$a = v^2/R, \tag{1.16}$$

as we have seen before.

## 1-7 Scalar product of vectors

Now let us examine a little further the properties of vectors. It is easy to see that the *length* of a step in space would be the same in any coordinate system. That is, if a particular step $\mathbf{r}$ is represented by $x$, $y$, $z$, in one coordinate system, and by $x'$, $y'$, $z'$ in another coordinate system, surely the distance $r = |\mathbf{r}|$ would be the same in both. Now

$$r = \sqrt{x^2 + y^2 + z^2}$$

and also

$$r' = \sqrt{x'^2 + y'^2 + z'^2}.$$

So what we wish to verify is that these two quantities are equal. It is much more convenient not to bother to take the square root, so let us talk about the square of the distance; that is, let us find out whether

$$x^2 + y^2 + z^2 = x'^2 + y'^2 + z'^2. \tag{1.17}$$

It had better be—and if we substitute Eq. (1.5) we do indeed find that it is. So we see that there are other kinds of equations which are true for any two coordinate systems.

## Vectors

Something new is involved. We can produce a new quantity, a function of $x$, $y$, and $z$, called a *scalar function*, a quantity which has no direction but which is the same in both systems. Out of a vector we can make a scalar. We have to find a general rule for that. It is clear what the rule is for the case just considered: add the squares of the components. Let us now define a new thing, which we call $\mathbf{a} \cdot \mathbf{a}$. This is not a vector, but a scalar; it is a number that is the same in all coordinate systems, and it is defined to be the sum of the squares of the three components of the vector:

$$\mathbf{a} \cdot \mathbf{a} = a_x^2 + a_y^2 + a_z^2. \tag{1.18}$$

Now you say, "But with what axes?" It does not depend on the axes, the answer is the same in *every* set of axes. So we have a new *kind* of quantity, a new *invariant* or *scalar* produced by one vector "squared." If we now define the following quantity for any two vectors $\mathbf{a}$ and $\mathbf{b}$:

$$\mathbf{a} \cdot \mathbf{b} = a_x b_x + a_y b_y + a_z b_z, \tag{1.19}$$

we find that this quantity, calculated in the primed and unprimed systems, also stays the same. To prove it we note that it is true of $\mathbf{a} \cdot \mathbf{a}$, $\mathbf{b} \cdot \mathbf{b}$, and $\mathbf{c} \cdot \mathbf{c}$, where $\mathbf{c} = \mathbf{a} + \mathbf{b}$. Therefore the sum of the squares $(a_x + b_x)^2 + (a_y + b_y)^2 + (a_z + b_z)^2$ will be invariant:

$$(a_x + b_x)^2 + (a_y + b_y)^2 + (a_z + b_z)^2 = \\ (a_{x'} + b_{x'})^2 + (a_{y'} + b_{y'})^2 + (a_{z'} + b_{z'})^2. \tag{1.20}$$

If both sides of this equation are expanded, there will be cross products of just the type appearing in Eq. (1.19), as well as the sums of squares of the components of $\mathbf{a}$ and $\mathbf{b}$. The invariance of terms of the form of Eq. (1.18) then leaves the cross product terms (1.19) invariant also.

The quantity $\mathbf{a} \cdot \mathbf{b}$ is called the *scalar product* of two vectors, $\mathbf{a}$ and $\mathbf{b}$, and it has many interesting and useful properties. For instance, it is easily proved that

$$\mathbf{a} \cdot (\mathbf{b} + \mathbf{c}) = \mathbf{a} \cdot \mathbf{b} + \mathbf{a} \cdot \mathbf{c}. \tag{1.21}$$

## Six Not-So-Easy Pieces

Also, there is a simple geometrical way to calculate $\mathbf{a} \cdot \mathbf{b}$, without having to calculate the components of $\mathbf{a}$ and $\mathbf{b}$: $\mathbf{a} \cdot \mathbf{b}$ is the product of the length of $\mathbf{a}$ and the length of $\mathbf{b}$ times the cosine of the angle between them. Why? Suppose that we choose a special coordinate system in which the $x$-axis lies along $\mathbf{a}$; in those circumstances, the only component of $\mathbf{a}$ that will be there is $a_x$, which is of course the whole length of $\mathbf{a}$. Thus Eq. (1.19) reduces to $\mathbf{a} \cdot \mathbf{b} = a_x b_x$ for this case, and this is the length of $\mathbf{a}$ times the component of $\mathbf{b}$ in the direction of $\mathbf{a}$, that is, $b \cos \theta$:

$$\mathbf{a} \cdot \mathbf{b} = ab \cos \theta.$$

Therefore, in that special coordinate system, we have proved that $\mathbf{a} \cdot \mathbf{b}$ is the length of $\mathbf{a}$ times the length of $\mathbf{b}$ times $\cos \theta$. But *if it is true in one coordinate system, it is true in all*, because $\mathbf{a} \cdot \mathbf{b}$ is independent of the coordinate system; that is our argument.

What good is the dot product? Are there any cases in physics where we need it? Yes, we need it all the time. For instance, in Chapter 4* the kinetic energy was called $\frac{1}{2}mv^2$, but if the object is moving in space it should be the velocity squared in the $x$-direction, the $y$-direction, and the $z$-direction, and so the formula for kinetic energy according to vector analysis is

$$\text{K.E.} = \tfrac{1}{2}m(\mathbf{v} \cdot \mathbf{v}) = \tfrac{1}{2}m(v_x^2 + v_y^2 + v_z^2). \tag{1.22}$$

Energy does not have direction. Momentum has direction; it is a vector, and it is the mass times the velocity vector.

Another example of a dot product is the work done by a force when something is pushed from one place to the other. We have not yet defined work, but it is equivalent to the energy change, the weights lifted, when a force $\mathbf{F}$ acts through a distance $\mathbf{s}$:

$$\text{Work} = \mathbf{F} \cdot \mathbf{s}. \tag{1.23}$$

It is sometimes very convenient to talk about the component of a vector in a certain direction (say the vertical direction because that is the direction of gravity). For such purposes, it is useful to invent

---

* of the original *Lectures on Physics*, vol. I.

## Vectors

what we call a *unit vector* in the direction that we want to study. By a unit vector we mean one whose dot product with itself is equal to unity. Let us call this unit vector $\mathbf{i}$; then $\mathbf{i} \cdot \mathbf{i} = 1$. Then, if we want the component of some vector in the direction of $\mathbf{i}$, we see that the dot product $\mathbf{a} \cdot \mathbf{i}$ will be $a \cos \theta$, i.e., the component of $\mathbf{a}$ in the direction of $\mathbf{i}$. This is a nice way to get the component; in fact, it permits us to get *all* the components and to write a rather amusing formula. Suppose that in a given system of coordinates, $x$, $y$, and $z$, we invent three vectors: $\mathbf{i}$, a unit vector in the direction $x$; $\mathbf{j}$, a unit vector in the direction $y$; and $\mathbf{k}$, a unit vector in the direction $z$. Note first that $\mathbf{i} \cdot \mathbf{i} = 1$. What is $\mathbf{i} \cdot \mathbf{j}$? When two vectors are at right angles, their dot product is zero. Thus

$$\mathbf{i} \cdot \mathbf{i} = 1$$
$$\mathbf{i} \cdot \mathbf{j} = 0 \qquad \mathbf{j} \cdot \mathbf{j} = 1 \qquad\qquad (1.24)$$
$$\mathbf{i} \cdot \mathbf{k} = 0 \qquad \mathbf{j} \cdot \mathbf{k} = 0 \qquad \mathbf{k} \cdot \mathbf{k} = 1$$

Now with these definitions, any vector whatsoever can be written this way:

$$\mathbf{a} = a_x \mathbf{i} + a_y \mathbf{j} + a_z \mathbf{k}. \qquad (1.25)$$

By this means we can go from the components of a vector to the vector itself.

This discussion of vectors is by no means complete. However, rather than try to go more deeply into the subject now, we shall first learn to use in physical situations some of the ideas so far discussed. Then, when we have properly mastered this basic material, we shall find it easier to penetrate more deeply into the subject without getting too confused. We shall later find that it is useful to define another kind of product of two vectors, called the vector product, and written as $\mathbf{a} \times \mathbf{b}$. However, we shall undertake a discussion of such matters in a later chapter.

# Two

# SYMMETRY IN
# PHYSICAL LAWS

## 2-1 *Symmetry operations*

▶ The subject of this chapter is what we may call *symmetry in physical laws*. We have already discussed certain features of symmetry in physical laws in connection with vector analysis (Chapter 1), the theory of relativity (which follows in Chapter 4), and rotation (Chapter 20*).

Why should we be concerned with symmetry? In the first place, symmetry is fascinating to the human mind, and everyone likes objects or patterns that are in some way symmetrical. It is an interesting fact that nature often exhibits certain kinds of symmetry in the objects we find in the world around us. Perhaps the most symmetrical object imaginable is a sphere, and nature is full of spheres—stars, planets, water droplets in clouds. The crystals found in rocks exhibit many different kinds of symmetry, the study of which tells us some important things about the structure of solids. Even the animal and vegetable worlds show some degree of symmetry, although the symmetry of a flower or of a bee is not as perfect or as fundamental as is that of a crystal.

But our main concern here is not with the fact that the *objects* of

---

* of the original *Lectures on Physics*, vol. I.

nature are often symmetrical. Rather, we wish to examine some of the even more remarkable symmetries of the universe—the symmetries that exist in the *basic laws themselves* which govern the operation of the physical world.

First, what *is* symmetry? How can a physical *law* be "symmetrical"? The problem of defining symmetry is an interesting one and we have already noted that Weyl gave a good definition, the substance of which is that a thing is symmetrical if there is something we can do to it so that after we have done it, it looks the same as it did before. For example, a symmetrical vase is of such a kind that if we reflect or turn it, it will look the same as it did before. The question we wish to consider here is what we can do to physical phenomena, or to a physical situation in an experiment, and yet leave the result the same. A list of the known operations under which various physical phenomena remain invariant is shown in Table 2-1.

## 2-2 Symmetry in space and time

The first thing we might try to do, for example, is to *translate* the phenomenon in space. If we do an experiment in a certain region, and then build another apparatus at another place in space (or move the original one over) then, whatever went on in one apparatus, in a certain order in time, will occur in the same way if we

*Table 2-1.*  Symmetry Operations

Translation in space
Translation in time
Rotation through a fixed angle
Uniform velocity in a straight line (Lorentz transformation)
Reversal of time
Reflection of space
Interchange of identical atoms or identical particles
Quantum-mechanical phase
Matter-antimatter (charge conjugation)

## Symmetry in Physical Laws

have arranged the same condition, with all due attention to the restrictions that we mentioned before: that all of those features of the environment which make it not behave the same way have also been moved over—we talked about how to define how much we should include in those circumstances, and we shall not go into those details again.

In the same way, we also believe today that *displacement in time* will have no effect on physical laws. (That is, *as far as we know today*—all of these things are as far as we know today!) That means that if we build a certain apparatus and start it at a certain time, say on Thursday at 10:00 A.M., and then build the same apparatus and start it, say, three days later in the same condition, the two apparatuses will go through the same motions in exactly the same way as a function of time no matter what the starting time, provided again, of course, that the relevant features of the environment are also modified appropriately in *time*. That symmetry means, of course, that if one bought General Motors stock three months ago, the same thing would happen to it if he bought it now!

We have to watch out for geographical differences too, for there are, of course, variations in the characteristics of the earth's surface. So, for example, if we measure the magnetic field in a certain region and move the apparatus to some other region, it may not work in precisely the same way because the magnetic field is different, but we say that is because the magnetic field is associated with the earth. We can imagine that if we move the whole earth and the equipment, it would make no difference in the operation of the apparatus.

Another thing that we discussed in considerable detail was rotation in space: if we turn an apparatus at an angle it works just as well, provided we turn everything else that is relevant along with it. In fact, we discussed the problem of symmetry under rotation in space in some detail in Chapter 1, and we invented a mathematical system called *vector analysis* to handle it as neatly as possible.

On a more advanced level we had another symmetry—the symmetry under uniform velocity in a straight line. That is to say—a rather remarkable effect—that if we have a piece of apparatus working a certain way and then take the same apparatus and put it in a car, and move the whole car, plus all the relevant surroundings, at a uniform velocity in a straight line, then so far as the phenomena inside the car are concerned there is no difference: all the laws of physics appear the same. We even know how to express this more technically, and that is that the mathematical equations of the physical laws must be unchanged under a *Lorentz transformation*. As a matter of fact, it was a study of the relativity problem that concentrated physicists' attention most sharply on symmetry in physical laws.

Now the above-mentioned symmetries have all been of a geometrical nature, time and space being more or less the same, but there are other symmetries of a different kind. For example, there is a symmetry which describes the fact that we can replace one atom by another of the same kind; to put it differently, there *are* atoms of the same kind. It is possible to find groups of atoms such that if we change a pair around, it makes no difference—the atoms are identical. Whatever one atom of oxygen of a certain type will do, another atom of oxygen of that type will do. One may say, "That is ridiculous, that is the *definition* of equal types!" That may be merely the definition, but then we still do not know whether there *are* any "atoms of the same type"; the *fact* is that there are many, many atoms of the same type. Thus it does mean something to say that it makes no difference if we replace one atom by another of the same type. The so-called elementary particles of which the atoms are made are also identical particles in the above sense—all electrons are the same; all protons are the same; all positive pions are the same; and so on.

After such a long list of things that can be done without changing the phenomena, one might think we could do practically anything; so let us give some examples to the contrary, just to see the difference. Suppose that we ask: "Are the physical laws symmetrical under a change of scale?" Suppose we build a certain piece of apparatus, and then build another apparatus five times bigger in every part, will it work exactly the same way? The answer is, in this

## Symmetry in Physical Laws

case, *no*! The wavelength of light emitted, for example, by the atoms inside one box of sodium atoms and the wavelength of light emitted by a gas of sodium atoms five times in volume is not five times longer, but is in fact exactly the same as the other. So the ratio of the wavelength to the size of the emitter will change.

Another example: we see in the newspaper, every once in a while, pictures of a great cathedral made with little matchsticks—a tremendous work of art by some retired fellow who keeps gluing matchsticks together. It is much more elaborate and wonderful than any real cathedral. If we imagine that this wooden cathedral were actually built on the scale of a real cathedral, we see where the trouble is; it would not last—the whole thing would collapse because of the fact that scaled-up matchsticks are just not strong enough. "Yes," one might say, "but we also know that when there is an influence from the outside, it also must be changed in proportion!" We are talking about the ability of the object to withstand gravitation. So what we should do is first to take the model cathedral of real matchsticks and the real earth, and then we know it is stable. Then we should take the larger cathedral and take a bigger earth. But then it is even worse, because the gravitation is increased still more!

Today, of course, we understand the fact that phenomena depend on the scale on the grounds that matter is atomic in nature, and certainly if we built an apparatus that was so small there were only five atoms in it, it would clearly be something we could not scale up and down arbitrarily. The scale of an individual atom is not at all arbitrary—it is quite definite.

The fact that the laws of physics are not unchanged under a change of scale was discovered by Galileo. He realized that the strengths of materials were not in exactly the right proportion to their sizes, and he illustrated this property that we were just discussing, about the cathedral of matchsticks, by drawing two bones, the bone of one dog, in the right proportion for holding up his weight, and the imaginary bone of a "super dog" that would be, say, ten or a hundred times bigger—that bone was a big, solid thing with quite different proportions. We do not know whether he ever carried the argument quite to the conclusion that the laws of nature must have a definite scale, but he was so impressed with this discovery that he considered it to be as important as the discovery of the laws of motion, because he published them both in the same volume, called "On Two New Sciences."

Another example in which the laws are not symmetrical, that we know quite well, is this: a system in rotation at a uniform angular velocity does not give the same apparent laws as one that is not rotating. If we make an experiment and then put everything in a space ship and have the space ship spinning in empty space, all alone at a constant angular velocity, the apparatus will not work the same way because, as we know, things inside the equipment will be thrown to the outside, and so on, by the centrifugal or coriolis forces, etc. In fact, we can tell that the earth is rotating by using a so-called Foucault pendulum, without looking outside.

Next we mention a very interesting symmetry which is obviously false, i.e., *reversibility in time*. The physical laws apparently cannot be reversible in time, because, as we know, all obvious phenomena are irreversible on a large scale: "The moving finger writes, and having writ, moves on." So far as we can tell, this irreversibility is due to the very large number of particles involved, and if we could see the individual molecules, we would not be able to discern whether the machinery was working forwards or backwards. To make it more precise: we build a small apparatus in which we know what all the atoms are doing, in which we can watch them jiggling. Now we build another apparatus like it, but which starts its motion in the final condition of the other one, with all the velocities precisely reversed. *It will then go through the same motions, but exactly in reverse.* Putting it another way: if we take a motion picture, with sufficient detail, of all the inner works of a piece of material and shine it on a screen and run it backwards, no physicist will be able to say, "That is against the laws of physics, that is doing something wrong!" If we do not see all the details, of course, the situation will be perfectly clear. If we see the egg splattering on the sidewalk and

## Symmetry in Physical Laws

the shell cracking open, and so on, then we will surely say, "That is irreversible, because if we run the moving picture backwards the egg will all collect together and the shell will go back together, and that is obviously ridiculous!" But if we look at the individual atoms themselves, the laws look completely reversible. This is, of course, a much harder discovery to have made, but apparently it is true that the fundamental physical laws, on a microscopic and fundamental level, are completely reversible in time!

### 2-3 Symmetry and conservation laws

The symmetries of the physical laws are very interesting at this level, but they turn out, in the end, to be even more interesting and exciting when we come to quantum mechanics. For a reason which we cannot make clear at the level of the present discussion—a fact that most physicists still find somewhat staggering, a most profound and beautiful thing, is that, in quantum mechanics, *for each of the rules of symmetry there is a corresponding conservation law*; there is a definite connection between the laws of conservation and the symmetries of physical laws. We can only state this at present, without any attempt at explanation.

The fact, for example, that the laws are symmetrical for translation in space when we add the principles of quantum mechanics, turns out to mean that *momentum is conserved*.

That the laws are symmetrical under translation in time means, in quantum mechanics, that *energy is conserved*.

Invariance under rotation through a fixed angle in space corresponds to the *conservation of angular momentum*. These connections are very interesting and beautiful things, among the most beautiful and profound things in physics.

Incidentally, there are a number of symmetries which appear in quantum mechanics which have no classical analog, which have no method of description in classical physics. One of these is as follows: If $\psi$ is the amplitude for some process or other, we know that the absolute square of $\psi$ is the probability that the process will

SIX NOT-SO-EASY PIECES

occur. Now if someone else were to make his calculations, not with this $\psi$, but with a $\psi'$ which differs merely by a change in phase (let $\Delta$ be some constant, and multiply $e^{i\Delta}$ times the old $\psi$), the absolute square of $\psi'$, which is the probability of the event, is then equal to the absolute square of $\psi$:

$$\psi' = \psi e^{i\Delta}; \qquad |\psi'|^2 = |\psi|^2. \tag{2.1}$$

Therefore the physical laws are unchanged if the phase of the wave function is shifted by an arbitrary constant. That is another symmetry. Physical laws must be of such a nature that a shift in the quantum-mechanical phase makes no difference. As we have just mentioned, in quantum mechanics there is a conservation law for every symmetry. The conservation law which is connected with the quantum-mechanical phase seems to be the *conservation of electrical charge*. This is altogether a very interesting business!

## 2-4 Mirror reflections

Now the next question, which is going to concern us for most of the rest of this chapter, is the question of symmetry under *reflection in space*. The problem is this: Are the physical laws symmetrical under reflection? We may put it this way: Suppose we build a piece of equipment, let us say a clock, with lots of wheels and hands and numbers; it ticks, it works, and it has things wound up inside. We look at the clock in the mirror. How it *looks* in the mirror is not the question. But let us actually *build* another clock which is exactly the same as the way the first clock looks in the mirror—every time there is a screw with a right-hand thread in one, we use a screw with a left-hand thread in the corresponding place of the other; where one is marked "2" on the face, we mark a "$\Sigma$" on the face of the other; each coiled spring is twisted one way in one clock and the other way in the mirror-image clock; when we are all finished, we have two clocks, both physical, which bear to each other the relation of an object and its mirror image, although they are both actual, material objects, we emphasize. Now the question is: If the two clocks are

## Symmetry in Physical Laws

started in the same condition, the springs wound to corresponding tightnesses, will the two clocks tick and go around, forever after, as exact mirror images? (This is a physical question, not a philosophical question.) Our intuition about the laws of physics would suggest that they *would*.

We would suspect that, at least in the case of these clocks, reflection in space is one of the symmetries of physical laws, that if we change everything from "right" to "left" and leave it otherwise the same, we cannot tell the difference. Let us, then, suppose for a moment that this is true. If it is true, then it would be impossible to distinguish "right" and "left" by any physical phenomenon, just as it is, for example, impossible to define a particular absolute velocity by a physical phenomenon. So it should be impossible, by any physical phenomenon, to define absolutely what we mean by "right" as opposed to "left," because the physical laws should be symmetrical.

Of course, the world does not *have* to be symmetrical. For example, using what we may call "geography," surely "right" can be defined. For instance, we stand in New Orleans and look at Chicago, and Florida is to our right (when our feet are on the ground!). So we can define "right" and "left" by geography. Of course, the actual situation in any system does not have to have the symmetry that we are talking about; it is a question of whether the *laws* are symmetrical—in other words, whether it is *against the physical laws* to have a sphere like the earth with "left-handed dirt" on it and a person like ourselves standing looking at a city like Chicago from a place like New Orleans, but with everything the other way around, so Florida is on the other side. It clearly seems not impossible, not against the physical laws, to have everything changed left for right.

Another point is that our definition of "right" should not depend on history. An easy way to distinguish right from left is to go to a machine shop and pick up a screw at random. The odds are it has a right-hand thread—not necessarily, but it is much more likely to have a right-hand thread than a left-hand one. This is a question of history or convention, or the way things happen to be, and is again

## SIX NOT-SO-EASY PIECES

not a question of fundamental laws. As we can well appreciate, everyone could have started out making left-handed screws!

So we must try to find some phenomenon in which "right hand" is involved fundamentally. The next possibility we discuss is the fact that polarized light rotates its plane of polarization as it goes through, say, sugar water. As we saw in Chapter 33,* it rotates, let us say, to the right in a certain sugar solution. That is a way of defining "right-hand," because we may dissolve some sugar in the water and then the polarization goes to the right. But sugar has come from living things, and if we try to make the sugar artificially, then we discover that it *does not* rotate the plane of polarization! But if we then take that same sugar which is made artificially and which does not rotate the plane of polarization, and put bacteria in it (they eat some of the sugar) and then filter out the bacteria, we find that we still have sugar left (almost half as much as we had before), and this time it does rotate the plane of polarization, but *the other way*! It seems very confusing, but is easily explained.

Take another example: One of the substances which is common to all living creatures and that is fundamental to life is protein. Proteins consist of chains of amino acids. Figure 2-1 shows a model of an amino acid that comes out of a protein. This amino acid is called alanine, and the molecular arrangement would look like that in Figure 2-1(a) if it came out of a protein of a real living thing. On the other hand, if we try to make alanine from carbon dioxide, ethane, and ammonia (and we *can* make it, it is not a complicated molecule), we discover that we are making equal amounts of this molecule and the one shown in Figure 2-1(b)! The first molecule, the one that comes from the living thing, is called *L-alanine*. The other one, which is the same chemically, in that it has the same kinds of atoms and the same connections of the atoms, is a "right-hand" molecule, compared with the "left-hand" L-alanine, and it is called *D-alanine*. The interesting thing is that when we make alanine at

* of the original *Lectures on Physics*, vol. I.

## Symmetry in Physical Laws

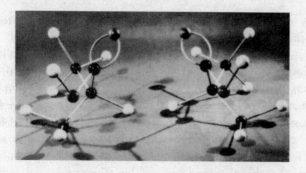

*Figure 2-1.* (a) L-alanine (left), and (b) D-alanine (right).

home in a laboratory from simple gases, we get an equal mixture of both kinds. However, the only thing that life uses is L-alanine. (This is not exactly true. Here and there in living creatures there is a special use for D-alanine, but it is very rare. All proteins use L-alanine exclusively.) Now if we make both kinds, and we feed the mixture to some animal which likes to "eat," or use up, alanine, it cannot use D-alanine, so it only uses the L-alanine; that is what happened to our sugar—after the bacteria eat the sugar that works well for them, only the "wrong" kind is left! (Left-handed sugar tastes sweet, but not the same as right-handed sugar.)

So it looks as though the phenomena of life permit a distinction between "right" and "left," or chemistry permits a distinction, because the two molecules are chemically different. But no, it does not! So far as physical measurements can be made, such as of energy, the rates of chemical reactions, and so on, the two kinds work exactly the same way if we make everything else in a mirror image too. One molecule will rotate light to the right, and the other will rotate it to the left in precisely the same amount, through the same amount of fluid. Thus, so far as physics is concerned, these two amino acids are equally satisfactory. So far as we understand things today, the fundamentals of the Schrödinger equation have it that the two molecules should behave in exactly corresponding ways, so that one is to the right as the other is to the left. Nevertheless, in life it is all one way!

It is presumed that the reason for this is the following. Let us suppose, for example, that life is somehow at one moment in a certain condition in which all the proteins in some creatures have left-handed amino acids, and all the enzymes are lopsided—every substance in the living creature is lopsided—it is not symmetrical. So when the digestive enzymes try to change the chemicals in the food from one kind to another, one kind of chemical "fits" into the enzyme, but the other kind does not (like Cinderella and the slipper, except that it is a "left foot" that we are testing). So far as we know, in principle, we could build a frog, for example, in which every molecule is reversed, everything is like the "left-hand" mirror image of a real frog; we have a left-hand frog. This left-hand frog would go on all right for a while, but he would find nothing to eat, because if he swallows a fly, his enzymes are not built to digest it. The fly has the wrong "kind" of amino acids (unless we give him a left-hand fly). So as far as we know, the chemical and life processes would continue in the same manner if everything were reversed.

If life is entirely a physical and chemical phenomenon, then we can understand that the proteins are all made in the same corkscrew only from the idea that at the very beginning some living molecules, by accident, got started and a few won. Somewhere, once, one organic molecule was lopsided in a certain way, and from this particular thing the "right" happened to evolve in our particular geography; a particular historical accident was one-sided, and ever since then the lopsidedness has propagated itself. Once having arrived at the state that it is in now, of course, it will always continue—all the enzymes digest the right things, manufacture the right things: when the carbon dioxide and the water vapor, and so on, go in the plant leaves, the enzymes that make the sugars make them lopsided because the enzymes are lopsided. If any new kind of virus or living thing were to originate at a later time, it would survive only if it could "eat" the kind of living matter already present. Thus it, too, must be of the same kind.

## Symmetry in Physical Laws

There is no conservation of the number of right-handed molecules. Once started, we could keep increasing the number of right-handed molecules. So the presumption is, then, that the phenomena in the case of life do not show a lack of symmetry in physical laws, but do show, on the contrary, the universal nature and the commonness of ultimate origin of all creatures on earth, in the sense described above.

### 2-5 Polar and axial vectors

Now we go further. We observe that in physics there are a lot of other places where we have "right-hand" and "left-hand" rules. As a matter of fact, when we learned about vector analysis we learned about the right-hand rules we have to use in order to get the angular momentum, torque, magnetic field, and so on, to come out right. The force on a charge moving in a magnetic field, for example, is $\mathbf{F} = q\mathbf{v} \times \mathbf{B}$. In a given situation, in which we know $\mathbf{F}$, $\mathbf{v}$, and $\mathbf{B}$, isn't that equation enough to define right-handedness? As a matter of fact, if we go back and look at where the vectors came from, we know that the "right-hand rule" was merely a convention; it was a trick. The original quantities, like the angular momenta and the angular velocities, and things of this kind, were not really vectors at all! They are all somehow associated with a certain plane, and it is just because there are three dimensions in space that we can associate the quantity with a direction perpendicular to that plane. Of the two possible directions, we chose the "right-hand" direction.

So if the laws of physics are symmetrical, we should find that if some demon were to sneak into all the physics laboratories and replace the word "right" for "left" in every book in which "right-hand rules" are given, and instead we were to use all "left-hand rules," uniformly, then it should make no difference whatever in the physical laws.

Let us give an illustration. There are two kinds of vectors. There are "honest" vectors, for example a step $\Delta\mathbf{r}$ in space. If in our apparatus there is a piece here and something else there, then in a

## SIX NOT-SO-EASY PIECES

mirror apparatus there will be the image piece and the image something else, and if we draw a vector from the "piece" to the "something else," one vector is the mirror image of the other (Figure 2-2). The vector arrow changes its head, just as the whole space turns inside out; such a vector we call a *polar vector*.

But the other kind of vector, which has to do with rotations, is of a different nature. For example, suppose that in three dimensions something is rotating as shown in Figure 2-3. Then if we look at it in a mirror, it will be rotating as indicated, namely, as the mirror image of the original rotation. Now we have agreed to represent the mirror rotation by the same rule, it is a "vector" which, on reflection, does *not* change about as the polar vector does, but is reversed relative to the polar vectors and to the geometry of the space; such a vector is called an *axial vector*.

Now if the law of reflection symmetry is right in physics, then it must be true that the equations must be so designed that if we change the sign of each axial vector and each cross-product of vectors, which would be what corresponds to reflection, nothing will happen. For instance, when we write a formula which says that the angular momentum is $L = r \times p$, that equation is all right, because if we change to a left-hand coordinate system, we change the sign of $L$, but $p$ and $r$ do not change; the cross-product sign is changed, since we must change from a right-hand rule to a left-hand rule. As another example, we know that the force on a charge moving in a magnetic field is $F = q v \times B$, but if we change from a right- to a left-handed system, since $F$ and $v$ are known to be polar vectors the sign change required by the cross-product must be cancelled by a sign change in $B$, which means that $B$ must be an

*Figure 2-2.* A step in space and its mirror image.

## Symmetry in Physical Laws

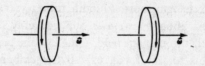

*Figure 2-3.* A rotating wheel and its mirror image. Note that the angular velocity "vector" is not reversed in direction.

axial vector. In other words, if we make such a reflection, **B** must go to − **B**. So if we change our coordinates from right to left, we must also change the poles of magnets from north to south.

Let us see how that works in an example. Suppose that we have two magnets, as in Figure 2-4. One is a magnet with the coils going around a certain way, and with current in a given direction. The other magnet looks like the reflection of the first magnet in a mirror—the coil will wind the other way, everything that happens inside the coil is exactly reversed, and the current goes as shown. Now, from the laws for the production of magnetic fields, which we do not know yet officially, but which we most likely learned in high school, it turns out that the magnetic field is as shown in the figure. In one case the pole is a south magnetic pole, while in the other magnet the current is going the other way and the magnetic field is reversed—it is a north magnetic pole. So we see that when we go from right to left we must indeed change from north to south!

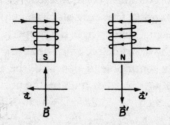

*Figure 2-4.* A magnet and its mirror image.

Never mind changing north to south; these too are mere conventions. Let us talk about *phenomena*. Suppose, now, that we have an electron moving through one field, going into the page. Then, if we use the formula for the force, $\mathbf{v} \times \mathbf{B}$ (remember the charge is minus), we find that the electron will deviate in the indicated direction according to the physical law. So the phenomenon is that we have a coil with a current going in a specified sense and an electron curves in a certain way—that is the physics—never mind how we label everything.

Now let us do the same experiment with a mirror: we send an electron through in a corresponding direction and now the force is reversed, if we calculate it from the same rule, and that is very good because the corresponding *motions* are then mirror images!

## 2-6 Which hand is right?

So the fact of the matter is that in studying any phenomenon there are always two right-hand rules, or an even number of them, and the net result is that the phenomena always look symmetrical. In short, therefore, we cannot tell right from left if we also are not able to tell north from south. However, it may seem that we *can* tell the north pole of a magnet. The north pole of a compass needle, for example, is one that points to the north. But of course that is again a local property that has to do with geography of the earth; that is just like talking about in which direction is Chicago, so it does not count. If we have seen compass needles, we may have noticed that the north-seeking pole is a sort of bluish color. But that is just due to the man who painted the magnet. These are all local, conventional criteria.

However, if a magnet were to have the property that if we looked at it closely enough we would see small hairs growing on its north pole but not on its south pole, if that were the general rule, or if there were *any* unique way to distinguish the north from the south pole of a magnet, then we could tell which of the two cases we actually had, and *that would be the end of the law of reflection symmetry*.

## Symmetry in Physical Laws

To illustrate the whole problem still more clearly, imagine that we were talking to a Martian, or someone very far away, by telephone. We are not allowed to send him any actual samples to inspect; for instance, if we could send light, we could send him right-hand circularly polarized light and say, "That is right-hand light—just watch the way it is going." But we cannot *give* him anything, we can only talk to him. He is far away, or in some strange location, and he cannot see anything we can see. For instance, we cannot say, "Look at Ursa major; now see how those stars are arranged. What we mean by 'right' is . . ." We are only allowed to telephone him.

Now we want to tell him all about us. Of course, first we start defining numbers, and say, "Tick, tick, *two*, tick, tick, tick, *three* . . . ," so that gradually he can understand a couple of words, and so on. After a while we may become very familiar with this fellow, and he says, "What do you guys look like?" We start to describe ourselves, and say, "Well, we are six feet tall." He says, "Wait a minute, what is six feet?" Is it possible to tell him what six feet is? Certainly! We say, "You know about the diameter of hydrogen atoms—we are 17,000,000,000 hydrogen atoms high!" That is possible because physical laws are not variant under change of scale, and therefore we *can* define an absolute length. And so we define the size of the body, and tell him what the general shape is—it has prongs with five bumps sticking out on the ends, and so on, and he follows us along, and we finish describing how we look on the outside, presumably without encountering any particular difficulties. He is even making a model of us as we go along. He says, "My, you are certainly very handsome fellows; now what is on the inside?" So we start to describe the various organs on the inside, and we come to the heart, and we carefully describe the shape of it, and say, "Now put the heart on the left side." He says, "Duhhh—the left side?" Now our problem is to describe to him which side the heart goes on without his ever seeing anything that we see, and without our ever sending any sample to him of what we mean by "right"—no standard right-handed object. Can we do it?

## 2-7 Parity is not conserved!

It turns out that the laws of gravitation, the laws of electricity and magnetism, nuclear forces, all satisfy the principle of reflection symmetry, so these laws, or anything derived from them, cannot be used. But associated with the many particles that are found in nature there is a phenomenon called *beta decay*, or *weak decay*. One of the examples of weak decay, in connection with a particle discovered in about 1954, posed a strange puzzle. There was a certain charged particle which disintegrated into three $\pi$-mesons, as shown schematically in Figure 2-5. This particle was called, for a while, a $\tau$-meson. Now in Figure 2-5 we also see another particle which disintegrates into *two* mesons; one must be neutral, from the conservation of charge. This particle was called a $\theta$-meson. So on the one hand we have a particle called a $\tau$, which disintegrates into three $\pi$-mesons, and a $\theta$, which disintegrates into two $\pi$-mesons. Now it was soon discovered that the $\tau$ and the $\theta$ are almost equal in mass; in fact, within the experimental error, they are equal. Next, the length of time it took for them to disintegrate into three $\pi$'s and two $\pi$'s was found to be almost exactly the same; they live the same length of time. Next, whenever they were made, they were made in the same proportions, say, 14 percent $\tau$'s to 86 percent $\theta$'s.

Anyone in his right mind realizes immediately that they must be the same particle, that we merely produce an object which has two different ways of disintegrating—not two different particles. This object that can disintegrate in two different ways has, therefore,

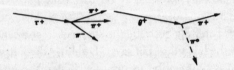

*Figure 2-5.* A schematic diagram of the disintegration of a $\tau^+$ and a
$\theta^+$ particle.

## Symmetry in Physical Laws

the same lifetime and the same production ratio (because this is simply the ratio of the odds with which it disintegrates into these two kinds).

However, it was possible to prove (and we cannot here explain at all *how*), from the principle of reflection symmetry in quantum mechanics, that it was *impossible* to have these both come from the same particle—the same particle *could not* disintegrate in both of these ways. The conservation law corresponding to the principle of reflection symmetry is something which has no classical analog, and so this kind of quantum-mechanical conservation was called the *conservation of parity*. So, it was a result of the conservation of parity or, more precisely, from the symmetry of the quantum-mechanical equations of the weak decays under reflection, that the same particle could not go into both, so it must be some kind of coincidence of masses, lifetimes, and so on. But the more it was studied, the more remarkable the coincidence, and the suspicion gradually grew that possibly the deep law of the reflection symmetry of nature may be false.

As a result of this apparent failure, the physicists Lee and Yang suggested that other experiments be done in related decays to try to test whether the law was correct in other cases. The first such experiment was carried out by Miss Wu from Columbia, and was done as follows. Using a very strong magnet at a very low temperature, it turns out that a certain isotope of cobalt, which disintegrates by emitting an electron, is magnetic, and if the temperature is low enough that the thermal oscillations do not jiggle the atomic magnets about too much, they line up in the magnetic field. So the cobalt atoms will all line up in this strong field. They then disintegrate, emitting an electron, and it was discovered that when the atoms were lined up in a field whose **B** vector points upward, most of the electrons were emitted in a downward direction.

If one is not really "hep" to the world, such a remark does not sound like anything of significance, but if one appreciates the problems and interesting things in the world, then he sees that it is a most dramatic discovery: When we put cobalt atoms in an extremely strong magnetic field, more disintegration electrons go down than up. Therefore if we were to put it in a corresponding experiment in a "mirror," in which the cobalt atoms would be lined up in the opposite direction, they would spit their electrons *up*, not *down*; the action is *unsymmetrical. The magnet has grown hairs!* The south pole of a magnet is of such a kind that the electrons in a $\beta$-disintegration tend to go away from it; that distinguishes, in a physical way, the north pole from the south pole.

After this, a lot of other experiments were done: the disintegration of the $\pi$ into $\mu$ and $\nu$; $\mu$ into an electron and two neutrinos; nowadays, the $\Lambda$ into proton and $\pi$; disintegration of $\Sigma$'s; and many other disintegrations. In fact, in almost all cases where it could be expected, all have been found *not* to obey reflection symmetry! Fundamentally, the law of reflection symmetry, at this level in physics, is incorrect.

In short, we can tell a Martian where to put the heart: we say, "Listen, build yourself a magnet, and put the coils in, and put the current on, and then take some cobalt and lower the temperature. Arrange the experiment so the electrons go from the foot to the head, then the direction in which the current goes through the coils is the direction that goes in on what we call the right and comes out on the left." So it is possible to define right and left, now, by doing an experiment of this kind.

There are a lot of other features that were predicted. For example, it turns out that the spin, the angular momentum, of the cobalt nucleus before disintegration is 5 units of $\hbar$, and after disintegration it is 4 units. The electron carries spin angular momentum, and there is also a neutrino involved. It is easy to see from this that the electron must carry its spin angular momentum aligned along its direction of motion, the neutrino likewise. So it looks as though the electron is spinning to the left, and that was also checked. In fact, it was checked right here at Caltech by Boehm and Wapstra, that the electrons spin mostly to the left.

## Symmetry in Physical Laws

(There were some other experiments that gave the opposite answer, but they were wrong!)

The next problem, of course, was to find the law of the failure of parity conservation. What is the rule that tells us how strong the failure is going to be? The rule is this: it occurs only in these very slow reactions, called weak decays, and when it occurs, the rule is that the particles which carry spin, like the electron, neutrino, and so on, come out with a spin tending to the left. That is a lopsided rule; it connects a polar vector velocity and an axial vector angular momentum, and says that the angular momentum is more likely to be opposite to the velocity than along it.

Now that is the rule, but today we do not really understand the whys and wherefores of it. *Why* is this the right rule, what is the fundamental reason for it, and how is it connected to anything else? At the moment we have been so shocked by the fact that this thing is unsymmetrical that we have not been able to recover enough to understand what it means with regard to all the other rules. However, the subject is interesting, modern, and still unsolved, so it seems appropriate that we discuss some of the questions associated with it.

## 2-8 Antimatter

The first thing to do when one of the symmetries is lost is to immediately go back over the list of known or assumed symmetries and ask whether any of the others are lost. Now we did not mention one operation on our list, which must necessarily be questioned, and that is the relation between matter and antimatter. Dirac predicted that in addition to electrons there must be another particle, called the positron (discovered at Caltech by Anderson), that is necessarily related to the electron. All the properties of these two particles obey certain rules of correspondence: the energies are equal; the masses are equal; the charges are reversed; but, more important than anything, the two of them, when they come together, can annihilate each other and liberate their entire mass in the form of energy, say γ-rays. The positron is called an *antiparticle* to the electron, and these are the characteristics of a particle and its antiparticle. It was clear from Dirac's argument that all the rest of the particles in the world should also have corresponding antiparticles. For instance, for the proton there should be an antiproton, which is now symbolized by a $\bar{p}$. The $\bar{p}$ would have a negative electrical charge and the same mass as a proton, and so on. The most important feature, however, is that a proton and an antiproton coming together can annihilate each other. The reason we emphasize this is that people do not understand it when we say there is a neutron and also an antineutron, because they say, "A neutron is neutral, so how *can* it have the opposite charge?" The rule of the "anti" is not just that it has the opposite charge, it has a certain set of properties, the whole lot of which are opposite. The antineutron is distinguished from the neutron in this way: if we bring two neutrons together, they just stay as two neutrons, but if we bring a neutron and an antineutron together, they annihilate each other with a great explosion of energy being liberated, with various π-mesons, γ-rays, and whatnot.

Now if we have antineutrons, antiprotons, and antielectrons, we can make antiatoms, in principle. They have not been made yet, but it is possible in principle. For instance, a hydrogen atom has a proton in the center with an electron going around outside. Now imagine that somewhere we can make an antiproton with a positron going around, would it go around? Well, first of all, the antiproton is electrically negative and the antielectron is electrically positive, so they attract each other in a corresponding manner—the masses are all the same; everything is the same. It is one of the principles of the symmetry of physics, the equations seem to show, that if a clock, say, were made of matter on one hand, and then we made the same clock of antimatter, it would run in this way. (Of course, if we put the clocks together, they would annihilate each other, but that is different.)

An immediate question then arises. We can build, out of matter,

## Symmetry in Physical Laws

two clocks, one which is "left-hand" and one which is "right-hand." For example, we could build a clock which is not built in a simple way, but has cobalt and magnets and electron detectors which detect the presence of $\beta$-decay electrons and count them. Each time one is counted, the second hand moves over. Then the mirror clock, receiving fewer electrons, will not run at the same rate. So evidently we can make two clocks such that the left-hand clock does not agree with the right-hand one. Let us make, out of matter, a clock which we call the standard or right-hand clock. Now let us make, also out of matter, a clock which we call the left-hand clock. We have just discovered that, in general, these two will *not* run the same way; prior to that famous physical discovery, it was thought that they would. Now it was also supposed that matter and antimatter were equivalent. That is, if we made an antimatter clock, right-hand, the same shape, then it would run the same as the right-hand matter clock, and if we made the same clock to the left it would run the same. In other words, in the beginning it was believed that *all four* of these clocks were the same; now of course we know that the right-hand and left-hand matter are not the same. Presumably, therefore, the right-handed antimatter and the left-handed antimatter are not the same.

So the obvious question is, which goes with which, if either? In other words, does the right-handed matter behave the same way as the right-handed antimatter? Or does the right-handed matter behave the same way as the left-handed antimatter? $\beta$-decay experiments, using positron decay instead of electron decay, indicate that this is the interconnection: matter to the "right" works the same way as antimatter to the "left."

Therefore, at long last, it is really true that right and left symmetry is still maintained! If we made a left-hand clock, but made it out of the other kind of matter, antimatter instead of matter, it would run in the same way. So what has happened is that instead of having two independent rules in our list of symmetries, two of these rules go together to make a new rule, which says that matter to the right is symmetrical with antimatter to the left.

So if our Martian is made of antimatter and we give him instructions to make this "right" handed model like us, it will, of course, come out the other way around. What would happen when, after much conversation back and forth, we each have taught the other to make space ships and we meet halfway in empty space? We have instructed each other on our traditions, and so forth, and the two of us come rushing out to shake hands. Well, if he puts out his left hand, watch out!

## 2-9 Broken symmetries

The next question is, what can we make out of laws which are *nearly* symmetrical? The marvelous thing about it all is that for such a wide range of important, strong phenomena—nuclear forces, electrical phenomena, and even weak ones like gravitation—over a tremendous range of physics, all the laws for these seem to be symmetrical. On the other hand, this little extra piece says, "No, the laws are not symmetrical!" How is it that nature can be almost symmetrical, but not perfectly symmetrical? What shall we make of this? First, do we have any other examples? The answer is, we do, in fact, have a few other examples. For instance, the nuclear part of the force between proton and proton, between neutron and neutron, and between neutron and proton, is all exactly the same—there is a symmetry for nuclear forces, a new one, that we can interchange neutron and proton—but it evidently is not a general symmetry, for the electrical repulsion between two protons at a distance does not exist for neutrons. So it is not generally true that we can *always* replace a proton with a neutron, but only to a good approximation. Why *good*? Because the nuclear forces are much stronger than the electrical forces. So this is an "almost" symmetry also. So we do have examples in other things.

We have, in our minds, a tendency to accept symmetry as some kind of perfection. In fact it is like the old idea of the Greeks that circles were perfect, and it was rather horrible to believe that the planetary orbits were not circles, but only nearly circles. The differ-

## Symmetry in Physical Laws

ence between being a circle and being nearly a circle is not a small difference, it is a fundamental change so far as the mind is concerned. There is a sign of perfection and symmetry in a circle that is not there the moment the circle is slightly off—that is the end of it—it is no longer symmetrical. Then the question is why it is only *nearly* a circle—that is a much more difficult question. The actual motion of the planets, in general, should be ellipses, but during the ages, because of tidal forces, and so on, they have been made almost symmetrical. Now the question is whether we have a similar problem here. The problem from the point of view of the circles is if they were perfect circles there would be nothing to explain, that is clearly simple. But since they are only nearly circles, there is a lot to explain, and the result turned out to be a big dynamical problem, and now our problem is to explain why they are nearly symmetrical by looking at tidal forces and so on.

So our problem is to explain where symmetry comes from. Why is nature so nearly symmetrical? No one has any idea why. The only thing we might suggest is something like this: There is a gate in Japan, a gate in Neiko, which is sometimes called by the Japanese the most beautiful gate in all Japan; it was built in a time when there was great influence from Chinese art. This gate is very elaborate, with lots of gables and beautiful carving and lots of columns and dragon heads and princes carved into the pillars, and so on. But when one looks closely he sees that in the elaborate and complex design along one of the pillars, one of the small design elements is carved upside down; otherwise the thing is completely symmetrical. If one asks why this is, the story is that it was carved upside down so that the gods will not be jealous of the perfection of man. So they purposely put an error in there, so that the gods would not be jealous and get angry with human beings.

We might like to turn the idea around and think that the true explanation of the near symmetry of nature is this: that God made the laws only nearly symmetrical so that we should not be jealous of His perfection!

# Three

# THE SPECIAL THEORY OF RELATIVITY

## 3-1 The principle of relativity

For over 200 years the equations of motion enunciated by Newton were believed to describe nature correctly, and the first time that an error in these laws was discovered, the way to correct it was also discovered. Both the error and its correction were discovered by Einstein in 1905.

Newton's Second Law, which we have expressed by the equation

$$F = d(mv)/dt,$$

was stated with the tacit assumption that $m$ is a constant, but we now know that this is not true, and that the mass of a body increases with velocity. In Einstein's corrected formula $m$ has the value

$$m = \frac{m_0}{\sqrt{1 - v^2/c^2}}, \tag{3.1}$$

where the "rest mass" $m_0$ represents the mass of a body that is not moving and $c$ is the speed of light, which is about $3 \times 10^5$ km $\cdot$ sec$^{-1}$ or about 186,000 mi $\cdot$ sec$^{-1}$.

For those who want to learn just enough about it so they can solve problems, that is all there is to the theory of relativity—it just changes Newton's laws by introducing a correction factor to the mass. From the formula itself it is easy to see that this mass increase is very small in ordinary circumstances. If the velocity is even as great as that of a satellite, which goes around the earth at 5 mi/sec, then $v/c = 5/186,000$: putting this value into the formula shows that the correction to the mass is only one part in two to three billion, which is nearly impossible to observe. Actually, the correctness of the formula has been amply confirmed by the observation of many kinds of particles, moving at speeds ranging up to practically the speed of light. However, because the effect is ordinarily so small, it seems remarkable that it was discovered theoretically before it was discovered experimentally. Empirically, at a sufficiently high velocity, the effect is very large, but it was not discovered that way. Therefore it is interesting to see how a law that involved so delicate a modification (at the time when it was first discovered) was brought to light by a combination of experiments and physical reasoning. Contributions to the discovery were made by a number of people, the final result of whose work was Einstein's discovery.

There are really two Einstein theories of relativity. This chapter is concerned with the Special Theory of Relativity, which dates from 1905. In 1915 Einstein published an additional theory, called the General Theory of Relativity. This latter theory deals with the extension of the Special Theory to the case of the law of gravitation; we shall not discuss the General Theory here.

The principle of relativity was first stated by Newton, in one of his corollaries to the laws of motion: "The motions of bodies included in a given space are the same among themselves, whether that space is at rest or moves uniformly forward in a straight line." This means, for example, that if a space ship is drifting along at a uniform speed, all experiments performed in the space ship and all the phenomena in the space ship will appear the same as if the ship were not moving, provided, of course, that one does not look outside. That is the meaning of the principle of relativity. This is a simple enough idea, and the only question is whether it is *true* that in all experiments performed inside a moving system the laws of physics will appear the same as they would if the system were

## The Special Theory of Relativity

standing still. Let us first investigate whether Newton's laws appear the same in the moving system.

Suppose that Moe is moving in the $x$-direction with a uniform velocity $u$, and he measures the position of a certain point, shown in Figure 3-1. He designates the "$x$-distance" of the point in his coordinate system as $x'$. Joe is at rest, and measures the position of the same point, designating its $x$-coordinate in his system as $x$. The relationship of the coordinates in the two systems is clear from the diagram. After time $t$ Moe's origin has moved a distance $ut$, and if the two systems originally coincided,

$$
\begin{aligned}
x' &= x - ut, \\
y' &= y, \\
z' &= z, \\
t' &= t.
\end{aligned}
\tag{3.2}
$$

If we substitute this transformation of coordinates into Newton's laws we find that these laws transform to the same laws in the primed system; that is, the laws of Newton are of the same form in a moving system as in a stationary system, and therefore it is impossible to tell, by making mechanical experiments, whether the system is moving or not.

The principle of relativity has been used in mechanics for a long time. It was employed by various people, in particular Huygens, to obtain the rules for the collision of billiard balls, in much the same

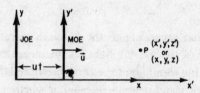

*Figure 3-1.* Two coordinate systems in uniform relative motion along their $x$-axes.

### Six Not-So-Easy Pieces

way as we used it in Chapter 10* to discuss the conservation of momentum. In the past century interest in it was heightened as the result of investigations into the phenomena of electricity, magnetism, and light. A long series of careful studies of these phenomena by many people culminated in Maxwell's equations of the electromagnetic field, which describe electricity, magnetism, and light in one uniform system. However, the Maxwell equations did *not* seem to obey the principle of relativity. That is, if we transform Maxwell's equations by the substitution of equations 3.2, *their form does not remain the same*; therefore, in a moving space ship the electrical and optical phenomena should be different from those in a stationary ship. Thus one could use these optical phenomena to determine the speed of the ship; in particular, one could determine the absolute speed of the ship by making suitable optical or electrical measurements. One of the consequences of Maxwell's equations is that if there is a disturbance in the field such that light is generated, these electromagnetic waves go out in all directions equally and at the same speed $c$, or 186,000 mi/sec. Another consequence of the equations is that if the source of the disturbance is moving, the light emitted goes through space at the same speed $c$. This is analogous to the case of sound, the speed of sound waves being likewise independent of the motion of the source.

This independence of the motion of the source, in the case of light, brings up an interesting problem:

Suppose we are riding in a car that is going at a speed $u$, and light from the rear is going past the car with speed $c$. Differentiating the first equation in (3.2) gives

$$dx'/dt = dx/dt - u,$$

which means that according to the Galilean transformation the apparent speed of the passing light, as we measure it in the car, should not be $c$ but should be $c - u$. For instance, if the car is going

* of the original *Lectures on Physics* vol. I.

### The Special Theory of Relativity

100,000 mi/sec, and the light is going 186,000 mi/sec, then apparently the light going past the car should go 86,000 mi/sec. In any case, by measuring the speed of the light going past the car (if the Galilean transformation is correct for light), one could determine the speed of the car. A number of experiments based on this general idea were performed to determine the velocity of the earth, but they all failed—they gave *no velocity at all*. We shall discuss one of these experiments in detail, to show exactly what was done and what was the matter; something *was* the matter, of course, something was wrong with the equations of physics. What could it be?

## 3-2 The Lorentz transformation

When the failure of the equations of physics in the above case came to light, the first thought that occurred was that the trouble must lie in the new Maxwell equations of electrodynamics, which were only 20 years old at the time. It seemed almost obvious that these equations must be wrong, so the thing to do was to change them in such a way that under the Galilean transformation the principle of relativity would be satisfied. When this was tried, the new terms that had to be put into the equations led to predictions of new electrical phenomena that did not exist at all when tested experimentally, so this attempt had to be abandoned. Then it gradually became apparent that Maxwell's laws of electrodynamics were correct, and the trouble must be sought elsewhere.

In the meantime, H. A. Lorentz noticed a remarkable and curious thing when he made the following substitutions in the Maxwell equations:

$$x' = \frac{x - ut}{\sqrt{1 - u^2/c^2}},$$
$$y' = y,$$
$$z' = z, \qquad (3.3)$$
$$t' = \frac{t - ux/c^2}{\sqrt{1 - u^2/c^2}},$$

namely, Maxwell's equations remain in the same form when this transformation is applied to them! Equations (3.3) are known as a *Lorentz transformation*. Einstein, following a suggestion originally made by Poincaré, then proposed that *all the physical laws* should be of such a kind that they *remain unchanged under a Lorentz transformation*. In other words, we should change, not the laws of electrodynamics, but the laws of mechanics. How shall we change Newton's laws so that *they* will remain unchanged by the Lorentz transformation? If this goal is set, we then have to rewrite Newton's equations in such a way that the conditions we have imposed are satisfied. As it turned out, the only requirement is that the mass $m$ in Newton's equations must be replaced by the form shown in Eq. (3.1). When this change is made, Newton's laws and the laws of electrodynamics will harmonize. Then if we use the Lorentz transformation in comparing Moe's measurements with Joe's, we shall never be able to detect whether either is moving, because the form of all the equations will be the same in both coordinate systems!

It is interesting to discuss what it means that we replace the old transformation between the coordinates and time with a new one, because the old one (Galilean) seems to be self-evident, and the new one (Lorentz) looks peculiar. We wish to know whether it is logically and experimentally possible that the new, and not the old, transformation can be correct. To find that out, it is not enough to study the laws of mechanics but, as Einstein did, we too must analyze our ideas of *space* and *time* in order to understand this transformation. We shall have to discuss these ideas and their implications for mechanics at some length, so we say in advance that the effort will be justified, since the results agree with experiment.

## 3-3 The Michelson-Morley experiment

As mentioned above, attempts were made to determine the absolute velocity of the earth through the hypothetical "ether" that was supposed to pervade all space. The most famous of these experiments is

## The Special Theory of Relativity

one performed by Michelson and Morley in 1887. It was 18 years later before the negative results of the experiment were finally explained, by Einstein.

The Michelson-Morley experiment was performed with an apparatus like that shown schematically in Figure 3-2. This apparatus is essentially comprised of a light source $A$, a partially silvered glass plate $B$, and two mirrors $C$ and $E$, all mounted on a rigid base. The mirrors are placed at equal distances $L$ from $B$. The plate $B$ splits an oncoming beam of light, and the two resulting beams continue in mutually perpendicular directions to the mirrors, where they are reflected back to $B$. On arriving back at $B$, the two beams are recombined as two superposed beams, $D$ and $F$. If the time taken for the light to go from $B$ to $E$ and back is the same as the time from $B$ to $C$ and back, the emerging beams $D$ and $F$ will be in phase and will reinforce each other, but if the two times differ slightly, the beams will be slightly out of phase and interference will result. If the apparatus is "at rest" in the ether, the times should be precisely equal, but if it is moving toward the right with a velocity $u$, there should be a difference in the times. Let us see why.

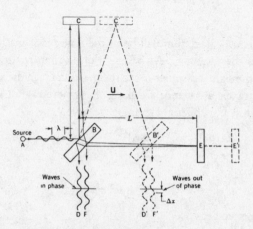

*Figure 3-2.* Schematic diagram of the Michelson-Morley experiment.

### SIX NOT-SO-EASY PIECES

First, let us calculate the time required for the light to go from $B$ to $E$ and back. Let us say that the time for light to go from plate $B$ to mirror $E$ is $t_1$, and the time for the return is $t_2$. Now, while the light is on its way from $B$ to the mirror, the apparatus moves a distance $ut_1$, so the light must traverse a distance $L + ut_1$, at the speed $c$. We can also express this distance as $ct_1$, so we have

$$ct_1 = L + ut_1, \quad \text{or} \quad t_1 = L/(c - u).$$

(This result is also obvious from the point of view that the velocity of light relative to the apparatus is $c - u$, so the time is the length $L$ divided by $c - u$.) In a like manner, the time $t_2$ can be calculated. During this time the plate $B$ advances a distance $ut_2$, so the return distance of the light is $L - ut_2$. Then we have

$$ct_2 = L - ut_2, \quad \text{or} \quad t_2 = L/(c + u).$$

Then the total time is

$$t_1 + t_2 = 2Lc/(c^2 - u^2).$$

For convenience in later comparison of times we write this as

$$t_1 + t_2 = \frac{2L/c}{1 - u^2/c^2}. \tag{3.4}$$

Our second calculation will be of the time $t_3$ for the light to go from $B$ to the mirror $C$. As before, during time $t_3$ the mirror $C$ moves to the right a distance $ut_3$ to the position $C'$; in the same time, the light travels a distance $ct_3$ along the hypotenuse of a triangle, which is $BC'$. For this right triangle we have

$$(ct_3)^2 = L^2 + (ut_3)^2$$

or

$$L^2 = c^2 t_3^2 - u^2 t_3^2 = (c^2 - u^2)t_3^2,$$

from which we get

$$t_3 = L/\sqrt{c^2 - u^2}.$$

## The Special Theory of Relativity

For the return trip from $C'$ the distance is the same, as can be seen from the symmetry of the figure; therefore the return time is also the same, and the total time is $2t_3$. With a little rearrangement of the form we can write

$$2t_3 = \frac{2L}{\sqrt{c^2 - u^2}} = \frac{2L/c}{\sqrt{1 - u^2/c^2}}. \tag{3.5}$$

We are now able to compare the times taken by the two beams of light. In expressions (3.4) and (3.5) the numerators are identical, and represent the time that would be taken if the apparatus were at rest. In the denominators, the term $u^2/c^2$ will be small, unless $u$ is comparable in size to $c$. The denominators represent the modifications in the times caused by the motion of the apparatus. And behold, these modifications are *not the same*—the time to go to $C$ and back is a little less than the time to $E$ and back, even though the mirrors are equidistant from $B$, and all we have to do is to measure that difference with precision.

Here a minor technical point arises—suppose the two lengths $L$ are not exactly equal? In fact, we surely cannot make them exactly equal. In that case we simply turn the apparatus 90 degrees, so that $BC$ is in the line of motion and $BE$ is perpendicular to the motion. Any small difference in length then becomes unimportant, and what we look for is a *shift* in the interference fringes when we rotate the apparatus.

In carrying out the experiment, Michelson and Morley oriented the apparatus so that the line $BE$ was nearly parallel to the earth's motion in its orbit (at certain times of the day and night). This orbital speed is about 18 miles per second, and any "ether drift" should be at least that much at some time of the day or night and at some time during the year. The apparatus was amply sensitive to observe such an effect, but no time difference was found—the velocity of the earth through the ether could not be detected. The result of the experiment was null.

The result of the Michelson-Morley experiment was very

puzzling and most disturbing. The first fruitful idea for finding a way out of the impasse came from Lorentz. He suggested that material bodies contract when they are moving, and that this foreshortening is only in the direction of the motion, and also, that if the length is $L_0$ when a body is at rest, then when it moves with speed $u$ parallel to its length, the new length, which we call $L_\parallel$ ($L$-parallel), is given by

$$L_\parallel = L_0\sqrt{1 - u^2/c^2}. \tag{3.6}$$

When this modification is applied to the Michelson-Morley interferometer apparatus the distance from $B$ to $C$ does not change, but the distance from $B$ to $E$ is shortened to $L\sqrt{1 - u^2/c^2}$. Therefore Eq. (3.5) is not changed, but the $L$ of Eq. (3.4) must be changed in accordance with Eq. (3.6). When this is done we obtain

$$t_1 + t_2 = \frac{(2L/c)\sqrt{1 - u^2/c^2}}{1 - u^2/c^2} = \frac{2L/c}{\sqrt{1 - u^2/c^2}}. \tag{3.7}$$

Comparing this result with Eq. (3.5), we see that $t_1 + t_2 = 2t_3$. So if the apparatus shrinks in the manner just described, we have a way of understanding why the Michelson-Morley experiment gives no effect at all. Although the contraction hypothesis successfully accounted for the negative result of the experiment, it was open to the objection that it was invented for the express purpose of explaining away the difficulty, and was too artificial. However, in many other experiments to discover an ether wind, similar difficulties arose, until it appeared that nature was in a "conspiracy" to thwart man by introducing some new phenomenon to undo every phenomenon that he thought would permit a measurement of $u$.

It was ultimately recognized, as Poincaré pointed out, that *a complete conspiracy is itself a law of nature!* Poincaré then proposed that there *is* such a law of nature, that it is not possible to discover an ether wind by *any* experiment; that is, there is no way to determine an absolute velocity.

## The Special Theory of Relativity

### 3-4 Transformation of time

In checking out whether the contraction idea is in harmony with the facts in other experiments, it turns out that everything is correct provided that the *times* are also modified, in the manner expressed in the fourth equation of the set (3.3). That is because the time $t_3$, calculated for the trip from $B$ to $C$ and back, is not the same when calculated by a man performing the experiment in a moving space ship as when calculated by a stationary observer who is watching the space ship. To the man in the ship the time is simply $2L/c$, but to the other observer it is $(2L/c)/\sqrt{1 - u^2/c^2}$ (Eq. 3.5). In other words, when the outsider sees the man in the space ship lighting a cigar, all the actions appear to be slower than normal, while to the man inside, everything moves at a normal rate. So not only must the lengths shorten, but also the time-measuring instruments ("clocks") must apparently slow down. That is, when the clock in the space ship records 1 second elapsed, as seen by the man in the ship, it shows $1/\sqrt{1 - u^2/c^2}$ second to the man outside.

This slowing of the clocks in a moving system is a very peculiar phenomenon, and is worth an explanation. In order to understand this, we have to watch the machinery of the clock and see what happens when it is moving. Since that is rather difficult, we shall take a very simple kind of clock. The one we choose is rather a silly kind of clock, but it will work in principle: it is a rod (meter stick) with a mirror at each end, and when we start a light signal between the mirrors, the light keeps going up and down, making a click every time it comes down, like a standard ticking clock. We build two such clocks, with exactly the same lengths, and synchronize them by starting them together; then they agree always thereafter, because they are the same in length, and light always travels with speed $c$. We give one of these clocks to the man to take along in his space ship, and he mounts the rod perpendicular to the direction of motion of the ship; then the length of the rod will not change. How do we know that perpendicular lengths do not change? The men

## SIX NOT-SO-EASY PIECES

can agree to make marks on each other's $y$-meter stick as they pass each other. By symmetry, the two marks must come at the same $y$- and $y'$-coordinates, since otherwise, when they get together to compare results, one mark will be above or below the other, and so we could tell who was really moving.

Now let us see what happens to the moving clock. Before the man took it aboard, he agreed that it was a nice, standard clock, and when he goes along in the space ship he will not see anything peculiar. If he did, he would know he was moving—if anything at all changed because of the motion, he could tell he was moving. But the principle of relativity says this is impossible in a uniformly moving system, so nothing has changed. On the other hand, when the external observer looks at the clock going by, he sees that the light, in going from mirror to mirror, is "really" taking a zigzag path, since the rod is moving sideways all the while. We have already analyzed such a zigzag motion in connection with the Michelson-Morley experiment. If in a given time the rod moves forward a distance proportional to $u$ in Figure 3-3, the distance the light

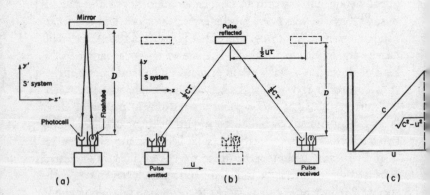

*Figure 3-3.* (a) A "light clock" at rest in the $S'$ system. (b) The same clock, moving through the $S$ system. (c) Illustration of the diagonal path taken by the light beam in a moving "light clock."

## The Special Theory of Relativity

travels in the same time is proportional to $c$, and the vertical distance is therefore proportional to $\sqrt{c^2 - u^2}$.

That is, it takes a *longer time* for light to go from end to end in the moving clock than in the stationary clock. Therefore the apparent time between clicks is longer for the moving clock, in the same proportion as shown in the hypotenuse of the triangle (that is the source of the square root expressions in our equations). From the figure it is also apparent that the greater $u$ is, the more slowly the moving clock appears to run. Not only does this particular kind of clock run more slowly, but if the theory of relativity is correct, any other clock, operating on any principle whatsoever, would also appear to run slower, and in the same proportion—we can say this without further analysis. Why is this so?

To answer the above question, suppose we had two other clocks made exactly alike with wheels and gears, or perhaps based on radioactive decay, or something else. Then we adjust these clocks so they both run in precise synchronism with our first clocks. When light goes up and back in the first clocks and announces its arrival with a click, the new models also complete some sort of cycle, which they simultaneously announce by some doubly coincident flash, or bong, or other signal. One of these clocks is taken into the space ship, along with the first kind. Perhaps *this* clock will not run slower, but will continue to keep the same time as its stationary counterpart, and thus disagree with the other moving clock. Ah no, if that should happen, the man in the ship could use this mismatch between his two clocks to determine the speed of his ship, which we have been supposing is impossible. *We need not know anything about the machinery* of the new clock that might cause the effect— we simply know that whatever the reason, it will appear to run slow, just like the first one.

Now if *all* moving clocks run slower, if no way of measuring time gives anything but a slower rate, we shall just have to say, in a certain sense, that *time itself* appears to be slower in a space ship. All the phenomena there—the man's pulse rate, his thought processes, the time he takes to light a cigar, how long it takes to grow up and get old—all these things must be slowed down in the same proportion, because he cannot tell he is moving. The biologists and medical men sometimes say it is not quite certain that the time it takes for a cancer to develop will be longer in a space ship, but from the viewpoint of a modern physicist it is nearly certain; otherwise one could use the rate of cancer development to determine the speed of the ship!

A very interesting example of the slowing of time with motion is furnished by mu-mesons (muons), which are particles that disintegrate spontaneously after an average lifetime of $2.2 \times 10^{-6}$ sec. They come to the earth in cosmic rays, and can also be produced artificially in the laboratory. Some of them disintegrate in midair, but the remainder disintegrate only after they encounter a piece of material and stop. It is clear that in its short lifetime a muon cannot travel, even at the speed of light, much more than 600 meters. But although the muons are created at the top of the atmosphere, some 10 kilometers up, yet they are actually found in a laboratory down here, in cosmic rays. How can that be? The answer is that different muons move at various speeds, some of which are very close to the speed of light. While from their own point of view they live only about 2 $\mu$sec, from our point of view they live considerably longer—enough longer that they may reach the earth. The factor by which the time is increased has already been given as $1/\sqrt{1 - u^2/c^2}$. The average life has been measured quite accurately for muons of different velocities, and the values agree closely with the formula.

We do not know why the meson disintegrates or what its machinery is, but we do know its behavior satisfies the principle of relativity. That is the utility of the principle of relativity—it permits us to make predictions, even about things that otherwise we do not know much about. For example, before we have any idea at all about what makes the meson disintegrate, we can still predict that when it is moving at nine-tenths of the speed of light, the apparent length of time that it lasts is $(2.2 \times 10^{-6})/\sqrt{1 - 9^2/10^2}$ sec; and our prediction works—that is the good thing about it.

*The Special Theory of Relativity*

## 3-5 The Lorentz contraction

Now let us return to the Lorentz transformation (3.3) and try to get a better understanding of the relationship between the $(x, y, z, t)$ and the $(x', y', z', t')$ coordinate systems, which we shall call the $S$ and $S'$ systems, or Joe and Moe systems, respectively. We have already noted that the first equation is based on the Lorentz suggestion of contraction along the $x$-direction; how can we prove that a contraction takes place? In the Michelson-Morley experiment, we now appreciate that the *transverse* arm $BC$ cannot change length, by the principle of relativity; yet the null result of the experiment demands that the *times* must be equal. So, in order for the experiment to give a null result, the longitudinal arm $BE$ must appear shorter, by the square root $\sqrt{1 - u^2/c^2}$. What does this contraction mean, in terms of measurements made by Joe and Moe? Suppose that Moe, moving with the $S'$ system in the $x$-direction, is measuring the $x'$-coordinate of some point with a meter stick. He lays the stick down $x'$ times, so he thinks the distance is $x'$ meters. From the viewpoint of Joe in the $S$ system, however, Moe is using a foreshortened ruler, so the "real" distance measured is $x'\sqrt{1 - u^2/c^2}$ meters. Then if the $S'$ system has travelled a distance $ut$ away from the $S$ system, the $S$ observer would say that the same point, measured in his coordinates, is at a distance $x = x'\sqrt{1 - u^2/c^2} + ut$, or

$$x' = \frac{x - ut}{\sqrt{1 - u^2/c^2}},$$

which is the first equation of the Lorentz transformation.

## 3-6 Simultaneity

In an analogous way, because of the difference in time scales, the denominator expression is introduced into the fourth equation of the Lorentz transformation. The most interesting term in that equation is the $ux/c^2$ in the numerator, because that is quite new and unexpected. Now what does that mean? If we look at the situation

SIX NOT-SO-EASY PIECES

carefully we see that events that occur at two separated places at the same time, as seen by Moe in $S'$, do *not* happen at the same time as viewed by Joe in $S$. If one event occurs at point $x_1$ at time $t_0$ and the other event at $x_2$ and $t_0$ (the same time), we find that the two corresponding times $t'_1$ and $t'_2$ differ by an amount

$$t'_2 = t'_1 = \frac{u(x_1 - x_2)/c^2}{\sqrt{1 - u^2/c^2}}.$$

This circumstance is called "failure of simultaneity at a distance," and to make the idea a little clearer let us consider the following experiment.

Suppose that a man moving in a space ship (system $S'$) has placed a clock at each end of the ship and is interested in making sure that the two clocks are in synchronism. How can the clocks be synchronized? There are many ways. One way, involving very little calculation, would be first to locate exactly the midpoint between the clocks. Then from this station we send out a light signal which will go both ways at the same speed and will arrive at both clocks, clearly, at the same time. This simultaneous arrival of the signals can be used to synchronize the clocks. Let us then suppose that the man in $S'$ synchronizes his clocks by this particular method. Let us see whether an observer in system $S$ would agree that the two clocks are synchronous. The man in $S'$ has a right to believe they are, because he does not know that he is moving. But the man in $S$ reasons that since the ship is moving forward, the clock in the front end was running away from the light signal, hence the light had to go more than halfway in order to catch up; the rear clock, however, was advancing to meet the light signal, so this distance was shorter. Therefore the signal reached the rear clock first, although the man in $S'$ thought that the signals arrived simultaneously. We thus see that when a man in a space ship thinks the times at two locations are simultaneous, equal values of $t'$ in his coordinate system must correspond to *different* values of $t$ in the other coordinate system!

## The Special Theory of Relativity

### 3-7 Four-vectors

Let us see what else we can discover in the Lorentz transformation. It is interesting to note that the transformation between the $x$'s and $t$'s is analogous in form to the transformation of the $x$'s and $y$'s that we studied in Chapter 1 for a rotation of coordinates. We then had

$$x' = x \cos \theta + y \sin \theta,$$
$$y' = y \cos \theta - x \sin \theta, \tag{3.8}$$

in which the new $x'$ mixes the old $x$ and $y$, and the new $y'$ also mixes the old $x$ and $y$; similarly, in the Lorentz transformation we find a new $x'$ which is a mixture of $x$ and $t$, and a new $t'$ which is a mixture of $t$ and $x$. So the Lorentz transformation is analogous to a rotation, only it is a "rotation" in *space and time*, which appears to be a strange concept. A check of the analogy to rotation can be made by calculating the quantity

$$x'^2 + y'^2 + z'^2 - c^2 t'^2 = x^2 + y^2 + z^2 - c^2 t^2. \tag{3.9}$$

In this equation the first three terms on each side represent, in three-dimensional geometry, the square of the distance between a point and the origin (surface of a sphere) which remains unchanged (invariant) regardless of rotation of the coordinate axes. Similarly, Eq. (3.9) shows that there is a certain combination which includes time, that is invariant to a Lorentz transformation. Thus, the analogy to a rotation is complete, and is of such a kind that vectors, i.e., quantities involving "components" which transform the same way as the coordinates and time, are also useful in connection with relativity.

Thus we contemplate an extension of the idea of vectors, which we have so far considered to have only space components, to include a time component. That is, we expect that there will be vectors with four components, three of which are like the components of an ordinary vector, and with these will be associated a fourth component, which is the analog of the time part.

This concept will be analyzed further in the next chapters, where we shall find that if the ideas of the preceding paragraph are applied to momentum, the transformation gives three space parts that are like ordinary momentum components, and a fourth component, the time part, which is the *energy*.

## 3-8 Relativistic dynamics

We are now ready to investigate, more generally, what form the laws of mechanics take under the Lorentz transformation. [We have thus far explained how length and time change, but not how we get the modified formula for $m$ (Eq. 3.1). We shall do this in the next chapter.] To see the consequences of Einstein's modification of $m$ for Newtonian mechanics, we start with the Newtonian law that force is the rate of change of momentum, or

$$\mathbf{F} = d(m\mathbf{v})/dt.$$

Momentum is still given by $mv$, but when we use the new $m$ this becomes

$$\mathbf{p} = m\mathbf{v} = \frac{m_0\mathbf{v}}{\sqrt{1 - v^2/c^2}}. \tag{3.10}$$

This is Einstein's modification of Newton's laws. Under this modification, if action and reaction are still equal (which they may not be in detail, but are in the long run), there will be conservation of momentum in the same way as before, but the quantity that is being conserved is not the old $mv$ with its constant mass, but instead is the quantity shown in (3.10), which has the modified mass. When this change is made in the formula for momentum, conservation of momentum still works.

Now let us see how momentum varies with speed. In Newtonian mechanics it is proportional to the speed and, according to (3.10),

## The Special Theory of Relativity

over a considerable range of speed, but small compared with $c$, it is nearly the same in relativistic mechanics, because the square-root expression differs only slightly from 1. But when $v$ is almost equal to $c$, the square-root expression approaches zero, and the momentum therefore goes toward infinity.

What happens if a constant force acts on a body for a long time? In Newtonian mechanics the body keeps picking up speed until it goes faster than light. But this is impossible in relativistic mechanics. In relativity, the body keeps picking up, not speed, but momentum, which can continually increase because the mass is increasing. After a while there is practically no acceleration in the sense of a change of velocity, but the momentum continues to increase. Of course, whenever a force produces very little change in the velocity of a body, we say that the body has a great deal of inertia, and that is exactly what our formula for relativistic mass says (see Eq. 3.10)—it says that the inertia is very great when $v$ is nearly as great as $c$. As an example of this effect, to deflect the high-speed electrons in the synchrotron that is used here at Caltech, we need a magnetic field that is 2000 times stronger than would be expected on the basis of Newton's laws. In other words, the mass of the electrons in the synchrotron is 2000 times as great as their normal mass, and is as great as that of a proton! That $m$ should be 2000 times $m_0$ means that $1 - v^2/c^2$ must be 1/4,000,000, and that means that $v^2/c^2$ differs from 1 by one part in 4,000,000, or that $v$ differs from $c$ by one part in 8,000,000, so the electrons are getting pretty close to the speed of light. If the electrons and light were both to start from the synchrotron (estimated as 700 feet away) and rush out to Bridge Lab, which would arrive first? The light, of course, because light always travels faster.\* How much earlier? That is too hard to tell—instead, we tell by what distance the light is ahead: it is about 1/1000 of an inch, or ¼ the thickness of a piece of paper!

---

\* The electrons would actually win the race versus *visible* light because of the index of refraction of air. A gamma ray would make out better.

When the electrons are going that fast their masses are enormous, but their speed cannot exceed the speed of light.

Now let us look at some further consequences of relativistic change of mass. Consider the motion of the molecules in a small tank of gas. When the gas is heated, the speed of the molecules is increased, and therefore the mass is also increased and the gas is heavier. An approximate formula to express the increase of mass, for the case when the velocity is small, can be found by expanding $m_0/\sqrt{1 - v^2/c^2} = m_0(1 - v^2/c^2)^{-1/2}$ in a power series, using the binomial theorem. We get

$$m_0(1 - v^2/c^2)^{-1/2} = m_0(1 + \tfrac{1}{2}v^2/c^2 + \tfrac{3}{8}v^4/c^4 + \cdots).$$

We see clearly from the formula that the series converges rapidly when $v$ is small, and the terms after the first two or three are negligible. So we can write

$$m \cong m_0 + \tfrac{1}{2}m_0 v^2 \left(\frac{1}{c^2}\right) \tag{3.11}$$

in which the second term on the right expresses the increase of mass due to molecular velocity. When the temperature increases the $v^2$ increases proportionately, so we can say that the increase in mass is proportional to the increase in temperature. But since $\tfrac{1}{2} m_0 v^2$ is the kinetic energy in the old-fashioned Newtonian sense, we can also say that the increase in mass of all this body of gas is equal to the increase in kinetic energy divided by $c^2$, or $\Delta m = \Delta(\text{K.E.})/c^2$.

## 3-9 Equivalence of mass and energy

The above observation led Einstein to the suggestion that the mass of a body can be expressed more simply than by the formula (3.1), if we say that the mass is equal to the total energy content divided by $c^2$. If Eq. (3.11) is multiplied by $c^2$ the result is

$$mc^2 = m_0 c^2 + \tfrac{1}{2}m_0 v^2 + \cdots. \tag{3.12}$$

Here, the term on the left expresses the total energy of a body, and we recognize the last term as the ordinary kinetic energy. Einstein

## The Special Theory of Relativity

interpreted the large constant term, $m_0 c^2$, to be part of the total energy of the body, an intrinsic energy known as the "rest energy."

Let us follow out the consequences of assuming, with Einstein, that *the energy of a body always equals* $mc^2$. As an interesting result, we shall find the formula (3.1) for the variation of mass with speed, which we have merely assumed up to now. We start with the body at rest, when its energy is $m_0 c^2$. Then we apply a force to the body, which starts it moving and gives it kinetic energy; therefore, since the energy has increased, the mass has increased—this is implicit in the original assumption. So long as the force continues, the energy and the mass both continue to increase. We have already seen (Chapter 13*) that the rate of change of energy with time equals the force times the velocity, or

$$\frac{dE}{dt} = \mathbf{F} \cdot \mathbf{v}. \tag{3.13}$$

We also have (Chapter 9*, Eq. 9.1) that $F = d(mv)/dt$. When these relations are put together with the definition of $E$, Eq. (3.13) becomes

$$\frac{d(mc^2)}{dt} = \mathbf{v} \cdot \frac{d(m\mathbf{v})}{dt}. \tag{3.14}$$

We wish to solve this equation for $m$. To do this we first use the mathematical trick of multiplying both sides by $2m$, which changes the equation to

$$c^2 (2m) \frac{dm}{dt} = 2mv \frac{d(mv)}{dt}. \tag{3.15}$$

We need to get rid of the derivatives, which can be accomplished by integrating both sides. The quantity $(2m)\, dm/dt$ can be recognized

---

* of the original *Lectures on Physics*, vol. I.

## SIX NOT-SO-EASY PIECES

as the time derivative of $m^2$, and $(2m\mathbf{v}) \cdot d(m\mathbf{v})/dt$ is the time derivative of $(mv)^2$. So, Eq. (3.15) is the same as

$$c^2 \frac{d(m^2)}{dt} = \frac{d(m^2 v^2)}{dt}. \tag{3.16}$$

If the derivatives of two quantities are equal, the quantities themselves differ at most by a constant, say $C$. This permits us to write

$$m^2 c^2 = m^2 v^2 + C. \tag{3.17}$$

We need to define the constant $C$ more explicitly. Since Eq. (3.17) must be true for all velocities, we can choose a special case where $v = 0$, and say that in this case the mass is $m_0$. Substituting these values into Eq. (3.17) gives

$$m_0^2 c^2 = 0 + C.$$

We can now use this value of $C$ in Eq. (3.17), which becomes

$$m^2 c^2 = m^2 v^2 + m_0^2 c^2. \tag{3.18}$$

Dividing by $c^2$ and rearranging terms gives

$$m^2 (1 - v^2/c^2) = m_0^2,$$

from which we get

$$m = m_0 / \sqrt{1 - v^2/c^2}. \tag{3.19}$$

This is the formula (3.1), and is exactly what is necessary for the agreement between mass and energy in Eq. (3.12).

Ordinarily these energy changes represent extremely slight changes in mass, because most of the time we cannot generate much energy from a given amount of material; but in an atomic bomb of explosive energy equivalent to 20 kilotons of TNT, for example, it can be shown that the dirt after the explosion is lighter by 1 gram than the initial mass of the reacting material, because of the energy that was released, i.e., the released energy had a mass of 1 gram, according to the relationship $\Delta E = \Delta(mc^2)$. This theory of equivalence of mass and energy has been beautifully verified by experiments in which matter is annihilated—converted totally to energy: An electron and a positron come together at rest, each with a rest mass $m_0$. When they come together they disintegrate and two gamma rays emerge, each with the measured energy of $m_0c^2$. This experiment furnishes a direct determination of the energy associated with the existence of the rest mass of a particle.

# Four

# RELATIVISTIC ENERGY AND MOMENTUM

## 4-1 Relativity and the philosophers

◢ In this chapter we shall continue to discuss the principle of relativity of Einstein and Poincaré, as it affects our ideas of physics and other branches of human thought.

Poincaré made the following statement of the principle of relativity: "According to the principle of relativity, the laws of physical phenomena must be the same for a fixed observer as for an observer who has a uniform motion of translation relative to him, so that we have not, nor can we possibly have, any means of discerning whether or not we are carried along in such a motion."

When this idea descended upon the world, it caused a great stir among philosophers, particularly the "cocktail-party philosophers," who say, "Oh, it is very simple: Einstein's theory says all is relative!" In fact, a surprisingly large number of philosophers, not only those found at cocktail parties (but rather than embarrass them, we shall just call them "cocktail-party philosophers"), will say, "That all is relative is a consequence of Einstein, and it has profound influences on our ideas." In addition, they say "It has been demonstrated in physics that phenomena depend upon your frame of reference." We hear that a great deal, but it is difficult to find out what it means. Probably the frames of reference that were originally referred to were the coordinate systems which we use in the analysis of the theory of relativity. So the fact that "things depend upon your frame of reference" is supposed to have had a profound effect on modern thought. One might well wonder why, because, after all, that things depend upon one's point of view is so simple an idea that it certainly cannot have been necessary to go to all the trouble of the physical relativity theory in order to discover it. That what one sees depends upon his frame of reference is certainly known to anybody who walks around, because he sees an approaching pedestrian first from the front and then from the back; there is nothing deeper in most of the philosophy which is said to have come from the theory of relativity than the remark that "A person looks different from the front than from the back." The old story about the elephant that several blind men describe in different ways is another example, perhaps, of the theory of relativity from the philosopher's point of view.

But certainly there must be deeper things in the theory of relativity than just this simple remark that "A person looks different from the front than from the back." Of course relativity is deeper than this, because *we can make definite predictions with it*. It certainly would be rather remarkable if we could predict the behavior of nature from such a simple observation alone.

There is another school of philosophers who feel very uncomfortable about the theory of relativity, which asserts that we cannot determine our absolute velocity without looking at something outside, and who would say, "It is obvious that one cannot measure his velocity without looking outside. It is self-evident that it is *meaningless* to talk about the velocity of a thing without looking outside; the physicists are rather stupid for having thought otherwise, but it has just dawned on them that this is the case. If only we philosophers had realized what the problems were that the physicists had, we could have decided immediately by brainwork that it is impossible to tell how fast one is moving without looking outside, and we could have made an enormous contribution to physics." These philosophers are always with us, struggling in the periphery to try to tell us something, but they never really understand the subtleties and depths of the problem.

Our inability to detect absolute motion is a result of *experiment* and not a result of plain thought, as we can easily illustrate. In the first place, Newton believed that it was true that one could not tell how fast he is going if he is moving with uniform velocity in a straight line. In fact, Newton first stated the principle of relativity, and one quotation made in the last chapter was a statement of Newton's. Why then did the philosophers not make all this fuss about "all is relative," or whatever, in Newton's time? Because it was not until Maxwell's theory of electrodynamics was developed that there were physical laws that suggested that one *could* measure his velocity without looking outside; soon it was found *experimentally* that one could *not*.

Now, *is* it absolutely, definitely, philosophically *necessary* that one should not be able to tell how fast he is moving without looking outside? One of the consequences of relativity was the development of a philosophy which said, "You can only define what you can measure! Since it is self-evident that one cannot measure a velocity without seeing what he is measuring it relative to, therefore it is clear that there is no *meaning* to absolute velocity. The physicists should have realized that they can talk only about what they can measure." But *that is the whole problem:* whether or not one *can define* absolute velocity is the same as the problem of whether or not one *can detect in an experiment*, without looking outside, whether he is moving. In other words, whether or not a thing is measurable is not something to be decided *a priori* by thought alone, but something that can be decided only by experiment. Given the fact that the velocity of light is 186,000 mi/sec, one will find few philosophers who will calmly state that it is self-evident that if light goes 186,000 mi/sec inside a car, and the car is going 100,000 mi/sec, that the light also goes 186,000 mi/sec past an observer on the ground. That is a shocking fact to them; the very ones who claim it is obvious find, when you give them a specific fact, that it is not obvious.

Finally, there is even a philosophy which says that one cannot detect *any* motion except by looking outside. It is simply not true in physics. True, one cannot perceive a *uniform* motion in a *straight line*, but if the whole room were *rotating* we would certainly know it, for everybody would be thrown to the wall—there would be all kinds of "centrifugal" effects. That the earth is turning on its axis can be determined without looking at the stars, by means of the so-called Foucault pendulum, for example. Therefore it is not true that "all is relative"; it is only *uniform velocity* that cannot be detected without looking outside. Uniform *rotation* about a fixed axis *can* be. When this is told to a philosopher, he is very upset that he did not really understand it, because to him it seems impossible that one should be able to determine rotation about an axis without looking outside. If the philosopher is good enough, after some time he may come back and say, "I understand. We really do not have such a thing as absolute rotation; we are really rotating *relative to the stars*, you see. And so some influence exerted by the stars on the object must cause the centrifugal force."

Now, for all we know, that is true; we have no way, at the present time, of telling whether there would have been centrifugal force if there were no stars and nebulae around. We have not been able to do the experiment of removing all the nebulae and then measuring our rotation, so we simply do not know. We must admit that the philosopher may be right. He comes back, therefore, in delight and says, "It is absolutely necessary that the world ultimately turn out to be this way: *absolute* rotation means nothing; it is only *relative* to the nebulae." Then we say to him, "*Now*, my friend, is it or is it not obvious that uniform velocity in a straight line, *relative to the nebulae*, should produce no effects inside a car?" Now that the motion is no longer absolute, but is a motion *relative to the nebulae*, it becomes a mysterious question, and a question that can be answered only by experiment.

What, then, *are* the philosophic influences of the theory of relativity? If we limit ourselves to influences in the sense of *what kind of new ideas and suggestions* are made to the physicist by the principle of relativity, we could describe some of them as follows. The first

## Relativistic Energy and Momentum

discovery is, essentially, that even those ideas which have been held for a very long time and which have been very accurately verified might be wrong. It was a shocking discovery, of course, that Newton's laws are wrong, after all the years in which they seemed to be accurate. Of course it is clear, not that the experiments were wrong, but that they were done over only a limited range of velocities, so small that the relativistic effects would not have been evident. But nevertheless, we now have a much more humble point of view of our physical laws—everything *can* be wrong!

Secondly, if we have a set of "strange" ideas, such as that time goes slower when one moves, and so forth, whether we *like* them or do *not* like them is an irrelevant question. The only relevant question is whether the ideas are consistent with what is found experimentally. In other words, the "strange ideas" need only agree with *experiment*, and the only reason that we have to discuss the behavior of clocks and so forth is to demonstrate that although the notion of the time dilation is strange, it is *consistent* with the way we measure time.

Finally, there is a third suggestion which is a little more technical but which has turned out to be of enormous utility in our study of other physical laws, and that is to *look at the symmetry of the laws* or, more specifically, to look for the ways in which the laws can be transformed and leave their form the same. When we discussed the theory of vectors, we noted that the fundamental laws of motion are not changed when we rotate the coordinate system, and now we learn that they are not changed when we change the space and time variables in a particular way, given by the Lorentz transformation. So this idea of studying the patterns or operations under which the fundamental laws are not changed has proved to be a very useful one.

## 4-2 The twin paradox

To continue our discussion of the Lorentz transformation and relativistic effects, we consider a famous so-called "paradox" of Peter and Paul, who are supposed to be twins, born at the same time. When they are old enough to drive a space ship, Paul flies away at very high speed. Because Peter, who is left on the ground, sees Paul going so fast, all of Paul's clocks appear to go slower, his heart beats go slower, his thoughts go slower, everything goes slower, from Peter's point of view. Of course, Paul notices nothing unusual, but if he travels around and about for a while and then comes back, he will be younger than Peter, the man on the ground! That is actually right; it is one of the consequences of the theory of relativity which has been clearly demonstrated. Just as the mu-mesons last longer when they are moving, so also will Paul last longer when he is moving. This is called a "paradox" only by the people who believe that the principle of relativity means that *all motion* is relative; they say, "Heh, heh, heh, from the point of view of Paul, can't we say that *Peter* was moving and should therefore appear to age more slowly? By symmetry, the only possible result is that both should be the same age when they meet." But in order for them to come back together and make the comparison, Paul must either stop at the end of the trip and make a comparison of clocks or, more simply, he has to come back, and the one who comes back must be the man who was moving, and he knows this, because he had to turn around. When he turned around, all kinds of unusual things happened in his space ship—the rockets went off, things jammed up against one wall, and so on—while Peter felt nothing.

So the way to state the rule is to say that *the man who has felt the accelerations*, who has seen things fall against the walls, and so on, is the one who would be the younger; that is the difference between them in an "absolute" sense, and it is certainly correct. When we discussed the fact that moving mu-mesons live longer, we used as an example their straight-line motion in the atmosphere. But we can also make mu-mesons in a laboratory and cause them to go in a curve with a magnet, and even under this accelerated motion, they last exactly as much longer as they do when they are moving in a straight line. Although no one has arranged an experiment explic-itly so that we can get rid of the paradox, one could compare a mu-meson which is left standing with one that had gone around a

## Relativistic Energy and Momentum

complete circle, and it would surely be found that the one that went around the circle lasted longer. Although we have not actually carried out an experiment using a complete circle, it is really not necessary, of course, because everything fits together all right. This may not satisfy those who insist that every single fact be demonstrated directly, but we confidently predict the result of the experiment in which Paul goes in a complete circle.

### 4-3 Transformation of velocities

The main difference between the relativity of Einstein and the relativity of Newton is that the laws of transformation connecting the coordinates and times between relatively moving systems are different. The correct transformation law, that of Lorentz, is

$$
\begin{aligned}
x' &= \frac{x - ut}{\sqrt{1 - u^2/c^2}}, \\
y' &= y, \\
z' &= z, \\
t' &= \frac{t - ux/c^2}{\sqrt{1 - u^2/c^2}}.
\end{aligned}
\tag{4.1}
$$

These equations correspond to the relatively simple case in which the relative motion of the two observers is along their common $x$-axes. Of course other directions of motion are possible, but the most general Lorentz transformation is rather complicated, with all four quantities mixed up together. We shall continue to use this simpler form, since it contains all the essential features of relativity.

Let us now discuss more of the consequences of this transformation. First, it is interesting to solve these equations in reverse. That is, here is a set of linear equations, four equations with four unknowns, and they can be solved in reverse, for $x, y, z, t$ in terms of $x', y', z', t'$. The result is very interesting, since it tells us how a system of coordinates "at rest" looks from the point of view of one that is "moving." Of course, since the motions are relative and of uniform velocity, the man who is "moving" can say, if he wishes, that

## SIX NOT-SO-EASY PIECES

it is really the other fellow who is moving and he himself who is at rest. And since he is moving in the opposite direction, he should get the same transformation, but with the opposite sign of velocity. That is precisely what we find by manipulation, so that is consistent. If it did not come out that way, we would have real cause to worry!

$$x = \frac{x' + ut'}{\sqrt{1 - u^2/c^2}},$$
$$y = y',$$
$$z = z', \qquad\qquad (4.2)$$
$$t = \frac{t' + ux'/c^2}{\sqrt{1 - u^2/c^2}}.$$

Next we discuss the interesting problem of the addition of velocities in relativity. We recall that one of the original puzzles was that light travels at 186,000 mi/sec in all systems, even when they are in relative motion. This is a special case of the more general problem exemplified by the following. Suppose that an object inside a space ship is going at 100,000 mi/sec and the space ship itself is going at 100,000 mi/sec; how fast is the object inside the space ship moving from the point of view of an observer outside? We might want to say 200,000 mi/sec, which is faster than the speed of light. This is very unnerving, because it is not supposed to be going faster than the speed of light! The general problem is as follows.

Let us suppose that the object inside the ship, from the point of view of the man inside, is moving with velocity $v$, and that the space ship itself has a velocity $u$ with respect to the ground. We want to know with what velocity $v_x$ this object is moving from the point of view of the man on the ground. This is, of course, still but a special case in which the motion is in the $x$-direction. There will also be a transformation for velocities in the $y$-direction, or for any angle; these can be worked out as needed. Inside the space ship the velocity is $v_{x'}$, which means that the displacement $x$ is equal to the velocity times the time:

$$x' = v_{x'}t'. \qquad\qquad (4.3)$$

## Relativistic Energy and Momentum

Now we have only to calculate what the position and time are from the point of view of the outside observer for an object which has the relation (4.2) between $x'$ and $t'$. So we simply substitute (4.3) into (4.2), and obtain

$$x = \frac{v_{x'} t' + ut'}{\sqrt{1 - u^2/c^2}}.\qquad(4.4)$$

But here we find $x$ expressed in terms of $t'$. In order to get the velocity as seen by the man on the outside, we must divide *his distance* by *his time*, not by the *other man's time*! So we must also calculate the *time* as seen from the outside, which is

$$t = \frac{t' + u(v_{x'} t')/c^2}{\sqrt{1 - u^2/c^2}}.\qquad(4.5)$$

Now we must find the ratio of $x$ to $t$, which is

$$v_x = \frac{x}{t} = \frac{u + v_{x'}}{1 + uv_{x'}/c^2},\qquad(4.6)$$

the square roots having cancelled. This is the law that we seek: the resultant velocity, the "summing" of two velocities, is not just the algebraic sum of two velocities (we know that it cannot be or we get in trouble), but is "corrected" by $1 + uv/c^2$.

Now let us see what happens. Suppose that you are moving inside the space ship at half the speed of light, and that the space ship itself is going at half the speed of light. Thus $u$ is $\frac{1}{2}c$ and $v$ is $\frac{1}{2}c$, but in the denominator $uv$ is one-fourth, so that

$$v = \frac{\frac{1}{2}c + \frac{1}{2}c}{1 + \frac{1}{4}} = \frac{4c}{5}.$$

So, in relativity, "half" and "half" does not make "one," it makes only "4/5." Of course low velocities can be added quite easily in the familiar way, because so long as the velocities are small compared with the speed of light we can forget about the $(1 + uv/c^2)$ factor; but things are quite different and quite interesting at high velocity.

Let us take a limiting case. Just for fun, suppose that inside the space ship the man was observing *light itself*. In other words, $v = c$,

## SIX NOT-SO-EASY PIECES

and yet the space ship is moving. How will it look to the man on the ground? The answer will be

$$v = \frac{u + c}{1 + uc/c^2} = c\,\frac{u + c}{u + c} = c.$$

Therefore, if something is moving at the speed of light inside the ship, it will appear to be moving at the speed of light from the point of view of the man on the ground too! This is good, for it is, in fact, what the Einstein theory of relativity was designed to do in the first place—so it had *better* work!

Of course, there are cases in which the motion is not in the direction of the uniform translation. For example, there may be an object inside the ship which is just moving "upward" with the velocity $v_{y'}$ with respect to the ship, and the ship is moving "horizontally." Now, we simply go through the same thing, only using $y$'s instead of $x$'s, with the result

$$y = y' = v_{y'}t',$$

so that if $v_{x'} = 0$,

$$v_y = \frac{y}{t} = v_{y'}\,\sqrt{1 - u^2/c^2}. \tag{4.7}$$

Thus a sidewise velocity is no longer $v_{y'}$, but $v_{y'}\sqrt{1 - u^2/c^2}$. We found this result by substituting and combining the transformation equations, but we can also see the result directly from the principle of relativity for the following reason (it is always good to look again to see whether we can see the reason). We have already (Figure 3-3) discussed how a possible clock might work when it is moving; the light appears to travel at an angle at the speed $c$ in the fixed system, while it simply goes vertically with the same speed in the moving system. We found that the *vertical component* of the velocity in the fixed system is less than that of light by the factor $\sqrt{1 - u^2/c^2}$ (see Eq. 3-3). But now suppose that we let a material particle go back and forth in this same "clock," but at some integral fraction $1/n$ of the speed of light (Figure 4-1). Then when the particle has gone back and forth once, the light will have gone exactly $n$ times. That is, each "click" of the "particle" clock will coincide with each $n$th

## Relativistic Energy and Momentum

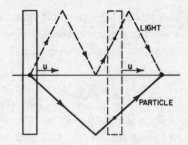

*Figure 4-1.* Trajectories described by a light ray and particle inside a
moving clock.

"click" of the light clock. *This fact must still be true when the whole
system is moving*, because the physical phenomenon of coincidence
will be a coincidence in any frame. Therefore, since the speed $c_y$ is
less than the speed of light, the speed $v_y$ of the particle must be
slower than the corresponding speed by the same square-root ratio!
That is why the square root appears in any vertical velocity.

## 4-4 Relativistic mass

We learned in the last chapter that the mass of an object increases
with velocity, but no demonstration of this was given, in the sense
that we made no arguments analogous to those about the way
clocks have to behave. However, we *can* show that, as a consequence of relativity plus a few other reasonable assumptions, the
mass must vary in this way. (We have to say "a few other assumptions" because we cannot prove anything unless we have some laws
which we assume to be true, if we expect to make meaningful
deductions.) To avoid the need to study the transformation laws of
force, we shall analyze a *collision*, where we need know nothing
about the laws of force, except that we shall assume the conservation of momentum and energy. Also, we shall assume that the
momentum of a particle which is moving is a vector and is always
directed in the direction of the velocity. However, we shall not

assume that the momentum is a *constant* times the velocity, as Newton did, but only that it is some *function* of velocity. We thus write the momentum vector as a certain coefficient times the vector velocity:

$$\mathbf{p} = m_v\mathbf{v}. \tag{4.8}$$

We put a subscript $v$ on the coefficient to remind us that it is a function of velocity, and we shall agree to call this coefficient $m_v$ the "mass." Of course, when the velocity is small, it is the same mass that we would measure in the slow-moving experiments that we are used to. Now we shall try to demonstrate that the formula for $m_v$ must be $m_0/\sqrt{1 - v^2/c^2}$, by arguing from the principle of relativity that the laws of physics must be the same in every coordinate system.

Suppose that we have two particles, like two protons, that are absolutely equal, and they are moving toward each other with exactly equal velocities. Their total momentum is zero. Now what can happen? After the collision, their directions of motion must be exactly opposite to each other, because if they are not exactly opposite, there will be a nonzero total vector momentum, and momentum would not have been conserved. Also they must have the same speeds, since they are exactly similar objects; in fact, they must have the same speed they started with, since we suppose that the energy is conserved in these collisions. So the diagram of an elastic collision, a reversible collision, will look like Figure 4-2(a): all the arrows are the same length, all the speeds are equal. We shall suppose that such collisions can always be arranged, that any angle $\theta$ can occur, and that any speed could be used in such a collision. Next, we notice that this same collision can be viewed differently by turning the axes, and just for convenience we *shall* turn the axes, so that the horizontal splits it evenly, as in Figure 4-2(b). It is the same collision redrawn, only with the axes turned.

Now here is the real trick: let us look at this collision from the point of view of someone riding along in a car that is moving with a speed equal to the horizontal component of the velocity of one particle.

## Relativistic Energy and Momentum

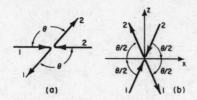

*Figure 4-2.* Two views of an elastic collision between equal objects moving at the same speed in opposite directions.

Then how does the collision look? It looks as though particle 1 is just going straight up, because it has lost its horizontal component, and it comes straight down again, also because it does not have that component. That is, the collision appears as shown in Fig. 4-3(a). Particle 2, however, was going the other way, and as we ride past it appears to fly by at some terrific speed and at a smaller angle, but we can appreciate that the angles before and after the collision are the *same*. Let us denote by $u$ the horizontal component of the velocity of particle 2, and by $w$ the vertical velocity of particle 1.

Now the question is, what is the vertical velocity $u \tan \alpha$? If we knew that, we could get the correct expression for the momentum, using the law of conservation of momentum in the vertical direction. Clearly, the horizontal component of the momentum is conserved: it is the same before and after the collision for both particles, and is zero for particle 1. So we need use the conservation law only for the upward velocity $u \tan \alpha$. But *we can* get the upward velocity, simply by looking at the same collision going the other way! If we look at the collision of Figure 4-3(a) from a car to the left moving with speed $u$, we see the same collision, except "turned over," as shown in Figure 4-3(b). Now particle 2 is the one that goes up and down with speed $w$, and particle 1 has picked up the horizontal speed $u$. Of course, now we *know* what the velocity $u \tan \alpha$ is: it is $w\sqrt{1 - u^2/c^2}$ (see Eq. 4.7). We know that the change in the vertical momentum of the vertically moving particle is

$$\Delta p = 2m_w w$$

SIX NOT-SO-EASY PIECES

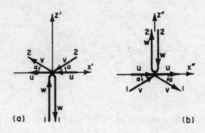

*Figure 4-3.* Two more views of the collision, from moving cars.

(2, because it moves up and back down). The obliquely moving particle has a certain velocity $v$ whose components we have found to be $u$ and $w\sqrt{1 - u^2/c^2}$, and whose mass is $m_v$. The change in *vertical* momentum of this particle is therefore $\Delta p' = 2m_v w \sqrt{1 - u^2/c^2}$ because, in accordance with our assumed law (4.8), the momentum component is always the mass corresponding to the magnitude of the velocity times the component of the velocity in the direction of interest. Thus in order for the total momentum to be zero the vertical momenta must cancel and the ratio of the mass moving with speed $v$ and the mass moving with speed $w$ must therefore be

$$\frac{m_w}{m_v} \sqrt{1 - u^2/c^2}. \tag{4.9}$$

Let us take the limiting case that $w$ is infinitesimal. If $w$ is very tiny indeed, it is clear that $v$ and $u$ are practically equal. In this case, $m_w \to m_0$ and $m_v \to m_u$. The grand result is

$$m_u = \frac{m_0}{\sqrt{1 - u^2/c^2}}. \tag{4.10}$$

It is an interesting exercise now to check whether or not Eq. (4.9) is indeed true for arbitrary values of $w$, assuming that Eq. (4.10) is the right formula for the mass. Note that the velocity $v$ needed in Eq. (4.9) can be calculated from the right-angle triangle:

$$v^2 = u^2 + w^2(1 - u^2/c^2).$$

## Relativistic Energy and Momentum

*Figure 4-4.* Two views of an inelastic collision between equally massive objects.

It will be found to check out automatically, although we used it only
in the limit of small $w$.

Now, let us accept that momentum is conserved and that the mass
depends upon the velocity according to (4.10) and go on to find what
else we can conclude. Let us consider what is commonly called an
*inelastic collision.* For simplicity, we shall suppose that two objects of
the same kind, moving oppositely with equal speeds $w$, hit each
other and stick together, to become some new, stationary object, as
shown in Figure 4-4(a). The mass $m$ of each corresponds to $w$, which,
as we know, is $m_0/\sqrt{1 - w^2/c^2}$. If we assume the conservation of
momentum and the principle of relativity, we can demonstrate an
interesting fact about the mass of the new object which has been
formed. We imagine an infinitesimal velocity $u$ at right angles to $w$
(we can do the same with finite values of $u$, but it is easier to
understand with an infinitesimal velocity), then look at this same
collision as we ride by in an elevator at the velocity $-u$. What we see
is shown in Figure 4-4(b). The composite object has an unknown
mass $M$. Now object 1 moves with an upward component of velocity
$u$ and a horizontal component which is practically equal to $w$, and so
also does object 2. After the collision we have the mass $M$ moving
upward with velocity $u$, considered very small compared with the
speed of light, and also small compared with $w$. Momentum must be
conserved, so let us estimate the momentum in the upward direction
before and after the collision. Before the collision we have $p \sim 2m_w u$,
and after the collision the momentum is evidently $p' = M_u u$, but $M_u$ is
essentially the same as $M_0$ because $u$ is so small. These momenta must
be equal because of the conservation of momentum, and therefore

$$M_0 = 2m_w. \tag{4.11}$$

*The mass of the object which is formed when two equal objects collide must be twice the mass of the objects which come together.* You might say, "Yes, of course, that is the conservation of mass." But not "Yes, of course," so easily, because *these masses have been enhanced* over the masses that they would be if they were standing still, yet they still contribute, to the total $M$, not the mass they have when standing still, but *more*. Astonishing as that may seem, in order for the conservation of momentum to work when two objects come together, the mass that they form must be greater than the rest masses of the objects, even though the objects are at rest after the collision!

## 4-5 Relativistic energy

In the last chapter we demonstrated that as a result of the dependence of the mass on velocity and Newton's laws, the changes in the kinetic energy of an object resulting from the total work done by the forces on it always comes out to be

$$\Delta T = (m_u - m_0)c^2 = \frac{m_0 c^2}{\sqrt{1 - u^2/c^2}} - m_0 c^2. \qquad (4.12)$$

We even went further, and guessed that the total energy is the total mass times $c^2$. Now we continue this discussion.

Suppose that our two equally massive objects that collide can still be "seen" inside $M$. For instance, a proton and a neutron are "stuck together," but are still moving about inside of $M$. Then, although we might at first expect the mass $M$ to be $2m_0$, we have found that it is not $2m_0$, but $2m_w$. Since $2m_w$ is what is put in, but $2m_0$ are the rest masses of the things inside, the *excess* mass of the composite object is equal to the kinetic energy brought in. This means, of course, that *energy has inertia*. In the last chapter we discussed the heating of a gas, and showed that because the gas molecules are moving and moving things are heavier, when we put energy into the gas its

## Relativistic Energy and Momentum

molecules move faster and so the gas gets heavier. But in fact the argument is completely general, and our discussion of the inelastic collision shows that the mass is there whether or not it is *kinetic* energy. In other words, if two particles come together and produce potential or any other form of energy; if the pieces are slowed down by climbing hills, doing work against internal forces, or whatever; then it is still true that the mass is the total energy that has been put in. So we see that the conservation of mass which we have deduced above is equivalent to the conservation of energy, and therefore there is no place in the theory of relativity for strictly inelastic collisions, as there was in Newtonian mechanics. According to Newtonian mechanics it is all right for two things to collide and so form an object of mass $2m_0$ which is in no way distinct from the one that would result from putting them together slowly. Of course we know from the law of conservation of energy that there is more kinetic energy inside, but that does not affect the mass, according to Newton's laws. But now we see that this is impossible; because of the kinetic energy involved in the collision, the resulting object will be *heavier*; therefore, it will be a *different* object. When we put the objects together gently they make something whose mass is $2m_0$; when we put them together forcefully, they make something whose mass is greater. When the mass is different, we can *tell* that it is different. So, necessarily, the conservation of energy must go along with the conservation of momentum in the theory of relativity.

This has interesting consequences. For example, suppose that we have an object whose mass $M$ is measured, and suppose something happens so that it flies into two equal pieces moving with speed $w$, so that they each have a mass $m_w$. Now suppose that these pieces encounter enough material to slow them up until they stop; then they will have mass $m_0$. How much energy will they have given to the material when they have stopped? Each will give an amount $(m_w - m_0)c^2$, by the theorem that we proved before. This much energy is left in the material in some form, as heat, potential energy, or whatever. Now $2m_w = M$, so the liberated energy is $E = (M - 2m_0)c^2$. This equation was used to estimate how much

SIX NOT-SO-EASY PIECES

energy would be liberated under fission in the atomic bomb, for example. (Although the fragments are not exactly equal, they are nearly equal.) The mass of the uranium atom was known—it had been measured ahead of time—and the atoms into which it split, iodine, xenon, and so on, all were of known mass. By masses, we do not mean the masses while the atoms are moving, we mean the masses when the atoms are *at rest*. In other words, both $M$ and $m_0$ are known. So by subtracting the two numbers one can calculate how much energy will be released if $M$ can be made to split in "half." For this reason poor old Einstein was called the "father" of the atomic bomb in all the newspapers. Of course, all that meant was that he could tell us ahead of time how much energy would be released if we told him what process would occur. The energy that should be liberated when an atom of uranium undergoes fission was estimated about six months before the first direct test, and as soon as the energy was in fact liberated, someone measured it directly (and if Einstein's formula had not worked, they would have measured it anyway), and the moment they measured it they no longer needed the formula. Of course, we should not belittle Einstein, but rather should criticize the newspapers and many popular descriptions of what causes what in the history of physics and technology. The problem of how to get the thing to occur in an effective and rapid manner is a completely different matter.

The result is just as significant in chemistry. For instance, if we were to weigh the carbon dioxide molecule and compare its mass with that of the carbon and the oxygen, we could find out how much energy would be liberated when carbon and oxygen form carbon dioxide. The only trouble here is that the differences in masses are so small that it is technically very difficult to do.

Now let us turn to the question of whether we should add $m_0c^2$ to the kinetic energy and say from now on that the total energy of an object is $mc^2$. First, if we can still *see* the component pieces of rest mass $m_0$ inside $M$, then we could say that some of the mass $M$ of the compound object is the mechanical rest mass of the parts, part of it is kinetic energy of the parts, and part of it is potential energy of the

## Relativistic Energy and Momentum

parts. But we have discovered, in nature, particles of various kinds which undergo reactions just like the one we have treated above, in which with all the study in the world, *we cannot see the parts inside*. For instance, when a $K$-meson disintegrates into two pions it does so according to the law (4.11), but the idea that a $K$ is made out of 2 $\pi$'s is a useless idea, because it also disintegrates into 3 $\pi$'s!

Therefore we have a *new idea*: we do not have to know what things are made of inside; we cannot and need not identify, inside a particle, which of the energy is rest energy of the parts into which it is going to disintegrate. It is not convenient and often not possible to separate the total $mc^2$ energy of an object into rest energy of the inside pieces, kinetic energy of the pieces, and potential energy of the pieces; instead, we simply speak of the *total energy* of the particle. We "shift the origin" of energy by adding a constant $m_0c^2$ to everything, and say that the total energy of a particle is the mass in motion times $c^2$, and when the object is standing still, the energy is the mass at rest times $c^2$.

Finally, we find that the velocity $v$, momentum $P$, and total energy $E$ are related in a rather simple way. That the mass in motion at speed $v$ is the mass $m_0$ at rest divided by $\sqrt{1 - v^2/c^2}$, surprisingly enough, is rarely used. Instead, the following relations are easily proved, and turn out to be very useful:

$$E^2 - P^2c^2 = m_0^2c^4 \tag{4.13}$$

and

$$Pc = Ev/c. \tag{4.14}$$

# Five

# SPACE-TIME

## 5-1 The geometry of space-time

The theory of relativity shows us that the relationships of positions and times as measured in one coordinate system and another are not what we would have expected on the basis of our intuitive ideas. It is very important that we thoroughly understand the relations of space and time implied by the Lorentz transformation, and therefore we shall consider this matter more deeply in this chapter.

The Lorentz transformation between the positions and times $(x, y, z, t)$ as measured by an observer "standing still," and the corresponding coordinates and time $(x', y', z', t')$ measured inside a "moving" space ship, moving with velocity $u$ are

$$x' = \frac{x - ut}{\sqrt{1 - u^2/c^2}},$$

$$y' = y,$$

$$z' = z, \tag{5.1}$$

$$t' = \frac{t - ux/c^2}{\sqrt{1 - u^2/c^2}}.$$

Let us compare these equations with Eq. (1.5), which also relates measurements in two systems, one of which in this instance is *rotated* relative to the other:

SIX NOT-SO-EASY PIECES

$$x' = x \cos \theta + y \sin \theta,$$
$$y' = y \cos \theta - x \sin \theta, \qquad (5.2)$$
$$z' = z.$$

In this particular case, Moe and Joe are measuring with axes having an angle $\theta$ between the $x'$- and $x$-axes. In each case, we note that the "primed" quantities are "mixtures" of the "unprimed" ones: the new $x'$ is a mixture of $x$ and $y$, and the new $y'$ is also a mixture of $x$ and $y$.

An analogy is useful: When we look at an object, there is an obvious thing we might call the "apparent width," and another we might call the "depth." But the two ideas, width and depth, are not *fundamental* properties of the object, because if we step aside and look at the same thing from a different angle, we get a different width and a different depth, and we may develop some formulas for computing the new ones from the old ones and the angles involved. Equations (5.2) are these formulas. One might say that a given depth is a kind of "mixture" of all depth and all width. If it were impossible ever to move, and we always saw a given object from the same position, then this whole business would be irrelevant—we would always see the "true" width and the "true" depth, and they would appear to have quite different qualities, because one appears as a subtended optical angle and the other involves some focusing of the eyes or even intuition; they would seem to be very different things and would never get mixed up. It is because we *can* walk around that we realize that depth and width are, somehow or other, just two different aspects of the same thing.

*Can we not look at the Lorentz transformations in the same way?* Here also we have a mixture—of positions and the time. A difference between a space measurement and a time measurement produces a new space measurement. In other words, in the space measurements of one man there is mixed in a little bit of the time, as seen by the other. Our analogy permits us to generate this idea: The "reality" of an object that we are looking at is somehow greater (speaking crudely and intuitively) than its "width" and its "depth"

## Space-Time

because *they* depend upon *how* we look at it; when we move to a new position, our brain immediately recalculates the width and the depth. But our brain does not immediately recalculate coordinates and time when we move at high speed, because we have had no effective experience of going nearly as fast as light to appreciate the fact that time and space are also of the same nature. It is as though we were always stuck in the position of having to look at just the width of something, not being able to move our heads appreciably one way or the other; if we could, we understand now, we would see some of the other man's time—we would see "behind," so to speak, a little bit.

Thus we shall try to think of objects in a new kind of world, of space and time mixed together, in the same sense that the objects in our ordinary space-world are real, and can be looked at from different directions. We shall then consider that objects occupying space and lasting for a certain length of time occupy a kind of a "blob" in a new kind of world, and that we look at this "blob" from different points of view when we are moving at different velocities. This new world, this geometrical entity in which the "blobs" exist by occupying position and taking up a certain amount of time, is called *space-time*. A given point $(x, y, z, t)$ in space-time is called an *event*. Imagine, for example, that we plot the $x$-positions horizontally, $y$ and $z$ in two other directions, both mutually at "right angles" and at "right angles" to the paper (!), and time, vertically. Now, how does a moving particle, say, look on such a diagram? If the particle is standing still, then it has a certain $x$, and as time goes on, it has the same $x$, the same $x$, the same $x$; so its "path" is a line that runs parallel to the $t$-axis (Figure 5-1 (a)). On the other hand, if it drifts outward, then as the time goes on $x$ increases (Figure 5-1 (b)). So a particle, for example, which starts to drift out and then slows up should have a motion something like that shown in Figure 5-1 (c). A particle, in other words, which is permanent and does not disintegrate is represented by a line in space-time. A particle which disintegrates would be represented by a forked line, because it would turn into two other things which would start from that point.

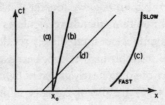

*Figure 5-1.* Three particle paths in space-time: (a) a particle at rest at $x = x_0$; (b) a particle which starts at $x = x_0$ and moves with constant speed; (c) a particle which starts at high speed but slows down.

What about light? Light travels at the speed $c$, and that would be represented by a line having a certain fixed slope (Figure 5-1 (d)).

Now according to our new idea, if a given event occurs to a particle, say if it suddenly disintegrates at a certain space-time point into two new ones which follow some new tracks, and this interesting event occurred at a certain value of $x$ and a certain value of $t$, then we would expect that, if this makes any sense, we just have to take a new pair of axes and turn them, and that will give us the new $t$ and the new $x$ in our new system, as shown in Figure 5-2(a). But this is wrong, because Eq. (5.1) is not *exactly* the same mathematical transformation as Eq. (5.2). Note, for example, the difference in sign between the two, and the fact that one is written in terms of cos $\theta$ and sin $\theta$, while the other is written with algebraic quantities. (Of course, it is not impossible that the algebraic quantities could be written as cosine and sine, but actually they cannot.) But still, the

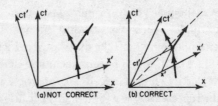

*Figure 5-2.* Two views of a disintegrating particle.

## Space-Time

two expressions *are* very similar. As we shall see, it is not really possible to think of space-time as a real, ordinary geometry because of that difference in sign. In fact, although we shall not emphasize this point, it turns out that a man who is moving has to use a set of axes which are inclined equally to the light ray, using a special kind of projection parallel to the $x'$- and $t'$-axes, for his $x'$ and $t'$, as shown in Figure 5-2(b). We shall not deal with the geometry, since it does not help much; it is easier to work with the equations.

## 5-2 Space-time intervals

Although the geometry of space-time is not Euclidean in the ordinary sense, there *is* a geometry which is very similar, but peculiar in certain respects. If this idea of geometry is right, there ought to be some functions of coordinates and time which are independent of the coordinate system. For example, under ordinary rotations, if we take two points, one at the origin, for simplicity, and the other one somewhere else, both systems would have the same origin, and the distance from here to the other point is the same in both. That is one property that is independent of the particular way of measuring it. The square of the distance is $x^2 + y^2 + z^2$. Now what about space-time? It is not hard to demonstrate that we have here, also, something which stays the same, namely, the combination $c^2t^2 - x^2 - y^2 - z^2$ is the same before and after the transformation:

$$c^2t'^2 - x'^2 - y'^2 - z'^2 = c^2t^2 - x^2 - y^2 - z^2. \qquad (5.3)$$

This quantity is therefore something which, like the distance, is "real" in some sense; it is called the *interval* between the two space-time points, one of which is, in this case, at the origin. (Actually, of course, it is the interval squared, just as $x^2 + y^2 + z^2$ is the distance squared.) We give it a different name because it is in a different geometry, but the interesting thing is only that some signs are reversed and there is a $c$ in it.

Let us get rid of the $c$; that is an absurdity if we are going to have a wonderful space with $x$'s and $y$'s that can be interchanged. One of the confusions that could be caused by someone with no experience would be to measure widths, say, by the angle subtended at the eye, and measure depth in a different way, like the strain on the muscles needed to focus them, so that the depths would be measured in feet and the widths in meters. Then one would get an enormously complicated mess of equations in making transformations such as (5.2), and would not be able to see the clarity and simplicity of the thing for a very simple technical reason, that the same thing is being measured in two different units. Now in Eqs. (5.1) and (5.3) nature is telling us that time and space are equivalent; time becomes space; *they should be measured in the same units*. What distance is a "second"? It is easy to figure out from (5.3) what it is. It is $3 \times 10^8$ meters, *the distance that light would go in one second*. In other words, if we were to measure all distances and times in the same units, seconds, then our unit of distance would be $3 \times 10^8$ meters, and the equations would be simpler. Or another way that we could make the units equal is to measure time in meters. What is a meter of time? A meter of time is the time it takes for light to go one meter, and is therefore $\frac{1}{3} \times 10^{-8}$ sec, or 3.3 billionths of a second! We would like, in other words, to put all our equations in a system of units in which $c = 1$. If time and space are measured in the same units, as suggested, then the equations are obviously much simplified. They are

$$x' = \frac{x - ut}{\sqrt{1 - u^2}},$$
$$y' = y,$$
$$z' = z, \tag{5.4}$$
$$t' = \frac{t - ux}{\sqrt{1 - u^2}},$$

$$t'^2 - x'^2 - y'^2 - z'^2 = t^2 - x^2 - y^2 - z^2. \tag{5.5}$$

If we are ever unsure or "frightened" that after we have this system with $c = 1$ we shall never be able to get our equations right again, the answer is quite the opposite. It is much easier to remember them

## Space-Time

without the $c$'s in them, and it is always easy to put the $c$'s back, by looking after the dimensions. For instance, in $\sqrt{1 - u^2}$, we know that we cannot subtract a velocity squared, which has units, from the pure number 1, so we know that we must divide $u^2$ by $c^2$ in order to make that unitless, and that is the way it goes.

The difference between space-time and ordinary space, and the character of an interval as related to the distance, is very interesting. According to formula (5.5), if we consider a point which in a given coordinate system had zero time, and only space, then the interval squared would be negative and we would have an imaginary interval, the square root of a negative number. Intervals can be either real or imaginary in the theory. The square of an interval may be either positive or negative, unlike distance, which has a positive square. When an interval is imaginary, we say that the two points have a *space-like interval* between them (instead of imaginary), because the interval is more like space than like time. On the other hand, if two objects are at the same place in a given coordinate system, but differ only in time, then the square of the time is positive and the distances are zero and the interval squared is positive; this is called a *time-like interval*. In our diagram of space-time, therefore, we would have a representation something like this: at 45° there are two lines (actually, in four dimensions these will be "cones," called light cones) and points on these lines are all at zero interval from the origin. Where light goes from a given point is always separated from it by a zero interval, as we see from Eq. (5.5). Incidentally, we have just proved that if light travels with speed $c$ in one system, it travels with speed $c$ in another, for if the interval is the same in both systems, i.e., zero in one and zero in the other, then to state that the propagation speed of light is invariant is the same as saying that the interval is zero.

## 5-3 Past, present, and future

The space-time region surrounding a given space-time point can be separated into three regions, as shown in Figure 5-3. In one region we have space-like intervals, and in two regions, time-like intervals.

SIX NOT-SO-EASY PIECES

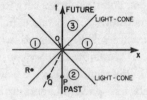

*Figure 5-3.* The space-time region surrounding a point at the origin.

Physically, these three regions into which space-time around a given point is divided have an interesting physical relationship to that point: a physical object or a signal can get from a point in region 2 to the event $O$ by moving along at a speed less than the speed of light. Therefore events in this region can affect the point $O$, can have an influence on it from the past. In fact, of course, an object at $P$ on the negative $t$-axis is precisely in the "past" with respect to $O$; it is the same space-point as $O$, only earlier. What happened there then, affects $O$ now. (Unfortunately, that is the way life is.) Another object at $Q$ can get to $O$ by moving with a certain speed less than $c$, so if this object were in a space ship and moving, it would be, again, the past of the same space-point. That is, in another coordinate system, the axis of time might go through both $O$ and $Q$. So all points of region 2 are in the "past" of $O$, and anything that happens in this region *can* affect $O$. Therefore region 2 is sometimes called the *affective past*, or affecting past; it is the locus of all events which can affect point $O$ in any way.

Region 3, on the other hand, is a region which we can affect *from* $O$, we can "hit" things by shooting "bullets" out at speeds less than $c$. So this is the world whose future can be affected by us, and we may call that the *affective future*. Now the interesting thing about all the rest of space-time, i.e., region 1, is that we can neither affect it now *from* $O$, nor can it affect us now *at* $O$, because nothing can go faster than the speed of light. Of course, what happens at $R$ *can* affect us *later* that is, if the sun is exploding "right now," it takes eight minutes before we know about it, and it cannot possibly affect us before then.

What we mean by "right now" is a mysterious thing which we cannot define and we cannot affect, but it can affect us later, or we could have affected it if we had done something far enough in the past. When we look at the star Alpha Centauri, we see it as it was four years ago; we might wonder what it is like "now." "Now" means at the same time from our special coordinate system. We can only see Alpha Centauri by the light that has come from our past, up to four years ago, but we do not know what it is doing "now"; it will take four years before what it is doing "now" can affect us. Alpha Centauri "now" is an idea or concept of our mind; it is not something that is really definable physically at the moment, because we have to wait to observe it; we cannot even define it right "now." Furthermore, the "now" depends on the coordinate system. If, for example, Alpha Centauri were moving, an observer there would not agree with us because he would put his axes at an angle, and his "now" would be a *different* time. We have already talked about the fact that simultaneity is not a unique thing.

There are fortune tellers, or people who tell us they can know the future, and there are many wonderful stories about the man who suddenly discovers that he has knowledge about the affective future. Well, there are lots of paradoxes produced by that because if we know something is going to happen, then we can make sure we will avoid it by doing the right thing at the right time, and so on. But actually there is no fortune teller who can even tell us the *present*! There is no one who can tell us what is really happening right now, at any reasonable distance, because that is unobservable. We might ask ourselves this question, which we leave to the student to try to answer: Would any paradox be produced if it were suddenly to become possible to know things that are in the space-like intervals of region 1?

SIX NOT-SO-EASY PIECES

## 5-4 More about four-vectors

Let us now return to our consideration of the analogy of the Lorentz transformation and rotations of the space axes. We have learned the utility of collecting together other quantities which have the same transformation properties as the coordinates, to form what we call *vectors*, directed lines. In the case of ordinary rotations, there are many quantities that transform the same way as $x$, $y$, and $z$ under rotation: for example, the velocity has three components, an $x$, $y$, and $z$ component; when seen in a different coordinate system, none of the components is the same, instead they are all transformed to new values. But, somehow or other, the velocity "itself" has a greater reality than do any of its particular components, and we represent it by a directed line.

We therefore ask: Is it or is it not true that there are quantities which transform, or which are related, in a moving system and in a nonmoving system, in the same way as $x$, $y$, $z$, and $t$? From our experience with vectors, we know that three of the quantities, like $x$, $y$, $z$, would constitute the three components of an ordinary space-vector, but the fourth quantity would look like an ordinary scalar under space rotation, because it does not change so long as we do not go into a moving coordinate system. Is it possible, then, to associate with some of our known "three-vectors" a fourth object, that we could call the "time component," in such a manner that the four objects together would "rotate" the same way as position and time in space-time? We shall now show that there is, indeed, at least one such thing (there are many of them, in fact): *the three components of momentum, and the energy as the time component, transform together* to make what we call a "four-vector." In demonstrating this, since it is quite inconvenient to have to write $c$'s everywhere, we shall use the same trick concerning units of the energy, the mass, and the momentum, that we used in Eq. (5.4). Energy and mass, for example, differ only by a factor $c^2$ which is merely a question of units, so we can say energy *is* the mass. Instead

## Space-Time

of having to write the $c^2$, we put $E = m$, and then, of course, if there were any trouble we would put in the right amounts of $c$ so that the units would straighten out in the last equation, but not in the intermediate ones.

Thus our equations for energy and momentum are

$$E = m = m_0/\sqrt{1 - v^2},$$
$$\mathbf{p} = m\mathbf{v} = m_0\mathbf{v}/\sqrt{1 - v^2}. \tag{5.6}$$

Also in these units, we have

$$E^2 - p^2 = m_0^2. \tag{5.7}$$

For example, if we measure energy in electron volts, what does a mass of 1 electron volt mean? It means the mass whose rest energy is 1 electron volt, that is, $m_0c^2$ is one electron volt. For example, the rest mass of an electron is $0.511 \times 10^6$ ev.

Now what would the momentum and energy look like in a new coordinate system? To find out, we shall have to transform Eq. (5.6), which we can do because we know how the velocity transforms. Suppose that, as we measure it, an object has a velocity $v$, but we look upon the same object from the point of view of a space ship which itself is moving with a velocity $u$, and in that system we use a prime to designate the corresponding thing. In order to simplify things at first, we shall take the case that the velocity $v$ is in the direction of $u$. (Later, we can do the more general case.) What is $v'$, the velocity as seen from the space ship? It is the composite velocity, the "difference" between $v$ and $u$. By the law which we worked out before,

$$v' = \frac{v - u}{1 - uv}. \tag{5.8}$$

Now let us calculate the new energy $E'$, the energy as the fellow in the space ship would see it. He would use the same rest mass, of course, but he would use $v'$ for the velocity. What we have to do is square $v'$, subtract it from one, take the square root, and take the reciprocal:

$$v'^2 = \frac{v^2 - 2uv + u^2}{1 - 2uv + u^2v^2},$$

$$1 - v'^2 = \frac{1 - 2uv + u^2v^2 - v^2 + 2uv - u^2}{1 - 2uv + u^2v^2}$$

$$= \frac{1 - v^2 - u^2 + u^2v^2}{1 - 2uv + u^2v^2}$$

$$= \frac{(1 - v^2)(1 - u^2)}{(1 - uv)^2}.$$

Therefore

$$\frac{1}{\sqrt{1 - v'^2}} = \frac{1 - uv}{\sqrt{1 - v^2}\sqrt{1 - u^2}}. \tag{5.9}$$

The energy $E'$ is then simply $m_0$ times the above expression. But we want to express the energy in terms of the unprimed energy and momentum, and we note that

$$E' = \frac{m_0 - m_0uv}{\sqrt{1 - v^2}\sqrt{1 - u^2}} = \frac{(m_0/\sqrt{1 - v^2}) - (m_0v/\sqrt{1 - v^2})u}{\sqrt{1 - u^2}},$$

or

$$E' = \frac{E - up_x}{\sqrt{1 - u^2}}, \tag{5.10}$$

which we recognize as being exactly of the same form as

$$t' = \frac{t - ux}{\sqrt{1 - u^2}}.$$

Next we must find the new momentum $p'_x$. This is just the energy $E$ times $v'$, and is also simply expressed in terms of $E$ and $p$:

$$p'_x = E'v' = \frac{m_0(1 - uv)}{\sqrt{1 - v^2}\sqrt{1 - u^2}} \cdot \frac{v - u}{(1 - uv)} = \frac{m_0v - m_0u}{\sqrt{1 - v^2}\sqrt{1 - u^2}}.$$

Thus

$$p'_x = \frac{p_x - uE}{\sqrt{1 - u^2}}, \tag{5.11}$$

### Space-Time

which we recognize as being of precisely the same form as

$$x' = \frac{x - ut}{\sqrt{1 - u^2}}.$$

Thus the transformations for the new energy and momentum in terms of the old energy and momentum are exactly the same as the transformations for $t'$ in terms of $t$ and $x$, and $x'$ in terms of $x$ and $t$: all we have to do is, every time we see $t$ in (5.4) substitute $E$, and every time we see $x$ substitute $p_x$, and then the equations (5.4) will become the same as Eqs. (5.10) and (5.11). This would imply, if everything works right, an additional rule that $p'_y = p_y$ and that $p'_z = p_z$. To prove this would require our going back and studying the case of motion up and down. Actually, we did study the case of motion up and down in the last chapter. We analyzed a complicated collision and we noticed that, in fact, the transverse momentum is *not* changed when viewed from a moving system; so we have already verified that $p'_y = p_y$ and $p'_z = p_z$. The complete transformation, then, is

$$p'_x = \frac{p_x - uE}{\sqrt{1 - u^2}},$$
$$p'_y = p_y,$$
$$p'_z = p_z \qquad (5.12)$$
$$E' = \frac{E - up_x}{\sqrt{1 - u^2}}.$$

In these transformations, therefore, we have discovered four quantities which transform like $x$, $y$, $z$, and $t$, and which we call the *four-vector momentum*. Since the momentum is a four-vector, it can be represented on a space-time diagram of a moving particle as an "arrow" tangent to the path, as shown in Figure 5-4. This arrow has a time component equal to the energy, and its space components represent its three-vector momentum; this arrow is more "real" than either the energy or the momentum, because those just depend on how we look at the diagram.

SIX NOT-SO-EASY PIECES

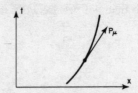

*Figure 5-4.* The four-vector momentum of a particle.

## 5-5 Four-vector algebra

The notation for four-vectors is different than it is for three-vectors. In the case of three-vectors, if we were to talk about the ordinary three-vector momentum we would write it **p**. If we wanted to be more specific, we could say it has three components which are, for the axes in question, $p_x$, $p_y$, and $p_z$, or we could simply refer to a general component as $p_i$, and say that $i$ could either be $x$, $y$, or $z$, and that these are the three components; that is, imagine that $i$ is any one of three directions, $x$, $y$, or $z$. The notation that we use for four-vectors is analogous to this: we write $p_\mu$ for the four-vector, and $\mu$ stands for the *four* possible directions $t$, $x$, $y$, or $z$.

We could, of course, use any notation we want; do not laugh at notations; invent them, they are powerful. In fact, mathematics is, to a large extent, invention of better notations. The whole idea of a four-vector, in fact, is an improvement in notation so that the transformations can be remembered easily. $A_\mu$, then, is a general four-vector, but for the special case of momentum, the $p_t$ is identified as the energy, $p_x$ is the momentum in the $x$-direction, $p_y$ is that in the $y$-direction, and $p_z$ is that in the $z$-direction. To add four-vectors, we add the corresponding components.

If there is an equation among four-vectors, then the equation is true for *each component*. For instance, if the law of conservation of three-vector momentum is to be true in particle collisions, i.e., if the sum of the momenta for a large number of interacting or colliding particles is to be a constant, that must mean that the sums of all momenta in the $x$-direction, in the $y$-direction, and in the $z$-

## Space-Time

direction, for all the particles, must each be constant. This law alone would be impossible in relativity because it is *incomplete*; it is like talking about only two of the components of a three-vector. It is incomplete because if we rotate the axes, we mix the various components, so we must include all three components in our law. Thus, in relativity, we must complete the law of conservation of momentum by extending it to include the *time* component. This is *absolutely necessary* to go with the other three, or there cannot be relativistic invariance. The *conservation of energy* is the fourth equation which goes with the conservation of momentum to make a valid four-vector relationship in the geometry of space and time. Thus the law of conservation of energy and momentum in four-dimensional notation is

$$\sum_{\substack{\text{particles} \\ \text{in}}} p_\mu = \sum_{\substack{\text{particles} \\ \text{out}}} p_\mu, \tag{5.13}$$

or, in a slightly different notation

$$\sum_i p_{i\mu} = \sum_j p_{j\mu}, \tag{5.14}$$

where $i = 1, 2, \ldots$ refers to the particles going into the collision, $j = 1, 2, \ldots$ refers to the particles coming out of the collision, and $\mu = x, y, z$, or $t$. You say, "In which axes?" It makes no difference. The law is true for each component, using *any* axes.

In vector analysis we discussed one other thing, the dot product of two vectors. Let us now consider the corresponding thing in space-time. In ordinary rotation we discovered there was an unchanged quantity $x^2 + y^2 + z^2$. In four dimensions, we find that the corresponding quantity is $t^2 - x^2 - y^2 - z^2$ (Eq. 5.3). How can we write that? One way would be to write some kind of four-dimensional thing with a square dot between, like $A_\mu \otimes B_\mu$; one of the notations which is actually used is

$$\sum_\mu{}' A_\mu A_\mu = A_t^2 - A_x^2 - A_y^2 - A_z^2. \tag{5.15}$$

The prime on $\Sigma$ means that the first term, the "time" term, is positive, but the other three terms have minus signs. This quantity, then, will be the same in any coordinate system, and we may call it the square of the length of the four-vector. For instance, what is the square of the length of the four-vector momentum of a single particle? This will be equal to $p_t^2 - p_x^2 - p_y^2 - p_z^2$ or, in other words, $E^2 - p^2$, because we know that $p_t$ is $E$. What is $E^2 - p^2$? It must be something which is the same in every coordinate system. In particular, it must be the same for a coordinate system which is moving right along with the particle, in which the particle is standing still. If the particle is standing still, it would have no momentum. So in that coordinate system, it is purely its energy, which is the same as its rest mass. Thus $E^2 - p^2 = m_0^2$. So we see that the square of the length of this vector, the four-vector momentum, is equal to $m_0^2$.

From the square of a vector, we can go on to invent the "dot product," or the product which is a scalar: if $a_\mu$ is one four-vector and $b_\mu$ is another four-vector, then the scalar product is

$$\sum{}' a_\mu b_\mu = a_t b_t = a_x b_x - a_y b_y - a_z b_z. \qquad (5.16)$$

It is the same in all coordinate systems.

Finally, we shall mention certain things whose rest mass $m_0$ is zero. A photon of light, for example. A photon is like a particle, in that it carries an energy and a momentum. The energy of a photon is a certain constant, called Planck's constant, times the frequency of the photon: $E = h\nu$. Such a photon also carries a momentum, and the momentum of a photon (or of any other particle, in fact) is $h$ divided by the wavelength: $p = h/\lambda$. But, for a photon, there is a definite relationship between the frequency and the wavelength: $\nu = c/\lambda$. (The number of waves per second, times the wavelength of each, is the distance that the light goes in one second, which, of course, is $c$.) Thus we see immediately that the energy of a photon must be the momentum times $c$, or if $c = 1$, *the energy and momentum are equal*. That is to say, the rest mass is zero. Let us look at that again; that is quite curious. If it is a particle of zero rest mass, what happens when it stops? *It never stops!* It always goes at the speed $c$. The usual formula for energy is $m_0/\sqrt{1 - v^2}$. Now can we say that $m_0 = 0$ and $v = 1$, so the energy is 0? We *cannot* say that it is zero; the photon really can (and does) have energy even though it has no rest mass, but this it possesses by perpetually going at the speed of light!

We also know that the momentum of any particle is equal to its total energy times its velocity: if $c = 1$, $p = vE$ or, in ordinary units, $p = vE/c^2$. For any particle moving at the speed of light, $p = E$ if $c = 1$. The formulas for the energy of a photon as seen from a moving system are, of course, given by Eq. (5.12), but for the momentum we must substitute the energy times $c$ (or times 1 in this case). The different energies after transformation means that there are different frequencies. This is called the Doppler effect, and one can calculate it easily from Eq. (5.12), using also $E = p$ and $E = hv$.

As Minkowski said, "Space of itself, and time of itself will sink into mere shadows, and only a kind of union between them shall survive."

# Six

# CURVED SPACE

## 6-1 Curved spaces with two dimensions

◆ According to Newton, everything attracts everything else with a force inversely proportional to the square of the distance from it, and objects respond to forces with accelerations proportional to the forces. They are Newton's laws of universal gravitation and of motion. As you know, they account for the motions of balls, planets, satellites, galaxies, and so forth.

Einstein had a different interpretation of the law of gravitation. According to him, space and time—which must be put together as space-time—are *curved* near heavy masses. And it is the attempt of things to go along "straight lines" in this curved space-time which makes them move the way they do. Now that is a complex idea—very complex. It is the idea we want to explain in this chapter.

Our subject has three parts. One involves the effects of gravitation. Another involves the ideas of space-time which we already studied. The third involves the idea of curved space-time. We will simplify our subject in the beginning by not worrying about gravity and by leaving out the time—discussing just curved space. We will talk later about the other parts, but we will concentrate now on the idea of curved space—what is meant by curved space, and, more specifically, what is meant by curved space in this application of Einstein. Now even that much turns out to be somewhat difficult in

111

three dimensions. So we will first reduce the problem still further and talk about what is meant by the words "curved space" in two dimensions.

In order to understand this idea of curved space in two dimensions you really have to appreciate the limited point of view of the character who lives in such a space. Suppose we imagine a bug with no eyes who lives on a plane, as shown in Figure 6-1. He can move only on the plane, and he has no way of knowing that there is any way to discover any "outside world." (He hasn't got your imagination.) We are, of course, going to argue by analogy. *We* live in a three-dimensional world, and we don't have any imagination about going off our three-dimensional world in a new direction; so we have to think the thing out by analogy. It is as though we were bugs living on a plane, and there was a space in another direction. That's why we will first work with the bug, remembering that he must live on his surface and can't get out.

As another example of a bug living in two dimensions, let's imagine one who lives on a sphere. We imagine that he can walk around on the surface of the sphere, as in Figure 6-2, but that he can't look "up," or "down," or "out."

Now we want to consider still a *third* kind of creature. He is also a bug like the others, and also lives on a plane, as our first bug did, but this time the plane is peculiar. The temperature is different at different places. Also, the bug and any rulers he uses are all made of

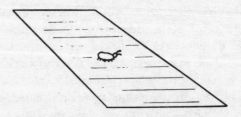

*Figure 6-1.* A bug on a plane surface.

## Curved Space

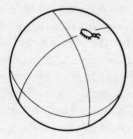

*Figure 6-2.* A bug on a sphere.

the same material which expands when it is heated. Whenever he puts a ruler somewhere to measure something the ruler expands immediately to the proper length for the temperature at that place. Wherever he puts any object—himself, a ruler, a triangle, or anything—the thing stretches itself because of the thermal expansion. Everything is longer in the hot places than it is in the cold places, and everything has the same coefficient of expansion. We will call the home of our third bug a "hot plate," although we will particularly want to think of a special kind of hot plate that is cold in the center and gets hotter as we go out toward the edges (Figure 6-3).

Now we are going to imagine that our bugs begin to study geometry. Although we imagine that they are blind so that they can't see any "outside" world, they can do a lot with their legs and feelers.

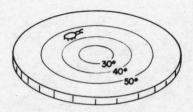

*Figure 6-3.* A bug on a hot plate.

They can draw lines, and they can make rulers, and measure off lengths. First, let's suppose that they start with the simplest idea in geometry. They learn how to make a straight line—defined as the shortest line between two points. Our first bug—see Figure 6-4—learns to make very good lines. But what happens to the bug on the sphere? He draws his straight line as the shortest distance—*for him*—between two points, as in Figure 6-5. It may look like a curve to us, but he has no way of getting off the sphere and finding out that there is "really" a shorter line. He just knows that if he tries any other path *in his world* it is always longer than his straight line. So we will let him have his straight line as the shortest arc between two points. (It is, of course an arc of a great circle.)

Finally, our third bug—the one in Figure 6-3—will also draw "straight lines" that look like curves to us. For instance, the shortest distance between *A* and *B* in Figure 6-6 would be on a curve like the one shown. Why? Because when his line curves out toward the warmer parts of his hot plate, the rulers get longer (from our omniscient point of view) and it takes fewer "yardsticks" laid end-to-end to get from *A* to *B*. So *for him* the line is straight—he has no way of knowing that there could be someone out in a strange three-dimensional world who would call a different line "straight."

We think you get the idea now that all the rest of the analysis will always be from the point of view of the creatures on the particular surfaces and not from *our* point of view. With that in mind let's see what the rest of their geometries looks like. Let's assume that the

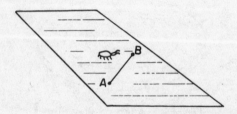

*Figure 6-4.* Making a "straight line" on a plane.

*Curved Space*

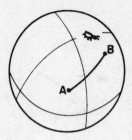

*Figure 6-5.* Making a "straight line" on a sphere.

bugs have all learned how to make two lines intersect at right angles. (You can figure out how they could do it.) Then our first bug (the one on the normal plane) finds an interesting fact. If he starts at the point *A* and makes a line 100 inches long, then makes a right angle and marks off another 100 inches, then makes another right angle and goes another 100 inches, then makes a third right angle and a fourth line 100 inches long, he ends up right at the starting point as shown in Figure 6-7(a). It is a property of his world—one of the facts of his "geometry."

Then he discovers another interesting thing. If he makes a triangle—a figure with three straight lines—the sum of the angles is equal to 180°, that is, to the sum of two right angles. See Figure 6-7(b).

Then he invents the circle. What's a circle? A circle is made this way: You rush off on straight lines in many many directions from a

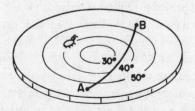

*Figure 6-6.* Making a "straight line" on the hot plate.

SIX NOT-SO-EASY PIECES

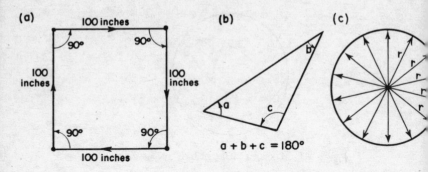

*Figure 6-7.* A square, triangle, and circle in a flat space.

single point, and lay out a lot of dots that are all the same distance from that point. See Figure 6-7(c). (We have to be careful how we define these things because we've got to be able to make the analogs for the other fellows.) Of course, it's equivalent to the curve you can make by swinging a ruler around a point. Anyway, our bug learns how to make circles. Then one day he thinks of measuring the distance around a circle. He measures several circles and finds a neat relationship: The distance around is always the same number times the radius $r$ (which is, of course, the distance from the center out to the curve). The circumference and the radius always have the same ratio—approximately 6.283—independent of the size of the circle.

Now let's see what our other bugs have been finding out about *their* geometries. First, what happens to the bug on the sphere when he tries to make a "square"? If he follows the prescription we gave above, he would probably think that the result was hardly worth the trouble. He gets a figure like the one shown in Figure 6-8. His end-point $B$ isn't on top of the starting point $A$. It doesn't work out to a closed figure at all. Get a sphere and try it. A similar thing would happen to our friend on the hot plate. If he lays out four straight lines of equal length—as measured with his expanding rulers—joined by right angles he gets a picture like the one in Figure 6-9.

*Curved Space*

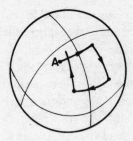

*Figure 6-8.* Trying to make a "square" on a sphere.

Now suppose that our bugs had each had their own Euclid who had told them what geometry "should" be like, and that they had checked him out roughly by making crude measurements on a *small* scale. Then as they tried to make accurate squares on a larger scale they would discover that something was wrong. The point is, that just by *geometrical measurements* they would discover that something was the matter with their space. We define a *curved space* to be a space in which the geometry is not what we expect for a plane. The geometry of the bugs on the sphere or on the hot plate is the geometry of a curved space. The rules of Euclidian geometry fail. And it isn't necessary to be able to lift yourself out of the plane in order to find out that the world that you live in is curved. It isn't necessary to circumnavigate the globe in order to find out that it is a ball. You can find out that you live

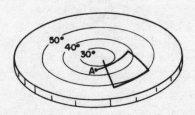

*Figure 6-9.* Trying to make a "square" on the hot plate.

SIX NOT-SO-EASY PIECES

on a ball by laying out a square. If the square is very small you will need a lot of accuracy, but if the square is large the measurement can be done more crudely.

Let's take the case of a triangle on a plane. The sum of the angles is 180 degrees. Our friend on the sphere can find triangles that are very peculiar. He can, for example, find triangles which have *three right angles*. Yes indeed! One is shown in Figure 6-10. Suppose our bug starts at the north pole and makes a straight line all the way down to the equator. Then he makes a right angle and another perfect straight line the same length. Then he does it again. For the very special length he has chosen he gets right back to his starting point, and also meets the first line with a right angle. So there is no doubt that for him this triangle has three right angles, or 270 degrees in the sum. It turns out that for him the sum of the angles of the triangle is *always* greater than 180 degrees. In fact, the excess (for the special case shown, the extra 90 degrees) is proportional to how much area the triangle has. If a triangle on a sphere is very small, its angles add up to very nearly 180 degrees, only a little bit over. As the triangle gets bigger the discrepancy goes up. The bug on the hot plate would discover similar difficulties with his triangles.

Let's look next at what our other bugs find out about circles. They make circles and measure their circumferences. For example,

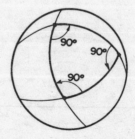

*Figure 6-10.* On a sphere a "triangle" can have three 90° angles.

## Curved Space

the bug on the sphere might make a circle like the one shown in Figure 6-11. And he would discover that the circumference is *less* than $2\pi$ times the radius. (You can see that because from the wisdom of our three-dimensional view it is obvious that what he calls the "radius" is a curve which is *longer* than the true radius of the circle.) Suppose that the bug on the sphere had read Euclid, and decided to predict a radius by dividing the circumference $C$ by $2\pi$, taking

$$r_{\text{pred}} = \frac{C}{2\pi}. \tag{6.1}$$

Then he would find that the measured radius was larger than the predicted radius. Pursuing the subject, he might define the difference to be the "excess radius," and write

$$r_{\text{meas}} - r_{\text{pred}} = r_{\text{excess}}, \tag{6.2}$$

and study how the excess radius effect depended on the size of the circle.

Our bug on the hot plate would discover a similar phenomenon. Suppose he was to draw a circle centered at the cold spot on the plate as in Figure 6-12. If we were to watch him as he makes the circle we would notice that his rulers are short near the center and get longer as they are moved outward—although the bug doesn't know it, of course. When he measures the circumference the ruler is

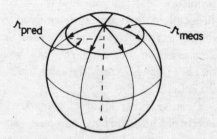

*Figure 6-11.* Making a circle on a sphere.

SIX NOT-SO-EASY PIECES

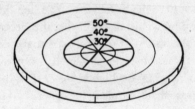

*Figure 6-12.* Making a circle on the hot plate.

long all the time, so he, too, finds out that the measured radius is longer than the predicted radius, $C/2\pi$. The hot-plate bug also finds an "excess radius effect." And again the size of the effect depends on the radius of the circle.

We will *define* a "curved space" as one in which these types of geometrical errors occur: The sum of the angles of a triangle is different from 180 degrees; the circumference of a circle divided by $2\pi$ is not equal to the radius; the rule for making a square doesn't give a closed figure. You can think of others.

We have given two different examples of curved space: the sphere and the hot plate. But it is interesting that if we choose the right temperature variation as a function of distance on the hot plate, the two *geometries* will be exactly the same. It is rather amusing. We can make the bug on the hot plate get exactly the same answers as the bug on the ball. For those who like geometry and geometrical problems we'll tell you how it can be done. If you assume that the length of the rulers (as determined by the temperature) goes in proportion to one plus some constant times the square of the distance away from the origin, then you will find that the geometry of that hot plate is exactly the same in all details* as the geometry of the sphere.

There are, of course, other kinds of geometry. We could ask about the geometry of a bug who lived on a pear, namely something which has a sharper curvature in one place and a weaker curvature

---

* except for the one point at infinity.

## Curved Space

in the other place, so that the excess in angles in triangles is more severe when he makes little triangles in one part of his world than when he makes them in another part. In other words, the curvature of a space can vary from place to place. That's just a generalization of the idea. It can also be imitated by a suitable distribution of temperature on a hot plate.

We may also point out that the results could come out with the opposite kind of discrepancies. You could find out, for example, that all triangles when they are made too large have the sum of their angles *less* than 180 degrees. That may sound impossible, but it isn't at all. First of all, we could have a hot plate with the temperature decreasing with the distance from the center. Then all the effects would be reversed. But we can also do it purely geometrically by looking at the two-dimensional geometry of the surface of a saddle. Imagine a saddle-shaped surface like the one sketched in Figure 6-13. Now draw a "circle" on the surface, defined as the locus of all points the same distance from a center. This circle is a curve that oscillates up and down with a scallop effect. So its circumference is larger than you would expect from calculating $2\pi r$. So $C/2\pi$ is now less than $r$. The "excess radius" would be negative.

Spheres and pears and such are all surfaces of *positive* curvatures; and the others are called surfaces of *negative* curvature. In general, a two-dimensional world will have a curvature which varies from place to place and may be positive in some places and negative in

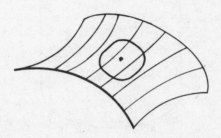

*Figure 6-13.* A "circle" on a saddle-shaped surface.

other places. In general, we mean by a curved space simply one in which the rules of Euclidean geometry break down with one sign of discrepancy or the other. The amount of curvature—defined, say, by the excess radius—may vary from place to place.

We might point out that, from our definition of curvature, a cylinder is, surprisingly enough, not curved. If a bug lived on a cylinder, as shown in Figure 6-14, he would find out that triangles, squares, and circles would all have the same behavior they have on a plane. This is easy to see, by just thinking about how all the figures will look if the cylinder is unrolled onto a plane. Then all the geometrical figures can be made to correspond exactly to the way they are in a plane. So there is no way for a bug living on a cylinder (assuming that he doesn't go all the way around, but just makes local measurements) to discover that his space is curved. In our technical sense, then, we consider that his space is *not* curved. What we want to talk about is more precisely called *intrinsic* curvature; that is, a curvature which can be found by measurements only in a local region. (A cylinder has no intrinsic curvature.) This was the

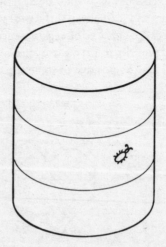

*Figure 6-14.* A two-dimensional space with zero intrinsic curvature.

sense intended by Einstein when he said that our space is curved. But we as yet only have defined a curved space in two dimensions; we must go onward to see what the idea might mean in three dimensions.

## 6-2 *Curvature in three-dimensional space*

We live in three-dimensional space and we are going to consider the idea that three-dimensional space is curved. You say, "But how can you imagine it being bent in any direction?" Well, we can't imagine space being bent in any direction because our imagination isn't good enough. (Perhaps it's just as well that we can't imagine too much, so that we don't get too free of the real world.) But we can still *define* a curvature without getting out of our three-dimensional world. All we have been talking about in two dimensions was simply an exercise to show how we could get a definition of curvature which didn't require that we be able to "look in" from the outside.

We can determine whether our world is curved or not in a way quite analogous to the one used by the gentlemen who live on the sphere and on the hot plate. We may not be able to distinguish between two such cases but we certainly can distinguish those cases from the flat space, the ordinary plane. How? Easy enough: We lay out a triangle and measure the angles. Or we make a great big circle and measure the circumference and the radius. Or we try to lay out some accurate squares, or try to make a cube. In each case we test whether the laws of geometry work. If they don't work, we say that our space is curved. If we lay out a big triangle and the sum of its angles exceeds 180 degrees, we can say our space is curved. Or if the measured radius of a circle is not equal to its circumference over $2\pi$, we can say our space is curved.

You will notice that in three dimensions the situation can be much more complicated than in two. At any one place in two dimensions there is a certain amount of curvature. But in three dimensions there can be *several components* to the curvature. If we

## SIX NOT-SO-EASY PIECES

lay out a triangle in some plane, we may get a different answer than if we orient the plane of the triangle in a different way. Or take the example of a circle. Suppose we draw a circle and measure the radius and it doesn't check with $C/2\pi$ so that there is some excess radius. Now we draw another circle at right angles—as in Figure 6-15. There's no need for the excess to be exactly the same for both circles. In fact, there might be a positive excess for a circle in one plane, and a defect (negative excess) for a circle in the other plane.

Perhaps you are thinking of a better idea: Can't we get around all of these components by using a *sphere* in three dimensions? We can specify a sphere by taking all the points that are the same distance from a given point in space. Then we can measure the surface area by laying out a fine scale rectangular grid on the surface of the sphere and adding up all the bits of area. According to Euclid the total area $A$ is supposed to be $4\pi$ times the square of the radius; so we can define a "predicted radius" as $\sqrt{A/4\pi}$. But we can also measure the radius directly by digging a hole to the center and measuring the distance. Again, we can take the measured radius minus the predicted radius and call the difference the radius excess.

$$r_{\text{excess}} = r_{\text{meas}} - \left(\frac{\text{measured area}}{4\pi}\right)^{1/2},$$

which would be a perfectly satisfactory measure of the curvature.

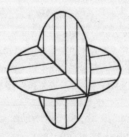

*Figure 6-15.* The excess radius may be different for circles with different orientations.

*Curved Space*

It has the great advantage that it doesn't depend upon how we orient a triangle or a circle.

But the excess radius of a sphere also has a disadvantage; it doesn't completely characterize the space. It gives what is called the *mean curvature* of the three-dimensional world, since there is an averaging effect over the various curvatures. Since it is an average, however, it does not solve completely the problem of defining the geometry. If you know only this number you can't predict all properties of the geometry of the space, because you can't tell what would happen with circles of different orientation. The complete definition requires the specification of six "curvature numbers" at each point. Of course the mathematicians know how to write all those numbers. You can read someday in a mathematics book how to write them all in a high-class and elegant form, but it is first a good idea to know in a rough way what it is that you are trying to write about. For most of our purposes the average curvature will be enough.*

## 6-3 Our space is curved

Now comes the main question. Is it true? That is, is the actual physical three-dimensional space we live in curved? Once we have enough imagination to realize the possibility that space might be curved, the human mind naturally gets curious about whether the real world is curved or not. People have made direct geometrical measurements to try to find out, and haven't found any deviations.

---

* We should mention one additional point for completeness. If you want to carry the hot-plate model of curved space over into three dimensions you must imagine that the length of the ruler depends not only on where you put it, but also on which orientation the ruler has when it is laid down. It is a generalization of the simple case in which the length of the ruler depends on where it is, but is the same if set north-south, or east-west, or up-down. This generalization is needed if you want to represent a three-dimensional space with any arbitrary geometry with such a model, although it happens not to be necessary for two dimensions.

SIX NOT-SO-EASY PIECES

On the other hand, by arguments about gravitation, Einstein discovered that space *is* curved, and we'd like to tell you what Einstein's law is for the amount of curvature, and also tell you a little bit about how he found out about it.

Einstein said that space is curved and that matter is the source of the curvature. (Matter is also the source of gravitation, so gravity is related to the curvature—but that will come later in the chapter.) Let us suppose, to make things a little easier, that the matter is distributed continuously with some density, which may vary, however, as much as you want from place to place.* The rule that Einstein gave for the curvature is the following: If there is a region of space with matter in it and we take a sphere small enough that the density $\rho$ of matter inside it is effectively constant, then the *radius excess* for the sphere is proportional to the mass inside the sphere. Using the definition of excess radius, we have

$$\text{Radius excess} = \sqrt{\frac{A}{4\pi}} - r_{\text{meas}} = \frac{G}{3c^2} \cdot M. \qquad (6.3)$$

Here, $G$ is the gravitational constant (of Newton's theory), $c$ is the velocity of light, and $M = 4\pi\rho r^3/3$ is the mass of the matter inside the sphere. This is Einstein's law for the mean curvature of space.

Suppose we take the earth as an example and forget that the density varies from point to point—so we won't have to do any integrals. Suppose we were to measure the surface of the earth very carefully, and then dig a hole to the center and measure the radius. From the surface area we could calculate the predicted radius we would get from setting the area equal to $4\pi r^2$. When we compared the predicted radius with the actual radius, we would find that the actual radius exceeded the predicted radius by the amount given in Eq. (6.3). The constant $G/3c^2$ is about $2.5 \times 10^{-29}$ cm per gram, so for each gram of material the measured radius is off by $2.5 \times 10^{-29}$ cm. Putting in the mass of the earth, which is about $6 \times 10^{27}$ grams, it

---

* Nobody—not even Einstein—knows how to do it if mass comes concentrated at points.

## Curved Space

turns out that the earth has 1.5 millimeters more radius than it should have for its surface area.* Doing the same calculation for the sun, you find that the sun's radius is one-half a kilometer too long.

You should note that the law says that the *average* curvature *above* the surface area of the earth is zero. But that does *not* mean that all the components of the curvature are zero. There may still be—and, in fact, there is—some curvature above the earth. For a circle in a plane there will be an excess radius of one sign for some orientations and of the opposite sign for other orientations. It just turns out that the average over a sphere is zero when there is no mass *inside* it. Incidentally, it turns out that there is a relation between the various components of the curvature and the *variation* of the average curvature from place to place. So if you know the average curvature everywhere, you can figure out the details of the curvature at each place. The average curvature above the earth varies with altitude, so the space there is curved. And it is that curvature that we see as a gravitational force.

Suppose we have a bug on a plane, and suppose that the "plane" has little pimples in the surface. Wherever there is a pimple the bug would conclude that his space has little local regions of curvature. We have the same thing in three dimensions. Wherever there is a lump of matter, our three-dimensional space has a local curvature—a kind of three-dimensional pimple.

If we make a lot of bumps on a plane there might be an overall curvature besides all the pimples—the surface might become like a ball. It would be interesting to know whether our space has a net average curvature as well as the local pimples due to the lumps of matter like the earth and the sun. The astrophysicists have been trying to answer that question by making measurements of galaxies at very large distances. For example, if the number of galaxies we see in a spherical shell at a large distance is different from what we

---

* Approximately, because the density is not independent of radius as we are assuming.

would expect from our knowledge of the radius of the shell, we would have a measure of the excess radius of a tremendously large sphere. From such measurements it is hoped to find out whether our whole universe is flat on the average, or round—whether it is "closed," like a sphere, or "open" like a plane. You may have heard about the debates that are going on about this subject. There are debates because the astronomical measurements are still completely inconclusive; the experimental data are not precise enough to give a definite answer. Unfortunately, we don't have the slightest idea about the overall curvature of our universe on a large scale.

## 6-4 Geometry in space-time

Now we have to talk about time. As you know from the special theory of relativity, measurements of space and measurements of time are interrelated. And it would be kind of crazy to have something happening to the space, without the time being involved in the same thing. You will remember that the measurement of time depends on the speed at which you move. For instance, if we watch a guy going by in a space ship we see that things happen more slowly for him than for us. Let's say he takes off on a trip and returns in 100 seconds flat *by our watches*; his watch might say that he had been gone for only 95 seconds. In comparison with ours, his watch—and all other processes, like his heart beat—have been running slow.

Now let's consider an interesting problem. Suppose you are the one in the space ship. We ask you to start off at a given signal and return to your starting place just in time to catch a later signal—at, say, exactly 100 seconds later according to *our* clock. And you are also asked to make the trip in such a way that *your* watch will show the *longest possible* elapsed time. How should you move? You should stand still. If you move at all your watch will read less than 100 seconds when you get back.

Suppose, however, we change the problem a little. Suppose we ask you to start at Point *A* on a given signal and go to point *B* (both fixed relative to us), and to do it in such a way that you arrive back just at the time of a second signal (say 100 seconds later according to our fixed clock). Again you are asked to make the trip in the way that lets you arrive with the latest possible reading on your watch. How would you do it? For which path and schedule will *your* watch show the greatest elapsed time when you arrive? The answer is that you will spend the longest time from *your* point of view if you make the trip by going at a uniform speed along a straight line. Reason: Any extra motions and any extra-high speeds will make your clock go slower. (Since the time deviations depend on the *square* of the velocity, what you lose by going extra fast at one place you can never make up by going extra slowly in another place.)

The point of all this is that we can use the idea to define "a straight line" in space-time. The analog of a straight line in space is for space-time a *motion* at uniform velocity in a constant direction.

The curve of shortest distance in space corresponds in space-time not to the path of shortest time, but to the one of *longest* time, because of the funny things that happen to signs of the *t*-terms in relativity. "Straight-line" motion—the analog of "uniform velocity along a straight line"—is then that motion which takes a watch from one place at one time to another place at another time in the way that gives the longest time reading for the watch. This will be our definition for the analog of a straight line in space-time.

## 6-5 Gravity and the principle of equivalence

Now we are ready to discuss the laws of gravitation. Einstein was trying to generate a theory of gravitation that would fit with the relativity theory that he had developed earlier. He was struggling along until he latched onto one important principle which guided him into getting the correct laws. That principle is based on the idea that when a thing is falling freely everything inside it seems weightless. For example, a satellite in orbit is falling freely in the earth's gravity, and an astronaut in it feels weightless. This idea, when stated with greater precision, is called *Einstein's principle of equivalence*. It depends on the fact that all objects fall with exactly the same acceleration no matter what their mass, or what they are made of. If we have a spaceship that is "coasting"—so it's in a free fall—and there is a man inside, then the laws governing the fall of the man and the ship are the same. So if he puts himself in the middle of the ship he will stay there. He doesn't fall *with respect to the ship*. That's what we mean when we say he is "weightless."

Now suppose you are in a rocket ship which is accelerating. Accelerating with respect to what? Let's just say that its engines are on and generating a thrust so that it is not coasting in a free fall. Also imagine that you are way out in empty space so that there are practically no gravitational forces on the ship. If the ship is accelerating with "1g" you will be able to stand on the "floor" and will feel your normal weight. Also if you let go of a ball, it will "fall" toward the floor. Why? Because the ship is accelerating "upward," but the ball has no forces on it, so it will not accelerate; it will get left behind. Inside the ship the ball will appear to have a downward acceleration of "1g."

Now let's compare that with the situation in a spaceship sitting at rest on the surface of the earth. *Everything is the same!* You would be pressed toward the floor, a ball would fall with an acceleration of 1g, and so on. In fact, how could you tell inside a space ship whether you are sitting on the earth or are accelerating in free space? According to Einstein's equivalence principle there is no way to tell if you only make measurements of what happens to things inside!

To be strictly correct, that is true only for one point inside the ship. The gravitational field of the earth is not precisely uniform, so a freely falling ball has a slightly different acceleration at different places—the direction changes and the magnitude changes. But if we imagine a strictly uniform gravitational field, it is completely imitated in every respect by a system with a constant acceleration. That is the basis of the principle of equivalence.

## 6-6 *The speed of clocks in a gravitational field*

Now we want to use the principle of equivalence for figuring out a strange thing that happens in a gravitational field. We'll show you something that happens in a rocket ship which you probably wouldn't have expected to happen in a gravitational field. Suppose we put a clock at the "head" of the rocket ship—that is, at the "front" end—and we put another identical clock at the "tail," as in Figure 6-16. Let's call the two clocks $A$ and $B$. If we compare these two clocks when the ship is accelerating, the clock at the head seems

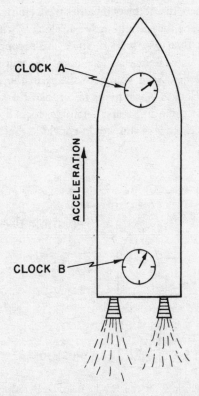

*Figure 6-16.* An accelerating rocket ship with two clocks.

to run fast relative to the one at the tail. To see that, imagine that the front clock emits a flash of light each second, and that you are sitting at the tail comparing the arrival of the light flashes with the ticks of clock $B$. Let's say that the rocket is in the position $a$ of Figure 6-17 when clock $A$ emits a flash, and at the position $b$ when the flash arrives at clock $B$. Later on the ship will be at position $c$ when the clock $A$ emits its next flash, and at position $d$ when you see it arrive at clock $B$.

The first flash travels the distance $L_1$ and the second flash travels the shorter distance $L_2$. It is a shorter distance because the ship is accelerating and has a higher speed at the time of the second flash. You can see, then, that if the two flashes were emitted from clock $A$ one second apart, they would arrive at clock $B$ with a separation somewhat less than one second, since the second flash doesn't spend as much time on the way. The same thing will also happen for all the later flashes. So if you were sitting in the tail you would conclude that clock $A$ was running faster than clock $B$. If you were to do the same thing in reverse—letting clock $B$ emit light and observing it at clock $A$—you would conclude that $B$ was running

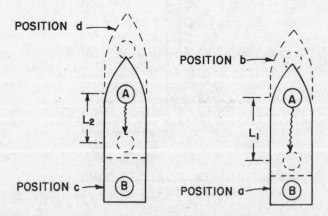

*Figure 6-17.* A clock at the head of an accelerating rocket ship appears to run faster than a clock at the tail.

*slower* than *A*. Everything fits together and there is nothing mysterious about it all.

But now let's think of the rocket ship at rest in the earth's gravity. *The same thing happens.* If you sit on the floor with one clock and watch another one which is sitting on a high shelf, it will appear to run faster than the one on the floor! You say, "But that is wrong. The times should be the same. With no acceleration there's no reason for the clocks to appear to be out of step." But they must if the principle of equivalence is right. And Einstein insisted that the principle *was* right, and went courageously and correctly ahead. He proposed that clocks at different places in a gravitational field must appear to run at different speeds. But if one always *appears* to be running at a different speed with respect to the other, then so far as the first is concerned the other *is* running at a different rate.

But now you see we have the analog for clocks of the hot ruler we were talking about earlier, when we had the bug on a hot plate. We imagined that rulers and bugs and everything changed lengths in the same way at various temperatures so they could never tell that their measuring sticks were changing as they moved around on the hot plate. It's the same with clocks in a gravitational field. Every clock we put at a higher level is seen to go faster. Heartbeats go faster, all processes run faster.

If they didn't you would be able to tell the difference between a gravitational field and an accelerating reference system. The idea that time can vary from place to place is a difficult one, but it is the idea Einstein used, and it is correct—believe it or not.

Using the principle of equivalence we can figure out how much the speed of a clock changes with height in a gravitational field. We just work out the apparent discrepancy between the two clocks in the accelerating rocket ship. The easiest way to do this is to use the result we found in Chapter 34 of Vol. I* for the Doppler effect. There, we found—see Eq. (34.14)*—that if $v$ is the *relative* velocity

* of the original *Lectures on Physics*.

of a source and a receiver, the *received* frequency $\omega$ is related to the *emitted* frequency $\omega_0$ by

$$\omega = \omega_0 \frac{1 + v/c}{\sqrt{1 - v^2/c^2}}. \tag{6.4}$$

Now if we think of the accelerating rocket ship in Figure 6-17 the emitter and receiver are moving with equal velocities at any one instant. But in the time that it takes the light signals to go from clock $A$ to clock $B$ the ship has accelerated. It has, in fact, picked up the additional velocity $gt$, where $g$ is the acceleration and $t$ is time it takes light to travel the distance $H$ from $A$ to $B$. This time is very nearly $H/c$. So when the signals arrive at $B$, the ship has increased its velocity by $gH/c$. The receiver always has this velocity *with respect to the emitter* at the instant the signal left it. So this is the velocity we should use in the Doppler shift formula, Eq. (6.4). Assuming that the acceleration and the length of the ship are small enough that this velocity is much smaller than $c$, we can neglect the term in $v^2/c^2$. We have that

$$\omega = \omega_0 \left(1 + \frac{gH}{c^2}\right). \tag{6.5}$$

So for the two clocks in the space ship we have the relation

$$(\text{Rate at the receiver}) = (\text{Rate of emission}) \left(1 + \frac{gH}{c^2}\right), \tag{6.6}$$

where $H$ is the height of the emitter *above* the receiver.

*From the equivalence principle the same result must hold for two clocks separated by the height H in a gravitational field with the free fall acceleration g.*

This is such an important idea we would like to demonstrate that it also follows from another law of physics—from the conservation of energy. We know that the gravitational force on an object is proportional to its mass $M$, which is related to its total internal energy $E$ by $M = E/c^2$. For instance, the masses of nuclei determined from the *energies* of nuclear reactions which transmute one nucleus into another agree with the masses obtained from atomic *weights*.

## Curved Space

Now think of an atom which has a lowest energy state of total energy $E_0$ and a higher energy state $E_1$, and which can go from the state $E_1$ to the state $E_0$ by emitting light. The frequency $\omega$ of the light will be given by

$$\hbar\omega = E_1 - E_0. \qquad (6.7)$$

Now suppose we have such an atom in the state $E_1$ sitting on the floor, and we carry it from the floor to the height $H$. To do that we must do some work in carrying the mass $m_1 = E_1/c^2$ up against the gravitational force. The amount of work done is

$$\frac{E_1}{c^2} gH. \qquad (6.8)$$

Then we let the atom emit a photon and go into the lower energy state $E_0$. Afterward we carry the atom back to the floor. On the return trip the mass is $E_0/c^2$; we get back the energy

$$\frac{E_0}{c^2} gH, \qquad (6.9)$$

so we have done a net amount of work equal to

$$\Delta U = \frac{E_1 - E_0}{c^2} gH. \qquad (6.10)$$

When the atom emitted the photon it gave up the energy $E_1 - E_0$. Now suppose that the photon happened to go down to the floor and be absorbed. How much energy would it deliver there? You might at first think that it would deliver just the energy $E_1 - E_0$. But that can't be right if energy is conserved, as you can see from the following argument. We started with the energy $E_1$ at the floor. When we finish, the energy at the floor level is the energy $E_0$ of the atom in its lower state plus the energy $E_{ph}$ received from the photon. In the meantime we have had to supply the additional energy $\Delta U$ of Eq. (6.10). If energy is conserved, the energy we end up with at the floor must be greater than we started with by just the work we have done. Namely, we must have that

SIX NOT-SO-EASY PIECES

$$E_{ph} + E_0 = E_1 + \Delta U,$$

or

$$E_{ph} = (E_1 - E_0) + \Delta U. \qquad (6.11)$$

It must be that the photon does *not* arrive at the floor with just the energy $E_1 - E_0$ it started with, but with a *little more energy*. Otherwise some energy would have been lost. If we substitute in Eq. (6.11) the $\Delta U$ we got in Eq. (6.10), we get that the photon arrives at the floor with the energy

$$E_{ph} = (E_1 - E_0) \left(1 + \frac{gH}{c^2}\right). \qquad (6.12)$$

But a photon of energy $E_{ph}$ has the frequency $\omega = E_{ph}/\hbar$. Calling the frequency of the *emitted* photon $\omega_0$—which is by Eq. (6.7) equal to $(E_1 - E_0)/\hbar$—our result in Eq. (6.12) gives again the relation of (6.5) between the frequency of the photon when it is absorbed on the floor and the frequency with which it was emitted.

The same result can be obtained in still another way. A photon of frequency $\omega_0$ has the energy $E_0 = \hbar\omega_0$. Since the energy $E_0$ has the gravitational mass $E_0/c^2$ the photon has a mass (*not* rest mass) $\hbar\omega_0/c^2$, and is "attracted" by the earth. In falling the distance $H$ it will gain an additional energy $(\hbar\omega_0/c^2)gH$, so it arrives with the energy

$$E = \hbar w_0 \left(1 + \frac{gH}{c^2}\right).$$

But its frequency after the fall is $E/\hbar$, giving again the result in Eq. (6.5). Our ideas about relativity, quantum physics, and energy conservation all fit together only if Einstein's predictions about clocks in a gravitational field are right. The frequency changes we are talking about are normally very small. For instance, for an altitude difference of 20 meters at the earth's surface the frequency difference is only about two parts in $10^{15}$. However, just such a change has recently been found experimentally using the Mössbauer effect.* Einstein was perfectly correct.

---

* R. V. Pound and G. A. Rebka, Jr., *Physical Review Letters* Vol. 4, p. 337 (1960).

*Curved Space*

## 6-7 The curvature of space-time

Now we want to relate what we have just been talking about to the idea of curved space-time. We have already pointed out that if the time goes at different rates in different places, it is analogous to the curved space of the hot plate. But it is more than an analogy; it means that space-time *is* curved. Let's try to do some geometry in space-time. That may at first sound peculiar, but we have often made diagrams of space-time with distance plotted along one axis and time along the other. Suppose we try to make a rectangle in space-time. We begin by plotting a graph of height $H$ versus $t$ as in Figure 6-18(a). To make the base of our rectangle we take an object which is *at rest* at the height $H_1$ and follow its world line for 100 seconds. We get the line $BD$ in part (b) of the figure which is parallel to the $t$-axis. Now let's take another object which is 100 feet above the first one at $t = 0$. It starts at the point $A$ in Figure 6-18(c). Now we follow its world line for 100 seconds as measured by a clock at $A$. The object goes from $A$ to $C$, as shown in part (d) of the figure. But notice that since time goes at a different rate at the two heights—we are assuming that there is a gravitational field—the two points $C$ and $D$ are not simultaneous. If we try to complete the square by drawing a line to the point $C'$ which is 100 feet above $D$ at the same time, as in Figure 6-18(e), the pieces don't fit. And that's what we mean when we say that space-time is curved.

## 6-8 Motion in curved space-time

Let's consider an interesting little puzzle. We have two identical clocks, $A$ and $B$, sitting together on the surface of the earth as in Figure 6-19. Now we lift clock $A$ to some height $H$, hold it there awhile, and return it to the ground so that it arrives at just the instant when clock $B$ has advanced by 100 seconds. Then clock $A$ will read something like 107 seconds, because it was running faster when it was up in the air. Now here is the puzzle. How should we

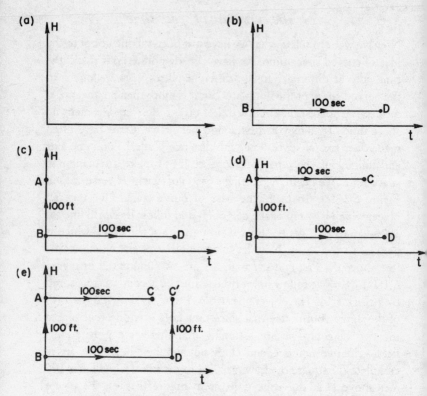

*Figure 6-18.* Trying to make a rectangle in space-time.

move clock *A* so that it reads the latest possible time—always assuming that it returns when *B* reads 100 seconds? You say, "That's easy. Just take *A* as high as you can. Then it will run as fast as possible, and be the latest when you return." Wrong. You forgot something—we've only got 100 seconds to go up and back. If we go very high, we have to go very fast to get there and back in 100 seconds. And you mustn't forget the effect of special relativity which causes moving clocks to *slow down* by the factor $\sqrt{1 - v^2/c^2}$. This relativity effect works in the direction of making clock *A* read

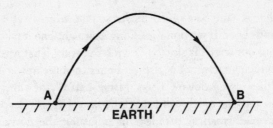

*Figure 6-19.* In a uniform gravitational field the trajectory with the maximum proper time for a fixed elapsed time is a parabola.

*less time* than clock B. You see that we have a kind of game. If we stand still with clock A we get 100 seconds. If we go up slowly to a small height and come down slowly we can get a little more than 100 seconds. If we go a little higher, maybe we can gain a little more. But if we go too high we have to move fast to get there, and we may slow down the clock enough that we end up with less than 100 seconds. What program of height versus time—how high to go and with what speed to get there, carefully adjusted to bring us back to clock B when it has increased by 100 seconds—will give us the largest possible time reading on clock A?

Answer: Find out how fast you have to throw a ball up into the air so that it will fall back to earth in exactly 100 seconds. The ball's motion—rising fast, slowing down, stopping, and coming back down—is exactly the right motion to make the time the maximum on a wrist watch strapped to the ball.

Now consider a slightly different game. We have two points A and B both on the earth's surface at some distance from one another. We play the same game that we did earlier to find what we call the straight line. We ask how we should go from A to B so that the time on our moving watch will be the longest—assuming we start at A on a given signal and arrive at B on another signal at B which we will say is 100 seconds later by a fixed clock. Now you say, "Well we found out before that the thing to do is to coast along a

## SIX NOT-SO-EASY PIECES

straight line at a uniform speed chosen so that we arrive at $B$ exactly 100 seconds later. If we don't go along a straight line it takes more speed, and our watch is slowed down." But wait! That was before we took gravity into account. Isn't it better to curve upward a little bit and then come down? Then during part of the time we are higher up and our watch will run a little faster? It is, indeed. If you solve the mathematical problem of adjusting the curve of the motion so that the elapsed time of the moving watch is the most it can possibly be, you will find that the motion is a parabola—the same curve followed by something that moves on a free ballistic path in the gravitational field, as in Figure 6-19. Therefore the law of motion in a gravitational field can also be stated: *An object always moves from one place to another so that a clock carried on it gives a longer time than it would on any other possible trajectory*—with, of course, the same starting and finishing conditions. The time measured by a moving clock is often called its "proper time." In free fall, the trajectory makes the proper time of an object a maximum.

Let's see how this all works out. We begin with Eq. (6.5) which says that the *excess* rate of the moving watch is

$$\frac{\omega_0 g H}{c^2}. \tag{6.13}$$

Besides this, we have to remember that there is a correction of the opposite sign for the speed. For this effect we know that

$$\omega = \omega_0 \sqrt{1 - v^2/c^2}.$$

Although the principle is valid for any speed, we take an example in which the speeds are always much less than $c$. Then we can write this equation as

$$\omega = \omega_0(1 - v^2/2c^2),$$

and the defect in the rate of our clock is

$$- \omega_0 \frac{v^2}{2c^2}. \tag{6.14}$$

### Curved Space

Combining the two terms in (6.13) and (6.14) we have that

$$\Delta\omega = \frac{\omega_0}{c^2}\left(gH - \frac{v^2}{2}\right).$$ (6.15)

Such a frequency shift of our moving clock means that if we measure a time $dt$ on a fixed clock, the moving clock will register the time

$$dt\left[1 + \left(\frac{gH}{c^2} - \frac{v^2}{2c^2}\right)\right].$$ (6.16)

The total time excess over the trajectory is the integral of the extra term with respect to time, namely

$$\frac{1}{c^2}\int\left(gH - \frac{v^2}{2}\right)dt,$$ (6.17)

which is supposed to be a maximum.

The term $gH$ is just the gravitational potential $\phi$. Suppose we multiply the whole thing by a constant factor $-mc^2$, where $m$ is the mass of the object. The constant won't change the condition for the maximum, but the minus sign will just change the maximum to a minimum. Equation (6.16) then says that the object will move so that

$$\int\left(\frac{mv^2}{2} - m\phi\right)dt = \text{a minimum}.$$ (6.18)

But now the integrand is just the difference of the kinetic and potential energies. And if you look in Chapter 19 of Volume II* you will see that when we discussed the principle of least action we showed that Newton's laws for an object in any potential could be written exactly in the form of Eq. (6.18).

### 6-9 Einstein's theory of gravitation

Einstein's form of the equations of motion—that the proper time should be a maximum in curved space-time—gives the same results

* of the original *Lectures on Physics*.

SIX NOT-SO-EASY PIECES

as Newton's laws for low velocities. As he was circling around the earth, Gordon Cooper's watch was reading later than it would have in any other path you could have imagined for his satellite.*

So the law of gravitation can be stated in terms of the ideas of the geometry of space-time in this remarkable way. The particles always take the longest proper time—in space-time a quantity analogous to the "shortest distance." That's the law of motion in a gravitational field. The great advantage of putting it this way is that the law doesn't depend on any coordinates, or any other way of defining the situation.

Now let's summarize what we have done. We have given you two laws for gravity:

(1) How the geometry of space-time changes when matter is present—namely, that the curvature expressed in terms of the excess radius is proportional to the mass inside a sphere, Eq. (6.3).

(2) How objects move if there are only gravitational forces—namely, that objects move so that their proper time between two end conditions is a maximum.

Those two laws correspond to similar pairs of laws we have seen earlier. We originally described motion in a gravitational field in terms of Newton's inverse square law of gravitation and his laws of motion. Now laws (1) and (2) take their places. Our new pair of laws also correspond to what we have seen in electrodynamics. There we had our law—the set of Maxwell's equations—which determines the fields produced by charges. It tells how the character of "space" is changed by the presence of charged matter, which is what law (1) does for gravity. In addition, we had a law about how

---

* Strictly speaking it is only a *local* maximum. We should have said that the proper time is larger than for any *nearby* path. For example, the proper time on an elliptical orbit around the earth need not be longer than on a ballistic path of an object which is shot to a great height and falls back down.

## Curved Space

particles move in the given fields—$d(m\mathbf{v})/dt = q(\mathbf{E} + \mathbf{v} \times \mathbf{B})$. This, for gravity, is done by law (2).

In the laws (1) and (2) you have a precise statement of Einstein's theory of gravitation—although you will usually find it stated in a more complicated mathematical form. We should, however, make one further addition. Just as time scales change from place to place in a gravitational field, so do the length scales. Rulers change lengths as you move around. It is impossible with space and time so intimately mixed to have something happen with time that isn't in some way reflected in space. Take even the simplest example: You are riding past the earth. What is "*time*" from *your* point of view is partly space from *our* point of view. So there must also be changes in space. It is the entire *space-time* which is distorted by the presence of matter, and this is more complicated than a change only in time scale. However, the rule that we gave in Eq. (6-3) is enough to determine completely all the laws of gravitation, provided that it is understood that this rule about the curvature of space applies not only from one man's point of view but is true for everybody. Somebody riding by a mass of material sees a different mass content because of the kinetic energy he calculates for its motion past him, and he must include the mass corresponding to that energy. The theory must be arranged so that everybody—no matter how he moves—will, when he draws a sphere, find that the excess radius is $G/3c^2$ times the total mass (or, better, $G/3c^4$ times the total energy content) inside the sphere. That this law—law (1)—should be true in any moving system is one of the great laws of gravitation, called *Einstein's field equation*. The other great law is (2)—that things must move so that the proper time is a maximum—and is called *Einstein's equation of motion*.

To write these laws in a complete algebraic form, to compare them with Newton's laws, or to relate them to electrodynamics is difficult mathematically. But it is the way our most complete laws of the physics of gravity look today.

Although they gave a result in agreement with Newton's mechanics for the simple example we considered, they do not always do so. The three discrepancies first derived by Einstein have been experimentally confirmed: The orbit of Mercury is not a fixed ellipse; starlight passing near the sun is deflected twice as much as you would think; and the rates of clocks depend on their location in a gravitational field. Whenever the predictions of Einstein have been found to differ from the ideas of Newtonian mechanics, Nature has chosen Einstein's.

Let's summarize everything that we have said in the following way. First, time and distance rates depend on the place in space you measure them and on the time. This is equivalent to the statement that space-time is curved. From the measured area of a sphere we can define a predicted radius, $\sqrt{A/4\pi}$, but the actual measured radius will have an excess over this which is proportional (the constant is $G/c^2$) to the total mass contained inside the sphere. This fixes the exact degree of the curvature of space-time. And the curvature must be the same no matter who is looking at the matter or how it is moving. Second, particles move on "straight lines" (trajectories of maximum proper time) in this curved space-time. This is the content of Einstein's formulation of the laws of gravitation.

# Index

146

*Index*

# *Index*

149

*Index*